The Broadway Musical

A Critical and Musical Survey

Second Edition

JOSEPH P. SWAIN

The Scarecrow Press, Inc.
Lanham, Maryland, and Oxford
2002

SCARECROW PRESS, INC.

Published in the United States of America
by Scarecrow Press, Inc.
A wholly owned subsidiary of
The Rowman & Littlefield Publishing Group, Inc.
4501 Forbes Boulevard, Suite 200, Lanham, Maryland 20706
www.scarecrowpress.com

PO Box 317
Oxford
OX2 9RU, UK

British Library Cataloguing in Publication Information Available

Library of Congress Cataloging-in-Publication Data
Swain, Joseph Peter.
  The Broadway musical : a critical and musical survey / Joseph P.
Swain. — 2nd ed.
      p. cm.
Includes index.
  ISBN 0-8108-4375-7 (alk. paper) — ISBN 0-8108-4376-5 (pbk. : alk.
paper)
  1. Musicals—United States—History and criticism. I. Title.
  ML2054 .S93 2002
  782.1'4'0973—dc21   2002004981

∞ ™ The paper used in this publication meets the minimum requirements of
American National Standard for Information Sciences—Permanence of
Paper for Printed Library Materials, ANSI/NISO Z39.48-1992.
Manufactured in the United States of America.

For Jan
who taught me
to love this music

Contents

Preface to the First Edition

The writer of the critical survey owes a good many debts, intellectual, practical, and personal, to those who have done essential groundwork in historical research and critical thinking and to those who have helped with the innumerable tasks that make the final work possible. In this sense criticism is never entirely original, for it depends on an environment composed of intellectual tradition and the works, in this case certain American musical plays, to which it calls attention.

Many good books and articles stand behind this book, but its principal formation comes chiefly from a select few. Joseph Kerman's *Opera as Drama* (New York: Vintage Books, 1956; rev. ed. London: Faber, 1989), still the best exposition of the notion of the composer as dramatist, contributed the main premise, which is that in the best examples of American musical theater the music acts as a dramatic agent. Francis Fergusson's *The Idea of a Theater* (Princeton, N.J., Princeton University Press, 1949) helped refine more precisely what that means, as did *The Life of the Drama* (New York: Atheneum, 1964), by Eric Bentley, which also acted as chief reference for the various traditional dramatic genres. The only historical survey of Broadway to investigate what makes a good musical is Lehman Engel's *The American Musical Theatre: A*

Consideration (New York: Macmillan, 1967), and although his arguments are not based on musical analysis, as is the case here, his observations are full of common sense and have much to teach. Other more
purely historical surveys of the American musical theater were relied
upon as essential references: Stanley Green's *The World of Musical Comedy* (New York: Barnes, 1974), Abe Laufe's *Broadway's Greatest Musicals*
(New York: Funk & Wagnall's, 1969) and Ethan Mordden's *Better Foot
Forward* (New York: Grossman, 1976) and Gerald Bordman's *American
Musical Theatre* (New York: Oxford University Press, 1977) are the
principal ones. Beyond those are many biographical books, works of
literary criticism, and articles of a specific nature which aided the writ
ing of particular chapters, and for these items the reader is referred to
the Notes for each chapter given at the end of the book. Missing even
from those lists are the hundreds of periodical reviews of shows, other
assorted newspaper features and interviews, and some writing in the
scholarly literature that were duly consulted but which proved irrelevant or had nothing to contribute to the issue at hand.

As sketchy as this bibliographical summary may be, the acknowl-
edgment of practical debts must be yet more inadequate, so many
are they who helped out with favors large and small. The research for
the book received an enormous boost at its outset from the National
Endowment for the Humanities, which supported the initial bibliographical collection with a Summer Research Stipend in 1986. The
Colgate University Research Council supported the work at a later
stage. To both of these institutions I am deeply grateful.

My chief aide in collecting bibliography was Ms. Susan M. Cooney.
Further help was provided by the reference staff at Case Library at Colgate University who patiently processed a large number of inter-library
loan requests in fine humor. In this new age of computers there is no
typist to thank, but the music department staff of Ms. Roberta Healy
and Ms. Marilyn Jones helped me with many other administrative tasks
and the entire department at Colgate gave me encouragement throughout the project. I must also thank Mr. Sheldon Meyer, Senior Vice-
President at Oxford University Press, and his able and professional
staff. Mr. Meyer supported this project enthusiastically when only two
chapters were drafted and made many valuable suggestions en route.

The heart and soul of this study—indeed the reason for writing it
when many other books on Broadway are available—are the musical

examples contained in it. The detailed analysis of these examples provides the lion's share of the evidence and illustration for the critical arguments. Appreciation is due all the agencies which own the reprint rights to this music (listed on the copyright page) for carrying out the necessary negotiations with understanding, fairness and efficiency. The one exception in this search for permissions was the Wren Music Co., which refused all permission to reprint the music and lyrics from *A Chorus Line* because of the critical nature of the attending discussion. I apologize to the reader for the inconvenience and somewhat convoluted writing the omission of those examples causes.

The examples were formatted using Dr. Keith A. Hamel's Notewriter, run on a Macintosh SE computer and printed with Macintosh's Laserwriter II NT. They were then reduced for final printing. In general I have copied the piano-vocal scores, the principal musical sources for this study, as closely as possible. Occasionally, in the interests of visual clarity, I omitted details of orchestration, stage directions, or other matters that have no bearing on the discussion, but in all cases I hoped to represent fairly the essence of what is heard in the theater in a format that keeps the discussion manageable.

Personal debts are harder to recognize sometimes but are no less real. The three most important ones I trace back to my undergraduate days at Dartmouth College. There two music teachers, Professors Steven J. Ledbetter and Charles Hamm, showed by the example of their own research in American music and, more important, by their wholesome open-mindedness to music of all sorts that a critical survey such as this was not beyond imagining. The last debt I trace to a young woman named Janice Lee, my classmate, best friend, now my wife of ten years, who insisted on dragging a high-brow music student again and again to musical theater productions to see and hear the magic there.

Joseph P. Swain
Hamilton, New York
Fall 1989

Preface to the Second Edition

There are three main reasons why a new, revised edition of *The Broadway Musical* seemed warranted. Most obviously, the musical theater tradition has aged another decade since the first edition appeared in 1990, and if one considers that the latest show discussed therein is Steven Sondheim's *Sweeney Todd* of 1979, a period more than twenty years has no representative. In particular, the international phenomenon of the "megamusical," which clearly stems from the Broadway tradition while at the same time magnifying its artistic and commercial premises, clearly demanded attention. Second, a new edition allows the recognition of a rapidly intensifying interest in the musical on the part of music and theater historians as well as the incorporation of their findings. Last, the project was encouraged by the many requests from faculty to find copies of the first edition, out of print since 1997, for their college courses.

This in no way means that the new edition has been transformed into a textbook. The book is written for exactly the same audience as the first edition: for all who love musical theater and want to understand how the songs act as dramatic agents in the best musical plays. While most of the new books on Broadway music are composer biographies and historical studies that give the reader a keen sense of the times when the songs and plays were composed, the focus here remains on the transcendent aesthetic values of the best musicals, those things that speak to us across the generations and apart from their origins. The stories of creation are fascinating—indeed, the pictures of Oscar Hammerstein II tutoring the teenaged Stephen Sondheim, Rex Harrison petrified with stage fright before the tryout of *My Fair Lady*, Michael Bennett drawing the book of *A Chorus Line* from an all-night bull session, and so many others have entered into American folklore—but they remain at the margins of what materially forms our experience of music drama when we hear these musicals today. That essential experience remains the subject of this book.

Naturally I have taken the opportunity to include the latest research and viewpoints of recent critics and to improve the writing wherever possible, but the first fourteen chapters appear much as they did before. The major changes come with the addition of one completely new essay, "Epic as Musical," on *Les Misérables* (Chapter 15) and a substantially revised epilogue (Chapter 16) that takes account of the altered cultural environment, production technology, and commercialization of the musical during the last two decades.

The most important books on Broadway's music since 1988 are Geoffrey Block's fine historical survey *Enchanted Evenings: The Broadway Musical from* Show Boat *to Sondheim* (New York: Oxford University Press, 1997), Stephen Banfield's comprehensive study *Sondheim's Broadway Musicals* (Ann Arbor, MI: University of Michigan Press, 1993), and Michael Walsh's *Andrew Lloyd Webber: His Life and Works* (New York: Harry N. Abrams, Inc., 1989). As in the first edition, the specific contributions of historians and biographers who are the advance guard of criticism are acknowledged in the notes.

I am once again grateful to those in the many agencies that handle copyrighted materials for their wise advice and cooperation and of course to the officers of Scarecrow Press who brought the project to light.

—Joseph P. Swain
Hamilton, New York
October 2001

Chapter 1

Introduction

The intention here is not to write a comprehensive history of the American musical theater, but to survey the achievements of its music as a dramatic element. In the best musical plays of the Broadway tradition, songs are embedded in a drama to which they contribute mightily. They are more than simple decorations or diversions. Rather, they establish characters, move the plot, intensify conflicts, and constitute other events that would be expected of a spoken play. Without the songs these plays would be considerably poorer, even incomprehensible.

The perspective adopted in this survey, then, is one as old as the very idea of combining music and drama. The music of a good musical play informs the drama that contains it, and the composer is a dramatist in his own right, more important sometimes than the person who writes the words. This perspective is perhaps best articulated in modern times by Joseph Kerman in his *Opera as Drama*,[1] a critical survey of serious opera of the European tradition.

Whether music in the theater can really be an essential dramatic force has been a matter of some contention. If drama is a product of words alone, then any musical adaptation must weaken the drama, because music is in general abstract, without explicit semantic reference.[2] "When drama takes on the abstract character of pure music or pure dance it ceases to be drama; when, as a compromise, it tries to combine the abstract with the concrete it is invariably the drama, the words, that suffer" writes theorist Eric Bentley.[3] But if actions are the stuff of drama, as Aristotle would have it, then words are just one way to articulate "the underlying structure of incident and character."[4] Anything else that can express the thread of the action has just as much right to dramatic representation as words. When the important actions are actions of feeling, or emotion, then music not only suffices, it sur passes the power of words to define the action. As Kerman has it:

> even the most passionate of speeches exists on a level of emotional reserve that music automatically passes. Music can be immediate and simple in the presentation of emotional states or shades. In an opera, people can give themselves over to sensibility; in a play nobody ever quite stops thinking.[5]

The broad semantic range typical of western music, the very quality that makes it unsuitable for conveying fact and idea, makes it an ideal symbol of psychological or emotional action. The first association of a musical phrase with a character or situation carries over throughout the drama, and so not only the overt actions of the characters but also their thoughts and states of feeling become sensible to the audience. That is the rationale behind the leitmotif, a fragment of music that comes to represent a character or object of importance. Bentley advises the dramatist to imitate action by finding "objective equivalents of subjective experience."[6] He means the subjective experience of the audience, but in music there is the equivalent of the character's experience as well, which in turn may be felt directly by the audience.

It is possible to deny music a dramatic role, then, only if one insists that drama is a product of words alone. Once anything else—stage gestures, facial expressions, lighting—is allowed to contribute, then music too must be admitted as a powerful and subtle analogue to the emotional and psychological action.

To understand how music performs as a significant dramatic element in the Broadway tradition, a musical analysis is needed that connects the songs in their detail with the dramatic elements of plot, character, and action. In the second act of Leonard Bernstein's *West Side Story*, for example, it is not enough to point out that when Maria persuades a bitter, bristling, and disillusioned Anita to intercede on behalf of the man who just killed her lover, a dramatic climax has occurred. Such persuasion seems incredible. On the other hand, any technical analysis of the music without reference to plot and character misses the essential meaning of the duet. In the contrasting section or "release" of Anita's opening solo, she sings the following:

Ex. 1-1 Bernstein and Sondheim, "A Boy Like That," mm. 18–20.

Her bitterness and hatred of Tony come through in the minor mode, accented offbeats, and the chromatic and diminished melodic intervals that her phrases outline. But why then should the same music be taken up by Maria when she enters?

Ex. 1-2 Bernstein and Sondheim, "A Boy Like That," mm. 38–40.

It fits because this is more than telling Anita that she is dead wrong. The song here makes explicit a serious accusation, that Anita's animosity is rooted in the shallowness of her own relationship with her lover Bernardo, a shallowness made painfully clear by the depth of Maria's commitment to Tony. Maria, in quoting this theme with the words "It's true for you, not for me" takes Anita's denial of love and turns it back on her. But this is confrontation, not persuasion. Persuasion begins with the onset of the last section of the duet:

Ex. 1-3 Bernstein and Sondheim, "A Boy Like That," mm. 68–72.

Maria's melody is much transformed and yet the same as before. Shorn of its chromatic anacrusis to the central G, the strong offbeats and the diminished intervals, and translated into the major mode, the song that once stood for the denial of love now becomes the expression of love. This transformation of the melody mirrors the change in Anita, and makes such a moving and drastic character change quite believable. Maria convinces her that the love she feels has a depth far beyond anything that Anita has known, and is therefore worth saving. She does this in terms that Anita understands, reshaping her own musical argument, as it were.

Musical gestures can take on dramatic meanings and functions because they have broad semantic ranges, unlike those of spoken words, which are much narrower and precise. Musical meanings become specific only when focused by a context, here the words of the libretto. The chromatic phrase in Example 1-1 reflects Anita's emotional state by its association with the text, whose meaning is obvious. But not just any musical gesture will do for a particular expression. The abstractness of music is limited by its home culture, which overlays various musical effects with meanings accumulated over many generations. Bitterness and hatred are not necessarily expressed by the minor mode and diminished intervals of Example 1-1, but those emotions are certainly within the expressive range of those effects; a composer would not use them to express love or joy except in the most contrived circumstances, or in a non-tonal idiom. The composer's art as a dramatist consists of choosing gestures appropriate for the expression required in a dramatic situation. These gestures then take on specific meaning when associated with the words in a musical texture. The most astonishing aspect of this scheme is that the music then amplifies incomparably the dramatic situation from which it takes its own meaning. There is a sort of feedback system that operates quite like certain other mechanisms of human perception.[7]

In short, the critical survey which this book comprises regards the traditional tools of composition—melody, its harmonization, change of key, rhythm, and texture—as elements of dramaturgy. This sort of analysis has never been applied to Broadway stage music before. There are fine surveys and histories of Broadway, to be sure, even ones in which dramatic criticism is the principal aim, but none have music as the principal focus of the criticism. Leaf through the pages of a volume by David Ewen, Stanley Green, Ethan Mordden, or Lehman Engel: there are no musical examples. This situation allows only the most general statements about the role that music can play; the particular musical solutions to dramatic problems and the rare moments of true musical-dramatic insight can only be recalled, never described. The direct analysis of music surely narrows the scope of this book—no one could discuss every important moment of every show in such detail—but in return it may provide a deeper understanding of the composer's craft as a dramatist.

One troubling question remains. Isn't this critical approach a bit lofty for Broadway? Is the popular tradition really worth this sort of attention?

It would be fair to say that the products of Broadway have not had much success in the annals of scholarly criticism. Before 1990 the musical theater received virtually no attention from serious music critics at all, and what little it did receive was patronizing at best. In his *The Playwright as Thinker* of 1946, Eric Bentley states that the dramatic content of one of the most renowned examples of American musical theater is essentially trivial:

> Perhaps Mr. Oscar Hammerstein is a fair specimen. His work *Oklahoma!* . . . has been "hailed" as establishing a new genre, praised in at least one literary quarterly, awarded a Pulitzer Prize by special dispensation, and compared, not unfavorably, with *The Magic Flute*. It was the outstanding theatrical success of the war

period; and it is entirely representative of current trends. In fact, it belongs with the "new Americanism" in being folksy and excessively, ostentatiously wholesome; also in being trite, cocksure, sentimental, and vacuous. On the stage it is decked out in gay color and from time to time enlivened by tricky dancing. But in all drama . . . color and dancing are only embellishments; in this case they are the embellishment of a scarecrow.[8]

If only the outline of the *Oklahoma!* story is recalled, this judgment might seem to be fair, but Mr. Bentley has not accounted for an essential element. In identifying the play as Hammerstein's, he disregards completely the contribution of the other dramatist, Richard Rodgers. This stems from his belief, somewhat muted in later writing, that music rarely contributes anything worthwhile to the drama of words. In its extreme form, it is a position that denies the claims that opera makes on dramatic art.

Even when it is agreed that any critical assessment of the American musical stage must include its music, it is entirely possible that the musical talent of Broadway is unequal to the ideal of music drama. In his speculation on the future of the musical stage in *Opera as Drama*, Kerman raises the possibility of popular musical theater as a source for new works of merit, but quickly dismisses such a thought:

Popular art has other channels. One of them is musical comedy. Theoretically this might serve as a proving-ground for art, just as *opera buffa* did in the eighteenth century; but in over a hundred years operetta and musical comedy have come forth with not a single serious dramatist . . .[9]

The context of this judgment, in particular Kerman's rather Olympian standards for "serious dramatists" as set out in his book, should perhaps be recalled. His pantheon admits but two members: Mozart and Verdi, and even their works have imperfections. Monteverdi, Handel, Gluck, Wagner, Debussy, Berg, and Stravinsky, among others, stand just outside the small inner circle. All others are simply undramatic.

The problem is complicated by two additional factors. One is the simple fact of popular success. The view from the beginning of the twenty-first century affords a perspective unavailable to Bentley and Kerman, namely, that there is now a repertoire of American musical theater pieces, a repertoire that has undergone a process of classicization just as other repertoires have done. From the thousands of shows composed in the last century, perhaps two or three dozen have survived to be regularly performed. Some critics recognize a golden age of the American musical theater centered on the decades of the 1940s and 1950s, when many of them were composed. This observation defines a group of important forerunners, including Jerome Kern, Cole Porter, George Gershwin, and Rodgers and Hart, and a period of decline setting in by the late 1960s. More important, the shows of the golden age are nearly three generations old by now, which means that their appeal has survived some rather radical changes in society and in the style of popular music. The rise of a repertoire that behaves like other serious repertoires in the culture is difficult to dismiss.

Even so, it was often dismissed because the music seems to be rooted in popular styles rather than "serious" or "cultivated" or "classical" styles. This origin is the second factor that complicates the judgment of Broadway's ultimate value.

Whether Broadway in modern times remains a purely popular tradition is open to question, but that its origins are popular is undeniable. The theatrical elements were entirely drawn from the traditions of vaudeville, burlesque, and popular stage plays; the theater songs of the early 1910s and 1920s were written by the same men who composed for the publishers of Tin Pan Alley. Both Jerome Kern and George Gershwin began their careers as song pluggers in music publishing houses. The training of many of even the greatest talents of Broadway was of such a happenstance nature that their musical facility was limited in ways that seem incredible today. Richard Rodgers, who always composed at the piano, never learned enough technique to play classical chamber music, despite an effort with formal lessons in the middle of his career.[10] Irving Berlin, it is said, composed all his songs in the key of F-sharp. He had to hire a musical secretary to transpose them to more suitable keys afterward.[11]

On the other hand, elements of the art music tradition of the West can be discerned creeping into Broadway from the late 1910s onward, a harbinger of the increasingly serious intentions of certain composers. Victor Herbert was a fine classical cellist, and the principal operetta composers of the 1920s, Sigmund Romberg and Rudolf Friml, were trained in Europe. Gershwin had formal training in harmony and counterpoint, although not before he was well established on Broadway, and of course his *Porgy and Bess* is known as an "opera" in the serious sense. Cole Porter studied with Vincent d'Indy in Paris. Such examples proliferate later in the century: Leonard Bernstein's brilliant career need not be detailed here, but it is less well known that Stephen Sondheim studied composition with Milton Babbitt, or that Andrew Lloyd Webber was trained from boyhood in classical horn, violin, and piano.

Certainly there were some who viewed the domination of the Broadway tradition by popular interests as a constraint so overwhelming that any artistic value must be choked off. Bentley admitted the possibility of a dramatic art admired by both critic and public:

> Until the modern period great drama has possessed not only those deeper and subtler qualities which reveal themselves to the careful analyst and which constitute its greatness, it has also possessed more generally available qualities. It has appealed on different levels. It has appealed to the connoisseur and the public.[12]

But his overall assessment of the state of modern theater was that "it is almost inconceivable that any drama could satisfy the canons of the most exacting criticism and also be popular."[13] The "commodity theater," as he termed it, appeals to the lowest common denominator in its audience and therefore excludes the deep and the subtle aspects of dramatic art.

In an absolute sense he is right about Broadway. The tyranny of the financial motive in the early decades is there for all to see, in the endless parade of mindless "formula" shows, in the reliance on such superficial devices as chorus lines and comedy routines quite unrelated to any story, and in the producers' resistance to the slightest innovation. The style of Broadway's music is eclectic by nature, able to absorb and put to dramatic use a variety of different sorts of music, but its contributing sources then were always popular. Experimentation with the new and various styles of art music coming out of Europe early in the twentieth century was impossible. These developments progressed at a rapid rate and left the entire world of popular music far behind for the first time in the history of western music. If high art resided only in those cultivated developments of Debussy, Schoenberg, and Stravinsky, then certainly Broadway must have been cut off from such ambitions.

But Stravinsky argued, "The more art is controlled, limited, worked over, the more it is free."[14] Because they had to please their public, and were thus denied the advances and pretensions of the European avant-garde, Broadway composers were left free to continue to explore the possibilities of a musical style which in learned circles had become old-fashioned and, in the individualistic world of the twentieth century, unacceptable. They were free to draw on the newer popular styles of jazz and rock. The most ingenious of these composers found that they could sell their creations without sacrificing their dramatic ideals. And there were substantial departures from the norm, amid the tight-fisted producers and unsophisticated public. *Porgy and Bess* was produced and did run for several months; *Oklahoma!* did begin without a chorus number; *Carousel* did have a few odd-sounding chords during its prelude and did kill off its main character. Gradually, the Broadway composers came to realize that if their musical dramaturgy was convincing enough, they could include most anything they wanted.

Stravinsky's point that conscious limitations of art can paradoxically liberate the artist is well to keep in mind, but such limitations also have their price. The most important constraints imposed on Broadway by the popular tradition were the technical ones. Popular songs can be most expressive, and composers learned to make them dramatically effective as well, but their expressive and dramatic range is limited, first of all by their length and second by the musical languages to which they have recourse.

American popular songs are simple in form and are generally quite short. These features limit not so much what can be expressed, but to what degree it can be conveyed. It is vain to hope for the affective climaxes that one hears in the classical operas because there is not enough time to prepare them in a Broadway song. Mozart can prepare a climactic finale for twenty minutes, and Wagner for an entire act, but a theater song must make its point and quit within a very few minutes. Only by constructing musical relationships across the entire drama could Broadway composers create similar effects, and that level of composition was beyond all but a handful of the best musical plays of the tradition.

The tradition assimilated a number of different popular styles during the course of the century, but at its core was a rather simplified nineteenth-century Romanticism. Like its glorious ancestor, this style made expressive use of chromaticism and of the systematic delay of the cadence, but these were never developed to the extent heard in large Romantic classical works because of the limitations of popular taste and of the popular song form. Musical expressions and constructions based on melodic phrasing and motivic or thematic processes are common in Broadway songs, but extreme chromatic effects are not, and the tonal center is generally clear at any point. Composers were free to mix in elements of jazz and rock when those styles became popular, but they turned out to be useful only in certain types of dramatic situations.

That the Broadway tradition is in its roots and through much of its history a popular tradition, then, is a factor that has constrained the tradition in significant ways but has yet left room for achievement. The significance of the achievement can be seen in the resilience of the repertoire grown up over the last six decades and in the attraction that the tradition has had for such "serious" musicians as Gershwin, Bernstein, and Weill.

The popular nature of the tradition does not undermine the search for a real musical dramaturgy, although it may limit the scope of the dramaturgy. Certainly the composers themselves seemed to understand their role: Kern spoke of himself as the "musical clothier" of a dramatic situation,[15] and Rodgers and Hammerstein spent weeks and weeks discussing dramatic problems of organization before a single word or note was written. That Stephen Sondheim actually researched the historical and cultural setting of his *Pacific Overtures* (1976), as did Webber and Rice for their *Evita* (1979), indicates how much the dramatic acumen of the most serious composers has developed.

Yet, Richard Rodgers and Sondheim cannot be equated with Verdi and Wagner just because their ideals of musical drama are similar. There is an essential difference that lies not so much in whether there is success or failure as in what is attempted. The most compelling Broadway show has a certain sense of limited scope never heard in a masterwork of European opera. It is not that the show has failed; it simply did not try to do as much. Perhaps here the element of sophistication comes in at last. Paradoxically, it could be argued that such a show is more valuable than the second-rank opera of Bellini or Meyerbeer which sets higher artistic goals of much greater sophistication, but which fails to live up to them. Certainly many shows of Broadway hold the stage better.

An aesthetics of popular art is clearly wanted here. The small New England church, the Greek household vase, and "Greensleeves" have won high esteem for generations, but how are they to be compared to the Gothic cathedral, the temple sculpture, and the Dowland lute song?

The problem is reminiscent of certain ideas of Leonard Meyer about "value" and "greatness" which might offer at least a working solution.[16] His argument attempts to solve the difficulty musicians have when they recognize that a Chopin prelude seems to be a flawless and completely satisfying work, but one which cannot be compared with the Beethoven "Hammerklavier" Sonata. The Chopin, as perfect as it seems, simply does not attempt the same structural dimensions and content as the sonata. Yet no one derides the prelude for this inequity. Both have value because they both succeed in fulfilling the terms of their conceptions, but only the Beethoven piece is great, because its conception is great. Edward T. Cone argues similarly "that for fullest enjoyment we want the medium of an art to be saturated—used to the fullest extent in every dimension."[17] As with the short song forms of Broadway, what is at issue here is not what may be conveyed, but to what degree.

Broadway is worth criticizing because its best works can have this sort of value without attempting the dimension of the European operatic masterworks, what Francis Fergusson calls "the limited perfection of the minor dramatic genres."[18] The achievements are simpler and the expectations are smaller. The abiding popularity and undeniable position of these plays in American culture warrants a more serious look than they have been given in the past.

Any critical survey must be selective by nature. Because Broadway is an American tradition, one bias must be toward American works, until the most recent decades when the tradition becomes international.[19] So while Kurt Weill's *The Threepenny Opera* and Lionel Bart's *Oliver* are important works in Broadway's history, they do not originate in that tradition and so are set aside. In a similar vein, works which are important primarily because of some historical reason are not included unless they are musically valuable as well. Marc Blitzstein's *The Cradle Will Rock* and Galt MacDermott's *Hair* come to mind.

Even with these exclusions, too many plays remain to be discussed between two covers. The final list of musical plays to be discussed in detail has been drawn up to demonstrate not only the quality of dramatic achievement in the Broadway tradition but the variety of the achievement. The tradition has successfully adapted romantic novels, frame stories, Shakespeare plays, and classical myths. It has promoted religious experience in a theatrical setting, produced a morality play, and included the characteristics of various ethnic groups. All of these facets need to be included in the selection if the wide variety of dramatic achievement within the tradition is to be appreciated.

There are some plays whose quality so impressed their contemporary audiences that they influenced the course of the tradition in their own right. *Showboat* and *Oklahoma!* demanded their places for this reason. Others such as *Carousel* and *West Side Story* have been recognized by the rest of the world as worthy of presentation in their own languages, in their world fairs, and as part of operatic repertories, so that they required inclusion not by virtue of immediate recognition but by a more sustained admiration.

The rest were included because they turned a particular interest into drama very well, and because they represent certain key personalities of Broadway's history. Cole Porter's *Kiss Me, Kate* was neither the first nor the last to use a Shakespearean model, but it comes at the end of his long career and is by far his best show, and one which uses that model most explicitly. Like Porter, Frank Loesser wrote his own lyrics as well as music, and in *The Most Happy Fella*, for which he also adapted his own libretto, he realized one of the very few neglected musical plays of highest merit. The chapter on Lerner and Loewe includes two of their most famous plays, *My Fair Lady* and *Camelot*, because they both dramatize important western myths. George Gershwin's *Porgy and Bess* comes closest to the ideal of European opera. There are a number of plays using ethnic settings to choose from, but Bock's *Fiddler on the Roof* is the most famous and the first to make a dramatic issue of ethnic values.

The period of the last thirty years, being most recent, is most difficult to evaluate, and the choices were made with more an eye to qualities that make a play stand apart, with less confidence of esteem that will last for generations. Stephen Schwartz has had a good career and his *Godspell* is a dramatic presentation of a seemingly antidramatic subject. Hamlisch's *A Chorus Line* has a novel approach to plot, and its complete commercial success makes it difficult to ignore, like the historical dramas of Webber and Rice. Most problematic of all perhaps is the work of Stephen Sondheim, whose work has such astonishing variety that choosing a single play of his is bound to be a misrepresentation. His setting of a thrilling story in *Sweeney Todd*, however, offers dramatic problems and solutions that are particularly engaging. Finally, *Les Misérables* must find a place here if only for its heroic attempt to dramatize epic.

Some readers will be disappointed in the lack of any consistent attempt to fix the most "authentic" version of each play through an examination of original sources, orchestra parts, conductors' scores, and other documents. Apart from the simple consideration that any such attempt would expand the book beyond all practicality and usefulness, the fact is that judging authenticity, of any music but particularly theater music, is an enormously complex issue. Leaving aside the technical matters, there is the basic question of what is to be considered, in general terms, the "authentic" version, even if every different stage of creation could be reconstructed. Is it to include all the composer's songs for a play, including those later discarded with his consent? Should it be the show before out-of-town tryouts, or the one that opened in New York, after changes and cuts were made? What if later changes came about at a later date? The problem has been visited anew with a recent recording of Jerome Kern's landmark musical, *Show Boat*, which includes all the music Kern ever wrote for it, including about forty minutes that he and Oscar Hammerstein agreed had to go well before the play opened in New York.[20] In only two cases, *Porgy and Bess* and *Carousel*, has it been necessary to include concerns of origin and authenticity in these essays, since in only those two plays are essential critical matters affected by them. In all the others the quest for the authentic version has proved irrelevant. After all, the American musical theater is a living tradition. There is no need to authenticate any of these plays in order to justify their production today; on the contrary, these musicals live on despite cutting, orchestration simplified down to a single upright piano, and singing that ranges from the unbearable to the operatic. The best musical plays of Broadway clearly own qualities which transcend the particular versions in which they are performed. Those qualities are the concern of this survey.

For this reason, the illustrating musical examples are taken, with appropriate permission of course, from the standard published piano-vocal scores. These are the most accessible and most efficient documents of the music, and are therefore the sources of most contemporary productions.

All of the plays included in the study are well known, or indeed, renowned. Bentley's arguments about commercial art notwithstanding, continual admiration for a play sustained over generations seems more trustworthy than the esteem of an individual writer.

This is not to say that the selected plays are to be accepted as unqualified artistic successes. Certainly the most compelling moments in these plays warrant attention if the variety of dramatic achievement is to be understood, but none of these plays is without significant weaknesses or flaws. The evaluation of these flaws can be just as instructive, in terms of the overall assessment of the American music theater, as the analysis of the high points. The opposite perspectives of success and failure enhance an understanding of musical dramaturgy. Beyond the serious recognition of the value in the Broadway tradition, it is this sort of understanding that this book seeks to promote.

Chapter 2

First Maturity

> It is my opinion that the musical numbers should carry
> the action of the play and should be representative of the
> personalities of the characters who sing them.[1]

> *Jerome Kern*

In virtually every historical study of the American musical theater, *Show Boat* is recognized as an important landmark. It is the summit of Jerome Kern's career as a stage composer, and the first critical success of the young lyricist Oscar Hammerstein II, who would follow it with many more in the coming decades. The comments of Wilfred Sargeant, classical violinist turned New Yorker critic, in reviewing the 1954 revival by the New York City Opera, reflect the general consensus:

> The work is, of course, a masterpiece of its kind, and a much more genuine example of American musical theatre than most self-consciously American operas that I can recall. Its tunes remain entirely enchanting, and, as musical shows or light operas go, it has a very effective book—a far more effective one than, for example, that classic of the species "Die Fledermaus.[2]

The journalists, writing about particular performances, point to the outstanding individual characteristics of the show: the quality of the music, the lyrics, the realism of the plot, the unabashed American character. Serious historians of Broadway have a different reason that is more fundamental and yet subsumes all of the above characteristics. *Show Boat* is the first American musical that integrates the elements of a musical theater into a credible drama. The songs, the generous amount of instrumental music, the dancing, the crowd scenes, all arise from events in a rather serious plot. Nothing is extraneous.

The play grew out of the novel *Show Boat* by Edna Ferber, who although little remembered today was once a highly popular novelist. She wrote *Show Boat* after having spent some time living on an active showboat that played the Mississippi in the mid-1920s. The book was published in 1926 and immediately became a best seller. Jerome Kern, an avid rare book collector who liked to keep abreast of literary developments, read it and saw its possibilities for the musical theater at once. He spoke to Ferber about it in person after meeting her at the theater, secured the rights, and then interested Hammerstein in the project. Best of all, he convinced the redoubtable Florenz Ziegfeld to produce it.

In retrospect it seems that the composition of *Show Boat* came about as the result of a series of fortunate coincidences. No other Broadway composer with sufficient clout to begin such an outlandish project would have looked twice at the novel. Kern in the mid-1920s was the dean of Broadway composers, and although his plays immediately preceding *Show Boat* are as unremarkable as those of his contemporaries, except perhaps for the quality of their music, it is clear that he had a much loftier conception of what the popular musical stage could be. He found a kindred spirit and an enormous talent in Hammerstein, who was to become one of the foremost lyricists of the Broadway stage for the next thirty years. Hammerstein had had his share of frivolous musical comedies, but gained valuable experience with some of the luminaries of the 1920s Broadway theater: Vincent Youmans (*Wildflower* of 1923), Rudolf Friml (*Rose Marie* of 1924), Sigmund Romberg (*The Desert Song* of 1926), and with Kern himself (*Sunny* of 1925). Together they fashioned a vision of musical theater unique for its day.

The fashioning required a prodigious amount of work. The novel, a rambling piece that takes in five decades, two cities, and thousands of miles, had to be streamlined to fit the conventions of the musical theater. An entire decade and many characters were cut out; other characters were combined into a single stage character, and in general the cast "around the showboat is much more consistent than in the novel, in which they come and go realistically."[3]

This sort of patient adaptation indicates how well Kern and Hammerstein understood their craft. Operas in general have smaller casts than spoken plays, since the dramatic action revolves around singing characters, and singing takes up much more time than speaking. A small cast is a prerequisite of significant character development in a musical play.

Composer and lyricist labored with revisions and improvements for nearly twelve months, a length of time unheard of in the 1920s. It opened at the Ziegfeld Theater on December 27, 1927 and ran for 572 performances.

The achievement of *Show Boat* impresses not only on its own terms, which it continually must do in order to last, but also in view of the reigning traditions of musical theater in the 1920s. There were two principal genres of musical theater: musical comedy and operetta.[4] They were as different in construction, tone, and effect as could be, but they both failed to contribute a single lasting work for the stage for the same reason. They failed to present their audiences with credible drama.

The musical comedy that flourished on Broadway in the early decades of the century was a casual and happenstance affair. Constructed as it was from traditions of vaudeville and burlesque combined with some of the procedures of European operetta, a musical comedy was little more than a succession of songs, comedy routines, and dance numbers that as often as not had nothing to do with the progression of a story. If one was fortunate enough to encounter a plot, it was with rare exceptions a silly situation comedy without any dramatic complications that might interfere with the various acts. That the New York Times critic in 1927 described *Show Boat*, which seems quite straightforward today, as "crammed with plot" gives some idea of the norm.[5] And even when there was a reasonable plot, the collaborators often took no notice of it. Jerome Kern, from early on in his career, stood out as somewhat odd because he demanded to know the entire story of the play before he began to compose the songs for it.

Indeed, from 1915 to 1918 he composed a series of shows for the small Princess Theater which combined small casts and simple plots with the aim of achieving significant continuity between story and song. Here Kern's reputation was made. If the very occasional revivals of some of the better "Princess" musicals reveal the awkwardness and strains of an adolescent growth, perhaps most of all in the plots of Guy

Bolton, it is growth nonetheless. Kern's dramatic instinct would eventually result in *Show Boat*, but the Broadway outside the Princess was
burdened by stifling conventions and contract requirements, and they
forced Kern to revert to older production standards in the early 1920s.
Oscar Hammerstein recalled his collaboration with Kern on the musical *Sunny* in 1925 this way:

> Our job was to tell a story with a cast that had been assembled as
> if for a revue. Charles Dillingham, the producer, had signed Cliff
> Edwards, who sang songs and played the ukelele and was known
> as Ukelele Ike. His contract required that he do his specialty
> between ten o'clock and ten fifteen! So we had to construct our
> story in such a way that Ukelele Ike could come out and perform
> during that time and still not interfere with the continuity. In
> addition to Marilyn Miller, the star, there was Jack Donahue, the
> famous dancing comedian, and there was Clifton Webb and Mary
> Hay, who were a leading dance team of the time, Joseph Cawthorn,
> a star comedian, Esther Howard, another, Paul Frawley, the lead-
> ing juvenile. In addition to the orchestra in the pit we had also to
> take care of George Olsen's Dance Band on the stage.[6]

To be sure, *Sunny* was a hit, which suggests that those producers knew
something about public expectations. On the other hand, *Show Boat*
too was a hit, which perhaps indicates that audiences will not hesitate
to embrace good theater when they have the chance to experience it.

The more serious operettas of Victor Herbert, Rudolf Friml, and
Sigmund Romberg, all Europeans with classical training, offered the
coherent plot and musical integration that the musical comedy lacked,
but undermined any significant dramatic effect by removing the story far
away from the real experience of the audience. They are typically historical fictions or fairy tales set in exotic places, such as a European court or
the Sahara desert, and involve disguised heroes, mistaken identities, and
the like. In its tone the operetta parallels nineteenth-century melodrama,
which, according to Eric Bentley, was designed to arouse a little bit of
anxiety in the audience without direct confrontation or involvement:

> One can see which elements of melodrama aroused anxiety: the
> hideous happenings of the plot, the terrible dangers, the wicked-
> ness of the world and of the villain. How were these things kept

under control? By a remoteness and exoticism, both of geography and style, which told the spectator: we don't mean you.[7]

In short, audiences were fascinated but seldom moved. It is an interesting point that not a few of the lasting musicals of the 1940s and 1950s are also set in exotic environments: *South Pacific, Brigadoon*, and *Fiddler on the Roof* come immediately to mind. Yet these avoid the trap that claimed nearly all American operettas. The difference is this: though these latter plays may be set in far away, even mythical, places and times, the dramatic issues in them do not depend on the exotic at all, but derive from the commonest of experiences. How many have wrestled with the sort of social prejudice that confronts Nellie and Lt. Cable, with the choice between security and the ultimate risk of loving that Charlie Dalrymple must make, and with the generation-gap problems of Tevye? At least, sympathy for such characters comes easily. It is much more difficult to take so seriously Margot Bonvalet's dilemma in *The Desert Song*, when she agonizes over loving a disguised outlawed revolutionary whom she has never really met.

The quality of the music in both of these genres is really not at issue. Victor Herbert, Romberg, and Friml, as well as Kern, Gershwin, Rodgers, and others wrote many, many songs which long outlasted the shows that first presented them. They were picked up by arrangers and jazz musicians to be played again and again as standards. The failure was entirely dramatic, a failure of courage, really, on the part of composers, librettists, and producers to confront their audiences with real dramatic situations. "Tea for Two" is a fine song by Vincent Youmans which has attracted listeners for generations, but if that is the deepest expression of love that the young couple in *No, No, Nannette* can manage, then no one need be surprised that the audience comes away merely amused, at best. The viewers were never seriously engaged.

Show Boat has had at least one revival in New York City in each decade since its first performance, and countless revivals elsewhere. It has attracted the attention of even serious opera companies; in 1954 it was performed by the New York City Opera, with Julius Rudel conducting, and in 1983 by the Houston Grand Opera.

With the exception of the first one in 1932, each major revival has occasioned revisions of the play, and some of these have been significant.

The 1946 revival cut three scenes, added Jerome Kern's last composition "Nobody Else But Me," and replaced his motivically constructed prologue to Act I with a traditional medley overture composed by orchestrator Robert Russell Bennett. The song was dropped thereafter, but this 1946 version is generally the one licensed and performed today.

Critical assessment by journalists has varied little in the seventy-five-year history of the show. There is some consensus in the later decades that the dialogue is dated and that there is some awkwardness in the plot, especially at the end, but all writers point to the continuing freshness and appeal of the music.

The one part of the musical that was never changed in any of its major revivals is the first scene of the first act, and it is this scene that is Kern's and Hammerstein's best achievement in musical dramaturgy. The musical theater has precious little time to establish its characters and main plot premises because musical expression takes up so much more time than speech. This scene's significant success is its integration of plot and character exposition with dramatic action, so that in barely fifteen minutes the audience is introduced to five main characters, three conflicts, two social norms, and a love story which is already developed in the music. All this is unified by a frame defined by the music.

The curtain rises to reveal the river levee at a Mississippi town crowded by black stevedores who are stacking bales of cotton. The showboat *Cotton Blossom* is moored upstage. The opening "crowd scene" was virtually required by the conventions of the 1920s; this one, however, is boldly unconventional in its immediate portrayal of racial inequity. After a brief introduction based on a chromatic leitmotif associated with the sheriff Vallon, the tempo becomes animato and the stevedores begin to sing:[8]

Ex. 2-1 Kern and Hammerstein, *Show Boat*, "Opening" (No. 1), mm. 13–20.

The musical setting for this uncompromising lyric is as simple as could be, employing mainly tonic and subdominant harmony, and yet Kern manages to evoke an ethnic flavor in the melody by recalling the "gapped" scale, missing the seventh step, on the word "Mississippi." The texture is enlivened somewhat when the women's chorus (the "gals") joins the men's with a contrasting section in G-sharp minor based on the same motives. The men sing a counterpoint of a work call motive beneath.

A cynical listener could well remark that the music does not come close to expressing the sentiment of the lyric. The melody is set in E major and its rhythm seems just too cheerful. This criticism must be dismissed, however, when the original tune returns, now sung by both men and women. Kern reharmonizes the refrain with a chromatic bass, whose "blue" sixth and seventh steps not only heighten the ethnic flavor of the chorus but express the black community's feeling of resignation about its position. This reharmonization is all the more effective for having been denied on the first hearing.

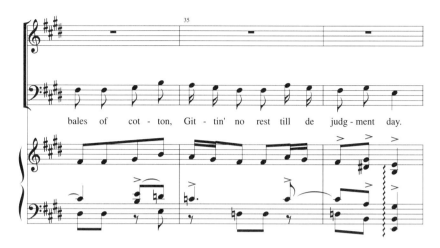

Ex. 2-2 Kern and Hammerstein, *Show Boat*, "Opening" (No. 1),
mm. 29–36.

The first musical section of the scene then concludes with another motive emphasizing the gapped scale (Ex. 2-3).

At this point the orchestra plays under a brief dialogue, in which the audience is introduced to Steve, the leading actor of the showboat troupe; Pete, the villianous engineer; and Queenie, the black cook. The orchestra plays a leitmotif which stands for Julie Laverne, the leading actress, even though she does not appear. The rationale for this is that Steve and Pete will soon quarrel over Julie, but on the whole, rapid introduction and alternation of motives in this interlude is rather clumsy.

Ex. 2-3 Kern and Hammerstein, *Show Boat*, "Opening" (No. 1),
mm. 37–44.

The crowd on stage is then increased by the entrance of a white women's chorus playing the local town beauties ("mincing misses" in the libretto) and a white men's chorus of "town beaux." The men begin with this salute. The slower rhythm and smoother lyricism of the tune makes a clear differentiation between the racial groups, which of course is Kern's purpose, but the new music is not without connections to the old. Clearly, the motive in measure 93 recalls the first black chorus tune (mm. 13–14) both in rhythm and in shape, and the sixth step of

Ex. 2-4 Kern and Hammerstein, *Show Boat*, "Opening" (No. 1),
mm. 93–101.

the scale is emphasized ("bevy") because of the following rest, again recalling the gapped scale so characteristic of the opening chorus. The women respond with the same tune, then modulate to F major, the mediant key to D-flat, the same relationship constructed by the E–G-sharp modulation of the black chorus.

When the music returns to D-flat, the beaux introduce a new melody.

Ex. 2-5 Kern and Hammerstein, *Show Boat*, "Opening" (No. 1), mm. 118–124.

Here the dotted rhythms so characteristic of the black chorus are reintroduced, but even the more lyrical first two measures recall the *Cotton Blossom* motive in its shape and emphasis on the sixth step of the scale.

These motivic connections are not frivolous. They make possible the climactic joining of the four singing groups that finishes the choral number of the first scene. As the white people sing in anticipation of the evening's show, Kern adds the black choruses singing a work call outlining a dissonant E minor seventh over a pedal of A. Finally all the

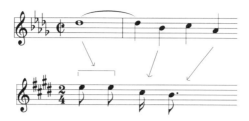

Fig. 2-1 Comparison of motives from Ex. 2–3 and Ex. 2–5.

singers are united by the *Cotton Blossom* motive. The ironic lyric maintains the distinction between the two social groups, but the ensemble makes musical sense because of Kern's careful preparation of the motivic material. In an audible way, the two groups, black and white, have shared the same material throughout.

The next section of this opening scene shows much less musical integration; its function is to introduce the main characters and conflicts as efficiently as possible. Hammerstein fashions the scene around a typical arrival of the show boat to a new river town. There is a parade and, once a crowd has gathered, a short presentation of the principal actors. This ploy familiarizes the audience with most of the main characters at a single stroke: Captain Andy, the troup leader; Parthy Ann, his shrewish wife; Julie, the leading lady; Frank and Ellie Chipley, the comic actors

Ex. 2-6 Kern and Hammerstein, *Show Boat*, "Opening" (No. 1),
mm. 142–149.

and dancers. In the course of the scene, the quarrel between Pete and
Steve over Julie erupts suddenly, and Pete is fired from troupe, and
leaves swearing revenge. Except for one chorus number for the admiring

townspeople ("Captain Andy"), the music here functions as a prop: the march of the parade, the dance music for the short presentation.

Two characters remain to be seen: Magnolia, Captain Andy's daughter, and Gaylord Ravenal, an aristocratic river gambler who will soon join the showboat troupe. They are introduced singly, in such a way that the audience instinctively and immediately recognizes them as the principals of the play.

Magnolia is only mentioned in dialogue at first, and, more importantly, is associated at once with a piece of music. A simple tune, played on the piano, is heard coming offstage from the interior of the *Cotton Blossom.*[9] One of the awestruck children asks of Parthy Ann:

Girl: Is that your little girl playing the piano?

Parthy: Yep—ain't so little any more—eighteen this comin' August.[10]

This occurs before the parade and quarrel. Shortly after Pete's departure, Ravenal strolls onstage to the accompaniment of a new theme in the orchestra, which is soon interrupted by the chromatic sheriff's motive when Vallon appears. He and Ravenal converse:

Vallon: Back in town, Gay?

Ravenal: For a short stay.

Vallon: Can't be more than twenty-four hours, you know.

Ravenal: Give me time, can't you? I haven't been twenty-four hours stepping off the gangplank to this wharf, have I? . . . I can get on just as quickly.

Vallon: No offense, Gay. Jest though I'd remind you in case of trouble—it'd be terrible to have you locked up—all the purty gals on the river front'd be cryin' their eyes out. Where you aim to go from here?

Ravenal: Who cares? Who cares where I go?

Vallon: Seegar?

(As he proffers it, Ravenal takes it, sniffs at it and raises his eyebrows disdainfully).

Ravenal: What did you call it?

Vallon: Seegar!

Ravenal: Optimist![11]

This exchange sketches Ravenal's character very quickly. He has no roots and is in some kind of legal trouble; he is also handsome, even dashing, and has aristocratic tastes. When Vallon leaves, Ravenal begins to sing a song which plays on these characteristics and begins the most important dramatic development of the first scene.

Ravenal begins by singing two four-bar periods which make up an antecendent phrase of a melody.

Ex. 2-7 Kern and Hammerstein, *Show Boat*, "Opening" (No. 1), mm. 351–358.

The harmonization of this antecedent could hardly be simpler, limited as it is to tonic and dominant harmony. The consequent phrase, which begins with exactly the same melodic gesture, takes quite a different turn.

Ex. 2-8 Kern and Hammerstein, *Show Boat*, "Opening" (No. 1),
mm. 359–370.

The plain authentic cadence in the third measure is now turned into a
more expressive deceptive cadence (V–vi), adding an urgent continuity
that requires an extra four-bar period at the end of the tune for its proper resolution. The antecedent phrase of eight bars is therefore balanced
by a convincing consequent of twelve. This added weight at the end

causes the listener to doubt Ravenal's rhetorical queries at the outset and to pay more attention to his wondering "where's the mate for me?" A change of character not at all implied by the lyric has been suggested quite firmly by the music.

Ravenal's musings are interrupted by the sound of a piano coming from the *Cotton Blossom*. The audience knows the tune already, and who is playing it, but Ravenal, ignorant of this, turns to listen. The first

Ex. 2-9 Kern and Hammerstein, *Show Boat*, "Opening" (No. 1), mm. 370–381.

encounter with Magnolia is made. The little tune is set in G major, in subdominant relation to Ravenal's melody. At this point, the orchestra takes up the phrase and effects a very distant modulation to F-sharp major (mm. 377–381). This cadence is turned into a dominant and Ravenal resumes his singing, taking up the piano motive in the key of B minor, the relative minor of his original D major, and immediately enters upon an expressive descending melodic sequence.

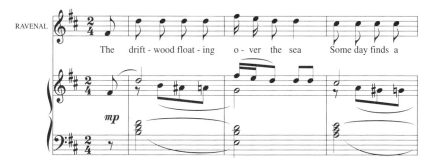

Ex. 2-10 Kern and Hammerstein, *Show Boat*, "Opening" (No. 1), mm. 386–394.

The sequence never really leaves the key of B minor, but since it is the descending minor scale that is heard, the pitches used are the same ones of Ravenal's original key of D. The piquant lowering of the A-sharp to A-natural in the very last phrase thus makes explicit what was already implied: a return to the local tonic.

Kern has turned again to the same procedure he used in Ravenal's first address, and made it more expansive. The harmonization of the orchestral transition and Ravenal's new phrases is so startling in comparison to the relatively simple harmonies heard earlier that the expression of his true feelings about the conflict of freedom and love is overwhelming and unmistakable. Moreover, because of the motivic connection with the little piano tune, the audience realizes the cause and solution of these longings even before he realizes them himself.

The A major chord, acting as dominant, makes the transition back to Ravenal's original theme for the song's conclusion.

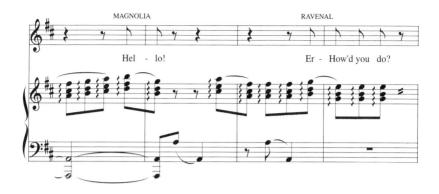

Ex. 2-11 Kern and Hammerstein, Showboat, "Opening" (No. 1), mm. 395–409.

Now the cadence in the third measure (m. 396–397) is made more expressive than ever by the use of the deceptive in minor (V-VI^7), undermining any remaining allegiance to the freedom about which he sings.

Ravenal is taken aback by her address; she seems naive, not knowing that she should wait for the gentleman to speak first. The interlude music behind their dialogue is neutral, except for a brief recapitulation of the piano tune, the modulation to the leading tone key by the strings, and the following sequence in minor, all of which reinforces the musical connections between the two characters. The audience learns that Magnolia wishes she were an actress, since actresses may make believe they are various exciting characters. She starts to leave because she realizes that she and Ravenal have not been properly introduced, but Ravenal suggests that they make believe, as actors do, that they have been introduced and that they have fallen in love at first sight!

Ex. 2-12 Kern and Hammerstein, *Show Boat*, "Make Believe" (No. 2),
mm. 5–37.

In its form, use of chromaticism, and melodic sequences, the song is a typical example of a popular song of Tin Pan Alley. Again, the musical interest is directed forward, toward the end, this time by careful placing of chromatic harmony. The first phrase has no trace of chromaticism; the second ("Others find . . .") introduces a touch, mostly in the interest of setting up an important dominant chord at the end. The emotional intensity is suddenly and forcefully increased at the beginning of the third phrase, however, when the opening motive is set with diminished harmony (VI+) instead of the vague tonic that began the song. This phrase too ends with chromatic alterations, but the most explicit chromatic writing is saved for the fourth and final phrase. The climactic lyric is set to rising chromatic lines both in bass and in the inner parts. The song ends with the same melody with which it began, now retaining its diminished harmony.

This emphasis on the end of the song encourages the audience to take Ravenal's last words more seriously than the first, as before in his soliloquy. Clearly his expressions of love are more than playacting, more than "make believe." To say so explicitly, as he does, however, is a breach of etiquette, and so even as he makes the cadence to his song, the music slips into a mild waltz and he begins to apologize. Magnolia, in her first musical entrance, however, interrupts his apology, finishing his melody by reminding him that they were only pretending to be

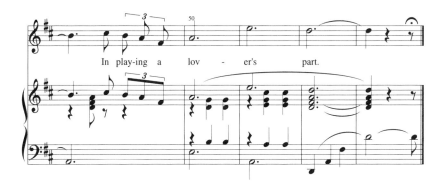

Ex. 2-13 Kern and Hammerstein, *Show Boat*, "Make Believe" (No. 2), mm. 37–53.

lovers. In this she shows a maturity far beyond her years. With consummate grace she has saved Ravenal, who as an aristocrat prides himself on his sense of propriety, from a very embarrassing situation. She relieves the situation further by elaborating on the joys of pretense, to a much lighter theme than Ravenal's waltz.

Ex. 2-14 Kern and Hammerstein, *Show Boat*, "Make Believe (No. 2),
mm. 53–69.

This theme recalls the music of the off-stage piano both in its melodic shape and its placement in the key subdominant to the principal key of "Make Believe." The music, then, succeeds in maintaining her ingenue character while resolving this difficult situation, since the little piano tune was her introduction to the action.

Ravenal, relieved, echoes her sentiments by repeating the new theme. This is the sort of quick, reflexive agreement that always occurs when two people are trying to paper over an obvious faux pas. The music now moves into a disjointed, accompanied recitative texture in which Magnolia reaffirms the rational basis for make believe. The real purpose of the passage seems to be to return to the original "Make Believe" tune, this time set a semitone higher than before.[12]

The recapitulation of "Make Believe" not only rounds out the form of this musical section but also fulfills a dramatic necessity by allowing Magnolia to offer her own love in the same terms as has Ravenal. These sentiments, of course, grow logically out of her excuses, but as before, the music contradicts the characters' professions of "make believe." After Magnolia sings the first two phrases (same as Ravenal in Ex. 2-12), Ravenal sings the third, and finally, both sing together in the fourth phrase, the one with the most intense rising chromaticism.

Ex. 2-15 Kern and Hammerstein, *Show Boat*, "Make Believe" (No. 2), mm. 111–119.[13]

During the climax of the chromatic progression, the two break into parts, and Magnolia rises to the high G, the highest sustained note of this section.

Although this duet is the center of the opening scene, it is not its conclusion. As soon as the lovers have finished singing, Vallon returns to escort Ravenal away for a conversation with the local magistrate. At the same time, Joe, a black stevedore, enters carrying a sack of flour. Magnolia, entirely enchanted, asks Joe whether he saw the young "gentleman" and he allows that he has seen many like him on the river. She runs off to tell her best friend Julie, and Joe muses to himself about what he has seen:

> Joe: Better ask de ol' man river what he thinks. He knows all 'bout dem boys . . . He knows all 'bout ever'thin.[14]

The introduction of Joe as the Everyman figure of the play is awkward perhaps, but his musical number is a superb conclusion to the first scene of *Show Boat*. His introductory quatrain is set to exactly the same music as the very beginning of the scene ("Niggers all work on de Mississippi . . ."), but the words are different, the tempo is greatly slowed, and with only strings accompanying, the tune seems quite transformed to the point that many would not recognize it as a recapitulation (Ex. 2-16). This is followed by the famous refrain (see Fig. 2-2, p. 49). The middle section of the refrain again recasts music from the opening number, this time the "gals'" song which is set in the mediant key.[15] This passage is dignified much more than its first occurrence by the slower tempo and by the transition back toward the tonic of C major. The moment of modulation (m.32, "jail") is made clear by the D minor chord, negating both the leading tone and supertonic of the mediant key of E minor, and is always dramatized by the singer. During the last phrase of the refrain, Joe is joined by the chorus of stevedores that opened the scene. Now the reference to that opening becomes explicit in the lyric:

> Joe: Niggers all work on de Mississippi
> Niggers all work while de white folks play.
> Pullin' dem boats from de dawn to sunset,
> Gitten' no rest till de Judgment Day
>
> Men: Don't look up an' don't look down,
> You don't dast make de white boss frown;
> Bend yo' knees an' bow yo' head,
> an pull dat rope until yo're dead. (etc.)

Ex. 2-16 Kern and Hammerstein, *Show Boat*, "Ol' Man River" (No. 3), mm. 25–32.

The music then returns to the refrain of "Ol' Man River" for a climactic choral rendition.

This song was almost instantly acclaimed by critics as the leitmotif for the entire play, and indeed it is used in just such a manner throughout the remainder. Its first occurrence, however, by recalling the essential themes and even the same performers from the play's beginning, provides a convincing structural close to this lengthy and dramatically ambitious opening scene. The musical recapitulations in "Ol' Man River," however, are not just a structural rounding for the scene, but constitute yet another dramatic development. Each theme is transformed in a simple yet effective way. The unavoidable impression at the scene's end is that although the love match is to be the primary dramatic focus, social injustice will provide a most serious backdrop for that story and affect its course in important ways.

Even if the song had not been placed in the larger musical context so effectively, "Ol' Man River" would still be counted as the most important musical achievement of the play. Certainly a number of technical details contribute to this impression: the mild syncopation in the main motive, the emphasis again on the sixth step, which gives the tune such an ethnic flavor, and the weak beat chords in the winds, which effectively paint the swell of the Mississippi. The real power of the song, however, derives from its overall melodic design, without which these details would seem like mere decorations.

Kern's melody is a triumph over the standard form for an American popular song, a form that has survived to some extent to the present day: A A B A. The advantages of such a form are immediately obvious; there is some repetition and some contrast. It is really an elaboration of the centuries-old ternary form (A B A). For dramatic uses, however, the form has one clear disadvantage, in that the song must end with the same music with which it began. In other words, a melodic idea conceived as a beginning must also function as an ending. In many examples less fortunate than "Ol' Man River" the effect is one of a static or even antidramatic emotion.

Clearly there must be some adjustment in the final phrase, and such adjustments were part of the expert songwriter's craft. Richard Rodgers often solved this problem by an extension of the phrase. Here is an example from Oklahoma!.

fix. *etc.*

I'm jist a fool when lights are low, I cain't be pris-sy and

quaint I ain't the type that c'n faint

Ex. 2-17 Rodgers and Hammerstein, *Oklahoma!*, "I Can't Say No",
mm. 22–29, 54–77.

The fourth phrase, based on the same melodic idea as the first, is more
than twice as long. The extension begins when the melodic course to
the fifth degree of the scale is delayed, first by changing the harmony so
that the tune goes up only to the fourth degree, and then by chromatic
elaborations on the notes around the fifth degree. This extension intensifies the comic effect of the song by making Ado Annie seem more flus-
tered and unstable than ever, because the chromaticism makes the
music seem unstable. More important, the extension turns what would
be a disappointing return into a climax. The dramatic development of
the character has moved forward in the face of a form that should com-
pel retreat.

Kern's solution is quite different from the device of extending the
final phrase. Instead, he incorporates into his melodic design subtle
changes which produce a climax in the final phrase without giving up
any sense of balanced proportion (see Fig. 2-2).

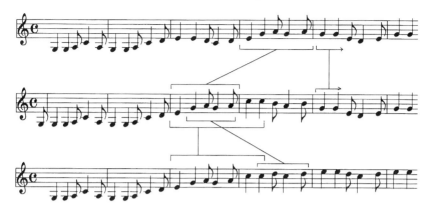

Fig. 2-2 Diagram comparing the first, second, and fourth phrases of
Kern and Hammerstein's "Ol' Man River."

The first phrase has a typical arch contour, rising a major ninth from
G up to A, the sixth degree of the scale. Quite untypical of a popular
melody is the motivic consistency of the phrase; every measure has
exactly the same rhythmic pattern until the cadence on the low C. The
second phrase, which is supposed to echo the first one according to
the A A B A pattern, does indeed sound the same. The diagram makes
clear, however, that Kern has shifted the fourth measure of the first
phrase to become the third measure of the second phrase. Thus, what
the listener takes to be the peak of the first phrase occurs earlier, and
this makes possible the continuation up to the high C on "soon forgotten." The subtlety of this alteration in the melody is such that one
barely notices any change at all. It is made possible by the motivic consistency, so that one measure seems so easily substituted for another.
The listener, already familiar with the melodic course up to the high A
in the first phrase, takes it as a matter of course in the second, even
though it is earlier. The original peak of the contour is replaced by a
smooth continuation that achieves an even higher peak at the same
point in time.

After the B section, or "release" (Ex. 2-16), the main melody returns.
Again the high A is reached by the third measure, and again the high C
seems to be the peak in the fourth. But in his most imaginative and yet
logical stroke yet, Kern does not reverse the contour; rather, he continues the upward motion to a high E and makes the final cadence on the
high C rather than the low one.

The climactic moment of "Ol' Man River" is generated from within, made possible by the extremely rare, if not unique, motivic consistency within each phrase. In this way Kern overcomes the inherent antidramatic nature of the form without doing away with it.

So ends the first scene of *Show Boat*. There are a number of other fine musical moments in the play, but Kern and Hammerstein never again attempt musical-dramatic integration on such a large scale. It is important to note, and characteristic of the American popular stage, that the one tragic moment of the first act, the dismissal of Julie and Steve on a miscegenation charge, has no operatic setting. There is only a response by the black chorus, a brief verse of "Misery," a lament which was cut down during tryouts. It will be a long time before Broadway musicians succeed in setting that sort of serious scene to music.

The remainder of the plot in the first act carries forward the love story, until the finale concludes with the wedding of Ravenal and Magnolia, attended by townspeople with great musical celebration. The second act, whose story takes place largely away from the *Cotton Blossom*, has been criticized on several counts. The plot concerns Ravenal's gambling problems, his general decline, and his eventual desertion of Magnolia and Kim, their daughter. There is no musical expression for this dissolution. Magnolia goes on to an acting career in her own right. Events bring her back to the *Cotton Blossom* for the finale, to be reunited by a series of coincidences with all her old acquaintances from the first act. Most improbably, Ravenal also appears and the old couple is reconciled at the play's end. Even Miles Kreuger, whose admiration for *Show Boat* produced a monograph study, finds little credibility in this finale:

> There is simply no way to rationalize the return of Ravenal. It is clearly an immature concession to musical comedy convention that in days to come Hammerstein himself would help abolish. It is very likely that, had *Show Boat* been adapted for the stage one decade later, Hammerstein would have adhered to Miss Ferber's elimination of the gambler and not permitted him to reappear.[16]

The weakness of the second act is underscored by the lack of new musical material. Only one dramatic number, "Why Do I Love You?", occurs after intermission. The remainder of the music consists of reprises, incidental music, and songs which might be called "prop songs."

A prop song is one which is sung because the character finds himself in a situation which demands or accommodates singing. It might be Don Giovanni serenading a lover, or Adelaide leading the Hot Box Girls at the local club. These songs are part of the scenery, like props, quite distinct from songs which are expressions of a character's emotions, and for which the operatic suspension of disbelief obtains. These appear quite frequently in European operas, and often the composer is at pains to show that the meaning of the character's singing is different. In *The Marriage of Figaro*, Susanna plays a guitar (with pizzicato accompaniment from the pit orchestra) while Cherubino sings his canzonet to the Countess, and Don Giovanni must play a mandolin when singing his second act serenade. Verdi creates a strong-beat, popular orchestral texture for the drinking song in the first act of *Otello*. These devices indicate that the character may no longer be expressing himself but is performing a song as part of the story.

The best example of the pure prop song in *Show Boat* is "After the Ball" which Magnolia sings as part of a night club act in Chicago. There is nothing in the music which further defines her character, emphasizes her emotional state, or brings the action along. She sings because singing is the action. To be sure, the choice of "After the Ball," a tremendously popular song by Charles K. Harris written at the turn of the century, was fortuitous for an audience in 1927, for it was assured of being immediately recognized and yet nostalgic. But these are sentiments of the audience, not of Magnolia.

In other cases, the distinction between what a character sings as a prop song and what he or she really feels is not so clear. In the first act, "Can't Help Lovin' Dat Man" is introduced as Julie's favorite song, purportedly a black folk song. In this sense it is a prop song; it is like a stage prop. However, the lyrics of this "folk song" reflect her own situation quite closely. She loves Steve, an untalented, rather lazy sort, in spite of herself. The same analysis would apply to "Bill" in the second act. This song is performed as part of a night club rehearsal, but in another sense Julie, who by this time has been deserted by Steve, is singing about herself in truth.

Despite such subtleties, an act of a musical that contains a high proportion of such prop songs cannot have the dramatic impact that operatic expression is supposed to have. Even in the ambiguous cases such as those mentioned, the expressive power of such songs must be weakened, because the audience can never be sure of how much of the sentiment belongs to the character.

Given the wide admiration that *Show Boat* has sustained, not only upon its opening in 1927 but through its first revival in 1932 and in the following decades, it is a wonder that this musical did not effect an instant reform of musical theater practice. Yet the next decade reveals only one work that seems to have learned some of the lessons taught by *Show Boat* well enough to survive—*Porgy and Bess*, and many would argue that Gershwin's magnum opus really stands outside the Broadway tradition. It is more puzzling still, considering that the teachers of the lesson, Jerome Kern and Oscar Hammerstein II, continued to work both separately and together and yet did not see such achievement again. There were innovations of the 1930s, to be sure, in the area of musical satire, such as Gershwin's *Of Thee I Sing* (1931), and in Weill's and Blitzstein's politically oriented works later in the decade. But in these the political themes dominated, and so did not last beyond the memory of their relevant targets.

One explanation often offered is that the Depression discouraged "serious" musicals because, in view of the conditions, audiences did not want to hear them. The financial constraints in turn discouraged producers from backing innovations and experiments, and it is certainly true that ticket prices were lower and runs shorter than in the 1920s. But the satirical musicals thrived on innovation and were quite successful, and *Porgy and Bess* was staged in the depths of the Depression (1935). Lehman Engel, considering what he regards as the pre-history of the mature American musical, has a deeper explanation:

> During these first forty years of *new* musicals in this country, men of enormous and fresh talent composed some of their best music and/or lyrics but, lacking models, what they accomplished, though successful for a time, is unfortunately unreproduceable today.[17]

It took a long time to learn the lessons of *Show Boat* simply because the lessons are so difficult. Remembering that even the most unpretentious types of operas are collaborative efforts, and remembering the failure rates of even the greatest opera composers, it seems less surprising that the fragile though real achievement of *Show Boat* was not repeated for some time, even by Kern and Hammerstein. There are so many things that must fall into place just right, and so many types of mature experience that must be coordinated.

The influence of *Show Boat* was perhaps subliminal or subconscious, but there is no doubt that members of the younger generation of stage composers, especially George Gershwin and Richard Rodgers, were impressed by the play, for it revealed what the Broadway stage could create if given the right materials and appropriate vision. It established a new set of dramatic ideals, ideals only approximated in the 1930s, but realized again and again thereafter.

Chapter 3
_____

America's Folk Opera

I think the music is so marvelous—I really don't believe I
wrote it.[1]

George Gershwin

By one of those curious coincidences of history, George Gershwin
was inspired to compose *Porgy and Bess* at about the same time and
in just the same way that Jerome Kern got his idea for *Show Boat*. After
a trying rehearsal of his newest musical comedy *Oh, Kay!* in the fall of
1926, Gershwin tried to fall asleep by reading DuBose Heyward's recent
novel, *Porgy*. Instead, as Heyward's wife Dorothy recounted later, he
"read himself wide awake" and became enthralled with the dramatic
prospects of the story. By four o'clock in the morning the composer was
writing to Heyward, inquiring if he might be interested in turning *Porgy*
into an opera.[2]

DuBose Heyward was an early figure in the Southern Renascence of
American literature and the foremost author of the so-called Charleston
writers.[3] *Porgy* was his first novel, published in 1925, and ultimately his
best known work. It portrays a black community in Charleston during
a summer around the turn of the century. The principal character,
Porgy, a crippled beggar who transports himself in a goat-drawn cart,
was modeled after a somewhat notorious figure of Heyward's native

Charleston known as "Goat Sammy." The plot of the book is extremely loose, "seemingly little more than a series of vignettes in structure."[4] One of its most unusual features is the recurrence of songs and spirituals sung by the community at large. For Heyward, these songs were the most economical means to his end of expressing the collective spirit of the community:

> The spiritual said everything for him [the black man] that he could not say in the new language that he found here—awe in the presence of death—his racial terror of being left alone—his escape from bondage into the new heaven—everything.[5]

It could have been these spirituals that attracted Gershwin, or perhaps Heyward's apparent success in getting at the heart of the black community, for Gershwin had already shown strong interest in black culture. In 1922, as part of a revue he was writing for *George White's Scandals*, he composed a twenty-minute one-act music drama called *Blue Monday*, with a libretto by G. B. "Buddy" DeSylva. The story, set in Harlem, involves two young men vying for the love of a woman and ends with the woman shooting her lover on suspicion of infidelity. The number was roundly criticized and White withdrew it after a single performance. A revival by Paul Whiteman in 1925 under the title *135th Street* proved no more successful. The critical consensus is that Gershwin, trying to set a soap opera libretto, had too little experience in serious dramatic composition.[6]

Despite Gershwin's and Heyward's initial enthusiasm for the new project, there was a hiatus of nine years between Gershwin's first reading of *Porgy* and the premiere of the opera in Boston in September 1935. The first obstacle was Dorothy Heyward, a playwright with several works to her credit, who told her astonished husband that she had already begun to turn the novel into a play, which eventually became a successful production of Broadway's Theatre Guild. This seemed to upset Gershwin not in the least. Dorothy recalls, "It was a great moment when George said there was plenty of room for both play and opera. And plenty of time. He wanted to spend years in study before composing his opera."[7] The last statement is no polite assurance on Gershwin's part. His detached estimation of his own talents and of his own music is a characteristic that recurs in almost all Gershwin biographical writing, and in 1926 the failure of *Blue Monday*, his only other attempt at serious music drama, could not have been far from his mind.

A second obstacle was Gershwin's own busy career. The late 1920s saw him engaged to write a series of musical comedies for the production team of Alex Aarons and Vinton Freedley, along with his brother Ira as lyricist and Guy Bolton as librettist.

> At first, it was the producers' intention to have these shows follow the bright, witty pattern of the old Princess Theatre attractions, only, according to Guy Bolton, on a larger scale. . . . Despite these intentions, the shows soon became star vehicles rather than closely coordinated book-and-music shows.[8]

However, a much more significant series of Gershwin musical plays opened in 1930, in collaboration with librettists George S. Kaufman and Morrie Ryskind, beginning with *Strike Up the Band*, and continuing with *Of Thee I Sing* (1931) and *Let'em Eat Cake* (1933). These are often called "satirical operettas," and in these works Gershwin makes a significant advance toward integrating the music with the story.

The most successful of the three was *Of Thee I Sing*. A story about a fictitious political campaign and presidential administration in which the main issue is "Love," the play successfully lampooned "hush-hush scandals, nonsensical debates, party politics, under-the-counter deals, political campaigns, and ridiculous bids for votes."[9] The play is undoubtedly an important landmark in the history of the American musical, running for 441 performances at the Music Box Theater, winning the 1932 Pulitzer Prize for Drama, becoming the first musical comedy to be published as a book, and attracting praise from all quarters for its musical and dramatic innovations. Despite all this, it has not survived in the repertoire, and critics are equally agreed about the reason, best explained by Lehman Engel:

> In *Of Thee I Sing* (1931) most of the comedy comes out of contemporary political situations. It worked well enough in its own time to win the Pulitzer Prize. Today it is meaningless, and the show, because it is built squarely on comedy, cannot be revived. It is significant that—and this is surely an important indication of modern-day artistry—the songs, *including* the lyrics, are not dated. The lyrics are universal and therefore enduring. Only the "comic" dialogue is entirely dated, and *Of Thee I Sing*, once funny because of it, is now impossible to revive because of it.[10]

Because of these shows, Gershwin did not begin work on *Porgy and Bess* until 1933. In retrospect, however, the delay must be considered most fortuitous, and the time between the initial inspiration and his actual composition well spent, for surely the satirical operettas constituted the most important part of the "study" he told DuBose Heyward that he wished to make. It should not be forgotten, too, that Gershwin was only twenty-eight years old when he read the novel, and that the gain in artistic maturity in those busy years was probably significant. Indeed, Stanley Green sees Gershwin's compositional oeuvre as an uninterrupted progression that, had he not died in 1937 of a brain tumor, had unlimited promise:

> His entire career had been the most steady, step-by-step advance of any theatre composer. There was some overlapping, but it is remarkable that his rise was so chronologically systematic—from revues (1920–1924), to musical comedies (1924–1930), to satirical comic operas (1931–1933), to an American folk-opera (1935).[11]

Gershwin himself seems to have realized that *Porgy and Bess* was to be his most important composition to date, representing an unprecedented attempt by a Broadway composer to write a serious music drama. As Heyward converted *Porgy* from stage play to opera libretto, along with certain lyric contributions from Ira Gershwin,[12] George spent eleven months composing the music (from February 1934 to January 1935), and nine more laborious months orchestrating it (from January to September 1935), a prodigious length of concentrated effort for any Broadway composer.[13] Because he refused to have the opera done in blackface, black professional singers were recruited from all over the country. There was even a special rehearsal in order to test the orchestrations, an aspect of Gershwin's compositions that had attracted criticism, and still does. Irving Kolodin observed the intense preparations and wrote:

> Watching this American folk-opera grow to perfected performance as a theatre work through months of careful rehearsal aimed to unify the drama and the music, the singing and the acting, has been an illuminating experience to a musician accustomed to the perfunctory and uncorrelated rehearsal generally accorded to the productions prepared for the conventional opera.[14]

After a triumphant tryout at the Colonial Theatre in Boston on September 20, 1935, the Theatre Guild presented *Porgy and Bess* to Broadway at the Alvin Theater on October 10, 1935, exactly eight years after the premiere of *Porgy* the stage play.

Except for an intensely symbolic analysis by Wilfrid Mellers,[15] most serious dramatic criticism of *Porgy and Bess* has been blunted and forestalled by preoccupation with three other matters.

The first is a concern over exactly what is the "authentic" version of the opera. This is a relatively recent concern, brought about by a history of revival that recorded various cut versions and spurred by a steadily growing appreciation of the opera's value. The first revival, a very successful production for Broadway by Cheryl Crawford in 1942, deleted many of the recitatives. Subsequent revivals in the 1950s restored much of this music but often altered the order of numbers given in Gershwin's piano-vocal score published in 1935. Thus, when in 1976 Lorin Maazel and the Cleveland Orchestra recorded all the music in Gershwin's original 1935 score, and the Houston opera produced a "complete" stage version, these events were hailed as events that, for the first time, revealed the true greatness of the opera.

As is often the case with matters of authenticity, however, especially in opera, the issue is rarely so simple. Ironically, the original production at the Alvin, under Gershwin's constant and direct supervision, was cut. Rouben Mamoulian, the production's director, wrote three years later that "*Porgy and Bess* as performed in New York was almost forty-five minutes shorter than the original score," which was sent to the publisher six months in advance of the premiere.[16] Excluded were the opening piano solo, known as the Jazzbo Brown music, the "Buzzard Song," Maria's denunciation of Sportin' Life in Act II, much of Porgy's solo and the following trio in Act III, and many other snippets from the score.[17]

Why did Gershwin cut music from his original score? Was the opera cut to make it conform to the normal length of a Broadway show, as *Show Boat* was, or were there deeper dramatic reasons? Was Gershwin convinced that they would improve the opera, or simply increase its chances for profit? Ewen writes, unfortunately without citation, that "these cuts hurt Gershwin, who loved every note; but, showman that he was, he accepted them willingly and often insisted on them."[18] But Todd Duncan, the original Porgy, recalls:

He was upset in Boston. My God, that opening night was killing. I think it was four hours. We performed the whole opera and we didn't get out until one o'clock or something. George didn't want one beautiful blessed note cut. He and Mamoulian and Smallens walked in the Boston Common all night long, fighting and fussing and talking about it. . . . all that last part that I sang, George Gershwin wrote for my voice. He wrote that after he met me and after he heard me. But it was just too much for one man to sing at the end of an opera . . .[19]

Charles Hamm's study reveals that cuts were made from the time of the first rehearsals, through the tryout in Boston, up to the New York premiere in October. According to rehearsal scores, they seem to have been the direct result of stage experience, and since Gershwin was in constant attendance during rehearsals, they must have had his approval, painful though they may have been to make.[20]

Such a multiplicity of versions places *Porgy and Bess* in the same confusing situation that obtains with a great many classical operas. There is a certain amount of authentic music that was removed or added at one time or another for one reason or another, usually with the composer's consent. One thinks of the cuts Beethoven made in the later versions of *Fidelio* and the extra solo arias Mozart put into his operas at the behest of irate singers. Knowing the precise reasons for such changes might make performance decisions today easier but will never remove entirely the need to make them. As with these other operas, the "complete" score of *Porgy and Bess* is something of a fiction. Naturally, the critic must be wary of this state of affairs, as it would be embarrassing to analyze some number as the key to the opera, only to find that Gershwin had cut it.[21] On the other hand, the precut score is Gershwin's first attempt to solve the dramatic problems, and as such must be considered a critical resource.

Is it an opera or a musical? This question was the focus of the reviews that followed the premiere and has not yet been dismissed. Olin Downes and Brooks Atkinson, writing for the music and drama columns of the *New York Times* of October 11, 1935, make typical comments:

The style is at one moment of opera and another of operetta or sheer Broadway entertainment.

Why commonplace remarks that carry no emotion have to be made in a chanting monotone is a problem [I] cannot fathom.

Turning "Porgy" into opera has resulted in a deluge of casual remarks that have to be thoughtfully intoned and that amazingly impede the action.[22]

Generally, the drama critics objected to recitative per se and the music critics to "Summertime," "I Got Plenty o' Nuttin'," and other tunes which seemed "too popular" for opera. Gershwin replied to both in the *New York Times* of October 20, 1935, writing that his recitatives were composed to the natural speech accents of blacks, and that "Nearly all of Verdi's operas contain what are known as 'song hits.' *Carmen* is almost a collection of song hits."[23]

Since it has been shown time and again that dramatic action can be created from any of the various genres subsumed under the various titles of "opera," "music drama," "operetta," "musical," and so forth, the classification of *Porgy and Bess*, as far as its dramatic artistry is concerned, is truly a trivial issue. As Engel so sensibly remarks:

> It has always seemed to me that this annoyance with *Porgy* is far more the product of semantics than of anything Gershwin put into his score. It is as if just calling *Porgy* by the name "Opera" serves to assail the sensibilities of those who believe that such a classification is a slur on the dignity of Wagner, Verdi, and Mozart.[24]

An issue much more serious but still related to the matter of classification has been the quality of the declamatory vocal writing in *Porgy and Bess*, including accompanied recitative, arioso, and the like. Opinions on this vary wildly, perhaps because there is little theory or consensus about what makes good recitative. At one end of the controversy there is Irving Kolodin, writing in 1935 that the declamatory writing is one of Gershwin's "most impressive accomplishments, for its adherence to the characteristics of the persons in the drama,"[25] and at the other end David Hamilton, in a review of the 1976 Cleveland recording, insisting that "in much of the scene music, there isn't any consistent idea of how to get from one place to another."[26] Even strident critics admit, however, that some of the most moving and dramatically important passages in the opera—such as Porgy's first speech, his subsequent invocation to the dice, and Bess's final plea to Crown in Act II—are composed in the declamatory style. If there are other awkward moments, if the declamatory music as a whole is not perfect, it is still absolutely necessary to set up the most striking moments:

> In *La Bohème, Otello, Louise, Die Meistersinger,* and all the others, there are many passages of recitative that in themselves might seem dull to this listener or that; but without the musical texture they create, many lyric passages that are not songs or arias would be impossible because—if there were no musical continuity—they would become small, isolated islands of music, unconnected, rootless, and even silly.[27]

And such passages in *Porgy and Bess* are essential not only for their lyricism and intrinsic beauty but for what music they contribute to the dramatic development.

Last, there is the most complex and politically sensitive question of the three: is *Porgy and Bess* a fair representation of black music and black culture?

Generally, the reaction of the black community has not been favorable through the years.[28] "The times are here to debunk Gershwin's lamp-black Negroisms," said Duke Ellington after the premiere, and Ralph Matthews seconded this opinion: "The singing, even down to the choral and ensemble numbers, has a conservatory twang."[29] As listeners have become more aware of the sensibilities of racial minorities, the undeniable stereotypical features of the opera have become even more glaring.

It is difficult to fault Gershwin for any conscious misrepresentation of the culture he tried to portray. He stayed for a month on Folly Island off the coast of South Carolina, close to a Gullah community, to hear its music and observe its religious celebrations, and he refused to accept a prestigious contract from the Metropolitan Opera for the premiere of the opera because a black cast would not have been allowed. These are not the actions of a dramatist who is interested in stereotypes. That the opera is in some ways still stereotypical shows not that Gershwin was racist, but that he was a child of his time, subject to its cultural prejudice and ignorance.

In the end, Gershwin did what any opera composer must do; he recast raw material into a unified musical-dramatic idiom. Hall Johnson, a black composer writing for *Opportunity* magazine in 1936, realized this even as he described characteristics that bothered him:

> [Gershwin] is an individual artist, as free to write about Negroes in his own way as any other composer to write about anything

else. The only thing a really creative artist can be expected to give us is an expression of *his own* reaction to a given stimulus. We are not compelled to agree with it or even like it.[30]

The social and political implications of *Porgy and Bess* for the black community are very real and quite complex, but ultimately they are irrelevant to any dramatic appraisal of the work. This may be difficult to swallow for some, and indeed, Gershwin's opera has been unjustly criticized on these terms. "Folk-lore subjects recounted by an outsider are only valid as long as the folk in question is unable to speak for itself, which is certainly not true of the American Negro in 1935," wrote Virgil Thomson in that year.[31] "Nor was it true of Spaniards and Spanish gypsies 60 years earlier, but one is grateful that such fine scruples did not keep Bizet from composing *Carmen*," retorted William Youngren.[32] There may not be a single opera that does not distort some social truth held today, but such defects lie apart from the musical-dramatic issues with which the composer is wrestling, and modern opera lovers forget politics as part of their suspension of disbelief that allows them to enter into the medium in the first place.

Consideration of the ethnic issue brings to the fore, ironically, the central musical-dramatic issue of *Porgy and Bess*: exactly what is a folk opera, and how do its characteristics affect the structure of the drama? By now it should be clear that a folk opera cannot be any sort of ethno-musicological tone poem of some exotic culture, because that kind of portrayal is not in the province of the opera composer and would not be dramatic even if it were. Rather, it must be an opera in which "the folk," taken as a group, acting together, becomes an important, if not central, character in the drama. Certainly it is this feature of *Porgy and Bess* which has impressed listeners perhaps more than any other. The opera has been compared with *Boris Godunov*, *Carmen*,[33] and operas of Janacek.[34] Composer Ned Rorem goes so far as to say that "so familiar are the seventeen arias that we forget they are almost incidental . . . as against the grand set of numbers of the group that accounts for three quarters of the opera."[35] And director Rouben Mamoulian was sensitive enough to realize how dramatic the chorus was supposed to be as he put the first production together. "Don't stand around like a chorus—break the formality of it all" he commanded again and again.[36]

The consequence of using "the folk" as an important character is that it can have but little dramatic action, because it is so deep and requires so much time for development. That is why Gershwin's opera and other "folk operas" seem almost undramatic, like a series of tableaux given on stage one after the other. The story of *Porgy and Bess* is studded with little scenes—self-contained "short stories"—that stand on the periphery of the main plot and often develop it not at all. Lawyer Frazier and his fake divorce and the scene of the street peddlers, both in Act II, are only two examples. Some are motivated by a rather obvious irony that is one of the main features of the original novel. Serena begs her husband Robbins in Act I not to play craps; he disdains her advice, and moments later violence erupting from the game kills him. Clara warns Jake not to go fishing during the time of "September storms"; by the end of that second act, a hurricane has drowned them both. Episodes such as these might be considered subplots, but a true subplot of an American musical extends throughout the play, and its purpose is to provide a dramatic counterpoint to the main plot and so extend its range. These "vignettes," to use Slavick's term, instead develop the community of Catfish Row as a character. Each one provides a different side of this complex character, and yet maintains and develops certain themes that apply to the community at large: superstition, a tenacious mutual support against the outside white world, and mutual dependence.

This peculiar character of the folk opera derives directly from the original novel. Its loose structure is characteristic of Heyward as "a chronicler or a memorialist,"[37] and the community is placed at the center of the conflicts.[38] The plot is considerably tightened in the stage version of *Porgy*, meaning that the connective love story is brought out, which in turn requires a fuller treatment of Bess. In the novel she is only the most important of many elements in Porgy's struggle; the reader does not even witness the critical seduction by Sportin' Life at the end. The stage version presents the sordid "happy dust" episode in full, except for Bess's surrender. Naturally, the opera requires an even more intense focus. The love story is now at the center of the drama in all its details, including her surrender at the end.

The result of these transformations is an opera in which the action, while not really tragic, has the exceedingly slow pace of tragedy. Every scene performs two functions. It develops the relationship of Porgy and Bess, and it develops the community as a dramatic character. Sometimes these functions are quite separated in time and action. The saucer burial scene (Act I, scene 2) is constructed as two discrete musical-dramatic sections. The first, organized around the key of G minor and the dirge refrain of "Gone, gone, gone," is a pure "folk scene" and contributes nothing to the Porgy-Bess relationship. Then the music changes to F major, and Bess jumps up to lead the mourners in the "Train" spiritual, and thus the one-time outcast is now accepted in some measure by the community. Other scenes integrate the two functions more fully. The second investigation scene (Act III, scene 2) presents a turning point in the love story when Porgy is taken to identify Crown's body, but includes also a humorous trio in which Serena and her two friends resist yet again the power of whites. Even the last scene, in which the community, now having been explored for three hours, is ready to play its most active dramatic role, even this scene begins with a lengthy and somewhat puzzling introduction in which people simply greet one another ("How are you dis very lovely mornin'?").[39]

The slow pace of the main plot is best revealed by how little actually happens between Porgy and Bess, especially at the beginning of the opera. In the first act, Porgy takes Bess into his room on Catfish Row after she flees the aftermath of her lover Crown's murder of Robbins. Later she is accepted by the community at Robbins's burial service. That is all that happens in the first act. The couple do not express love for one another until well into the second act. With Crown's return, a love triangle is formed and the action picks up. The remainder of this long act includes Bess's seduction by Crown and her reconciliation with Porgy. The final act has perhaps the most compressed action: Porgy murders Crown and is hauled off and held in jail for superstitiously refusing to identify the body; Bess yields once again to her drug addiction and leaves with Sportin' Life; Porgy returns to find her gone.

The treatment of this seemingly tragic story is quite different from that of most tragic operas in that, although the action is slow, the musical treatment of the important plot events is not extensive. The murders are brief, though violent, musical interludes; Sportin' Life needs only one round of "There's a Boat Dat's Leavin' Soon for New York" to lure Bess. To ensure that such brief moments are convincing is far from easy, and that they succeed so well is another sort of testament to Gershwin's artistry. Sportin' Life's seduction contains in its brassy tune all the allure of the city, while beneath, in its slithering chromatic bass, is barely masked the identity of the seducer. Similarly, "Summertime," the first song of the opera, seems to capture at once the essential spirituality of the community, especially when the chorus joins in harmony, so much so that through its several reprises it becomes their leitmotif. Such musical economy, however admirable, is a necessary constraint of the "folk opera" genre. To portray Catfish Row in depth requires a lot of time, time that cannot be spared for effulgent Wagnerian love duets.

Still, in terms of the music drama, the main plot must remain at the center of the musical action. How indeed does Gershwin's music define, develop, and sustain the *Porgy and Bess* relationship without losing track of "the folk"?

The inherent conflict in this dual purpose comes to the fore when Porgy is to make his first entrance. The opera has begun with a lengthy scene that introduces the Catfish Row community. Various small scenes are lit on various stage locations. Characters come and go. A crap game begins at center stage. Porgy comes to join it, but how is he to be distinguished as the principal character, and not just another member of the Row? Gershwin chooses a means as simple as it is effective. A command given while the orchestra is quiet,

Maria: You Scipio! Here come Porgy. Open the gate for him.

a trill, and then the music which began the opera is recapitulated for the first time, signaling that this character brings a new dramatic phase. Then there is a striking new theme, distinguished by the lowered third (G-natural) and a powerful accompaniment composed of parallel chromatic chords. This becomes Porgy's leitmotif:

Ex. 3-1 Gershwin, *Porgy and Bess*, Act I, Rehearsal 70, mm. 1–3.

With the protagonist established, Gershwin loses no time in moving the action musically. Porgy's first extended solo, a lyric arioso, defines the main dramatic theme:

Ex. 3-2 Gershwin, *Porgy and Bess*, Act I, Rehearsal 80, mm. 3–6, Rehearsal 81, mm. 1–10.

It is no overstatement to say that the action motivating the entire plot, then, is Porgy's struggle against loneliness. Even the love relationship is portrayed by both words and music to be the cure for this sickness and is therefore a secondary dramatic theme. For one thing, while Bess at several points declares her love for Porgy, he never does, at least not in so many words.[40] For another, *Porgy and Bess* owns a leitmotif technique that is Wagnerian in its method and in its intensity, and yet Bess is the only one of six major characters who has no distinctive theme. Her music adapts to the material of the man she is with—Crown, Porgy, or Sportin' Life—as if her fickle character is not capable of musical identity but instead must identify with his.[41]

The effectiveness of this arioso, its success in making the listener cognizant of its dramatic importance, is due to its singular texture. With its sustained polytonal accompaniment, articulating at once both C and A, and slow harmonic rhythm functioning only on the highest level, it is like nothing heard thus far, neither recitative nor song, but a deep and free expression of inner character.

Nothing at all happens between Porgy and Bess until after the murder, when Bess is searching desperately for a room to hide in. No one will take her in until she comes to Porgy. She goes inside and closes the door; not a word is sung or spoken, but the orchestra rises and ends the first scene by quoting the entire "loneliness" arioso (Rehearsal 156, 157). Clearly, Bess is to mean the end of Porgy's deepest longing.

The fullest and most explicit unification of Bess with the dramatic theme of Porgy's loneliness, however, comes with the great love duet of Act II, scene 1, "Bess, You Is My Woman Now," (Rehearsal 94–106). This, the couple's first real love scene, is set up, through the long preparation and an unusually empty stage, as one of the few dramatic climaxes of the opera. This is where the meaning of the relationship must be explicated by the music, and Gershwin does not fail.

The first connection with what has already transpired is the most obvious. The five-measure introduction to the main melody quotes the "Night time, day time" portion of the arioso (Rehearsal 94, mm. 3–5). Then Porgy begins:

Ex. 3-3 Gershwin, *Porgy and Bess*, Act II, Rehearsal 95, mm. 1–8,
Rehearsal 96, mm. 1–8, Rehearsal 97, mm. 1–4.

At this point Bess takes up the same melody in the key of D major for
twelve measures before taking a new turn:

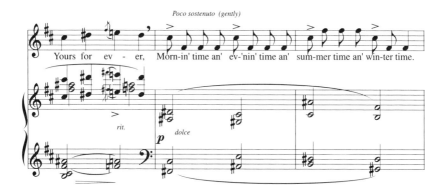

Ex. 3-4 Gershwin, *Porgy and Bess*, Act II, Rehearsal 99, mm. 5–8,
Rehearsal 100, mm. 1–6.

The new melody, so different and yet so fitting, is the complete "Night time, day time" melody, very slightly adapted, from the first-act arioso. It is then transposed down to lead into the climactic return of the first phrase, now in the key of F-sharp major for the first time. The tune is not quite the same; it refuses the octave syncopations and instead reiterates the gesture to the high A-sharp, amplifying the intensity. For this moment, setting Porgy's name, Gershwin provides a new accompaniment, a rising and falling chromatic figure that recalls the striking harmonization of Porgy's leitmotif (Ex. 3-1). Finally, there is the lovely codetta to the main tune. It is nothing more than an F-sharp arpeggiation, but its "Mornin' time an' ev'nin' time" text amplifies once more the relationship of this duet with the arioso.[42]

How economical these gestures are, and yet how broad their effect! In a brief twelve measures, Gershwin has justified the short introduction, which otherwise might have seemed forced, and made three long-range connections with the most important musical idea in the first act that clarify the relationship of Porgy and Bess even as the piece confirms it.

The place of "Bess, You Is My Woman Now" as the centerpiece of this scene is supported by a seemingly unrelated and much lighter song: Porgy's "I Got Plenty o' Nuttin'," which is heard near the beginning of the scene.

The song's harmonic pattern is first heard, played softly by the strings, behind Porgy's strangely moving invocation to the dice during the crap game in Act I. The song itself appears fully formed

in Act II, as Porgy's carefree response to the fisherman Jake's dec-
laration that he must take his boat out, even in the face of hurricane warnings, if he is to earn the money to give his children a
college education. We recall Porgy's luck in the crap game, and his
song seems the celebration of the far more significant stroke of the
same luck that has, in the interim, brought him Bess . . .[43]

If such a reading seems far-fetched at first, it becomes less so when the
scene ends with Bess departing for the community picnic and Porgy, left
alone, singing a reprise of "I Got Plenty o' Nuttin'." Now the song acts
as a musical frame for the whole scene, and the cause of its underlying
emotion by this point has surely been revealed.

Of course, the dramatic climax must depend on the effectiveness of
the music on its own terms, no matter how many and how subtle are the
leitmotifs. The very first phrase of "Bess, You Is My Woman Now" shows
Gershwin at the height of his lyric powers (Ex. 3-3). The first hint of
the coming depth of feeling is the lowered seventh step (A-flat) in the
second measure; it is only a hint because this chromatic alteration is
one of the commonplaces of this opera. But the phrase ending on the
long F (Rh. 95, m. 3) is interrupted by the two octave leaps, interrupted
because they are emphatic intervals and, more important, because they
come on the weak beats. The typical four-measure phrase ending is
therefore blurred. The sense of meter in the melody is weakened further
by the next measure, in which the repeated groupings of C-sharp and D
once more make accents against the meter.[44] Not until the high C (m. 7)
is the sense of strong beat restored, but Gershwin now substitutes harmonic and melodic tension for rhythmic, prolonging the tense supertonic with a series of dominant substitutions, harmonic articulations
that are quite necessary, that beautifully color Porgy's note before melt-
ing into the expected F dominant seventh at the end of the eighth measure, at exactly the place the listener expects.[45] Because Gershwin blurs
the sense of periodic phrasing in the fourth measure, its restoration with
this long dominant harmony is especially effective and beautiful.

The next phrase is half again as long, a rhapsodic extension based on
expressive intervals of the major seventh, then the major ninth, and
articulated by a passing modulation through D major and ending in F-
sharp major. Since the song began in B-flat, the changes of key reflect
the rising intensity of the duet. Bess steps back to the key of D major,

but, as noted, returns gloriously to the F-sharp tonality, which Porgy has already prepared, with the climactic gesture of her melody.[46]

And the connection with "the folk"? It is in the musical idiom itself. Gershwin's style has always been associated with American jazz, and in *Porgy and Bess* there are features of "native" black music as well.[47] The lowered seventh step of "Bess, You Is My Woman Now" (Ex. 3-3) might be described as a blue note, and the octave leaps that follow as typical jazz syncopations. Similarly there are the lowered third step and the bluesy chord progressions of Porgy's leitmotif (Ex. 3-1). And yet, these gestures, in their most important occurrences, have a function far beyond that of a simple jazz or folk flavoring that gives the opera a certain mood. They contribute to dramatic effect and to large-scale musical organization as well.[48] The effect of those octave leaps has already been noted; their syncopation is not just a taste of jazz, but blurs the sense of phrase so that a much more climactic phrase ending can occur later. Consider the haunting refrain of the saucer burial. The funereal setting prepares the audience to hear spirituals, and so it does, but no authentic spiritual contains such a nonfunctional chord progression. Its purpose, yes, is to recall the black spiritual, but also to prolong the fundamental key of G minor for this scene, which must last a long time. Notice that the upbeat ("He's a- ")

Ex. 3-5 Gershwin, *Porgy and Bess*, Act I, scene 2, mm. 4–7.

continues the preceding G minor harmony (i) and the phrase ends with a D major seventh (V²), leaving the listener with little option but to interpret the entire progression as some exotic passage in G, or, more fundamentally, as a simple i–V progression stretched out. The consequent phrase contains a resolution (V–i) in the same manner:

Ex. 3-6 Gershwin, *Porgy and Bess*, Act II, mm. 7–11.

This chromatic harmony succeeds beautifully because of Gershwin's essentially Romantic voice leading, which, as in Wagner, places the weight of organization on continuous melodic lines rather than on harmonic function. This voice leading not only makes for slower harmonic rhythm on the high level but allows Gershwin to fashion the local progressions to remind the listener of blues, jazz, or haunting spirituals such as this (Fig. 3-1).

The modulations in "Bess, You Is My Woman Now," while heightening the dramatic expression on stage, are also essentially Romantic in that they delay the strong melodic-harmonic cadence. The first great phrase ends on a half-cadence (Ex. 3-3), and thereafter the music changes key often enough to avoid the inexorable tendency toward the tonic, until the codetta can draw out the final chords over what is the couple's vow of fidelity, combined in counterpoint with all the principal motives and the single full cadence of the song.

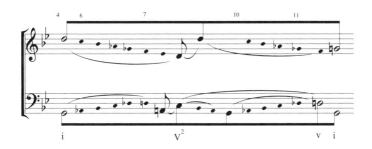

Fig. 3-1 Diagram showing high-level harmonic functions (large note heads) and linear voice leading (small note heads) in "Gone, gone, gone" refrain.

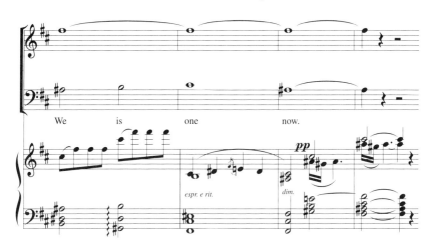

Ex. 3-7 Gershwin, *Porgy and Bess*, Act II, Rehearsal 105, mm. 3–7,
Rehearsal 106, mm. 1–6.

The duality of dramatic purpose of this folk opera, then, is accomplished through a musical idiom that has multiple effects at the same time. It colors the opera and develops the community as a character by recalling musical clichés and stereotypes but uses the idiom in a sophisticated fashion that accomplishes essential dramatic and structural purposes. In this way Gershwin develops the music drama without losing track of "the folk."

Controlling these simultaneous dramatic effects cannot be easy, and they are not always as unified as in the second act duet. In particular, the last scene of the opera—in which Porgy returns from jail, laden with gifts for his Bess and other friends on Catfish Row—has been criticized for not meeting the dramatic issues.[49] The aforementioned "greeting" scene is puzzling enough, but the real problem is the moment of Porgy's reception by the community. It begins confidently enough: they sing a variant of his leitmotif in welcome. But thereafter, Gershwin seems unsure how to set the long period between his arrival and his realization that Bess is gone. Admittedly, the musical expression of simultaneous yet contrary emotions is one of opera's most ticklish problems. Gershwin simply ignores the issue.

As Porgy recounts his jail experience for the community and begins to distribute gifts, the various members, of course, are very uncomfortable in the knowledge that the source of his joyful homecoming has already gone. This is the emotional conflict on stage: his joy, their despair. The music cannot reflect this. The orchestra moves from development of Porgy's leitmotif (Rehearsal 131, m. 5–Rehearsal 134, m. 5), to harmonica chords for Scipio's present of a mouth organ (Rehearsal 135–Rehearsal 137, m. 3), to "I Got Plenty o' Nuttin'" (Rehearsal 138–45) as he doles out other presents and tells everyone how he won the money to buy them, to "Bess, You Is My Woman Now," as he prepares to summon Bess. Even if one generously ascribes some sense to the use of "I Got Plenty" while the gift-giving goes on, the use of these themes here is a most superficial substitute for actual music drama, recalling the Broadway practice of calling for a reprise of a show's best song when there was nothing better to do. The tension of the crowd's mood against Porgy's is completely missing, and a significant opportunity for Gershwin is lost.[50]

The conclusion of the opera, containing the most radical transformation of the original story, is much more convincing. The novel ends by cutting out the community and showing only Porgy and Maria in an image as bleak as could be:

> She looked until she could bear the sight no longer; then she stumbled into her shop and closed the door, leaving Porgy and the goat alone in an irony of morning sunlight.[51]

In the stage version, the Heywards, thinking this ending quite undramatic, restore the community and have Porgy strike out for New York in search of Bess, but there is no question that this is a desperate gesture of despair. The departure is retained in the opera, but Gershwin transforms its significance entirely with the spiritual "Oh Lawd, I'm on My Way." Despite its accompanimental syncopated figure, which has been criticized as too casual for such a moment, this song, set in the opera's central key of E major, is an effective and moving summary of many of its elements. Musically, it contains the jazz vamp, the blues chromaticism, and of course, the spiritual idiom. In the drama it represents a final unification of the two main strands, the love relationship and the community at large as character, for here the spirit of the community has been changed, from despair to hope, on account of that love relationship. That change of heart and that unification seem to be implied in the construction of the piece, in the way that the emphasis on the tonic note and triad expresses the stalwart hope, and when the chorus joins in with Porgy after only a single phrase of solo. "The folk" at last becomes an active participant in the music drama.

From the vantage point of over sixty-five years of history, it seems that *Porgy and Bess* is one of those rare modern works, comparable perhaps to the master films of Chaplin, that make the leap from a local popular tradition into world-class art. Since its premiere, which was a financial failure,[52] its appeal to sophisticated opera audiences and popular musicians alike has only increased by leaps and bounds. Having already played in Copenhagen, Zurich, and Stockholm by 1950, and having been added to the regular seasonal repertory of the Zurich Stadttheater,[53] the opera truly arrived on the world stage with a four-year tour sponsored by the U.S. State Department from 1952 to 1956. This included triumphant performances in Berlin, Vienna, and the Soviet Union, and at La Scala in Milan.

It is quite clear that just this sort of leap was Gershwin's intention:

> I chose the form I have used for "Porgy and Bess" because I believe that music lives only when it is in serious form. When I wrote the "Rhapsody in Blue," I took "blues" and put them in a larger and more serious form. That was twelve years ago and the "Rhapsody in Blue" is very much alive whereas if I had taken the same themes and put them in songs they would have been gone years ago.[54]

The longevity Gershwin sought has indeed been achieved, but ironically, its "serious form" has limited *Porgy and Bess* to only superficial influence on subsequent Broadway productions, mostly in the form of musicals boasting black casts: *The Hot Mikado* (1939), *The Swing Mikado* (1939), *Cabin in the Sky* (1940), among others. The high-level harmonic organization and the whole idea of the folk opera has little application in the traditional musical play of Broadway, whose plot is usually much tighter and more directed, and divided into much smaller musical pieces. The long-range interconnections of motive, leitmotif, and dramatic character find no parallel until Leonard Bernstein. They were simply beyond the reach of all other Broadway composers.

Although the opera seems almost to step out of its native tradition, *Porgy and Bess* must be one of Broadway's most luminous moments. Criticisms made here and elsewhere hardly challenge the overall conception of the work and merely prove once more that there is no perfect opera. The famous opera historian Donald J. Grout is still quite right when he writes that "no work has yet risen to challenge the secure place of *Porgy and Bess* in the history of American opera."[55] For how many other works of art can appeal to so many levels of culture, and have done so? Perhaps more important in this age without a common musical language, how many have done so in the twentieth century?

Chapter 4

Second Maturity

> When a show works perfectly, it's because all the individual
> parts complement each other and fit together. . . . In a great
> musical, the orchestrations sound the way the costumes look.
> That's what made *Oklahoma!* work. . . . It was a work created
> by many that gave the impression of having been created
> by one.[1]
>
> *Richard Rodgers*

There are a number of reasons why a particular work of art might be considered a milestone in the history of its genre. It might introduce innovations of technique and style so convincing that they become highly influential. It might attract such wide acclaim that it cannot be ignored by the artists who come after, even if the acclaim eventually fades. It could stand as the first work of an important series, like the First Symphony of Beethoven. Or perhaps, in addition to all of these, it sets a new standard of artistry. All of these reasons can be found in the first musical play of Rodgers and Hammerstein, *Oklahoma!*

Almost from its first performance at the St. James Theater on March 31, 1943, *Oklahoma!* has been recognized as a new kind of musical play that denied its Broadway audiences many of their most cherished traditions. There was no opening chorus line, no chorus at all until midway through the first act, in fact. There was a rather serious ballet and other serious overtones, including a killing in the second act. The story, apparently so simple, seemed to engage the audience in a way that went beyond evening diversion. These departures, far from disappointing their viewers, were ratified by a commercial success that was unprecedented in the history of the musical theater. The original production of *Oklahoma!* at the St. James ran 2,248 performances, blasting the previous record for a musical play, 670 for *Irene* (1919).[2] The touring company played continuously for ten years, performing in Berlin, South Africa, Denmark, and Australia, and established the performance record at the Drury Lane Theatre in London.

Even if *Oklahoma!* had flopped, it would still be recorded in histories of Broadway as the first collaboration of Richard Rodgers, composer, and Oscar Hammerstein, lyricist and playwright, who, between the premiere of *Oklahoma!* and Hammerstein's death in 1960, dominated Broadway as no other team has done. When *Oklahoma!* was revived on Broadway in 1953, there were three other Rodgers and Hammerstein musicals playing there already in their opening runs: *South Pacific* (opened 1949), *The King and I* (1951), and *Me and Juliet* (1953). Replace the last with their earlier *Carousel* (1945, revived 1954), and the result is a quartet of the most outstanding achievements of the American musical theater. Their later years produced two more which, while not quite reaching that exalted level, are yet worthy of occasional revival: *The Flower Drum Song* (1958) and *The Sound of Music* (1959). The sheer number of their successes places them above any other single composer or lyricist; that this book devotes to them two chapters to everyone else's one is only a constrained reflection of the historical fact: their work is at the center of Broadway's "golden age."

Of course, *Oklahoma!* did not flop. It survives today not because of its supposed innovations, which, real or not, inevitably fade with time, nor because of its original appeal, nor its historical position, but because of its own integrity. Its solution to the problem of music and drama is quite different from *Show Boat*'s, but like the earlier play, *Oklahoma!* took that problem seriously and conjured up a dramatic presentation that has not yet ceased to satisfy.

Both Rodgers and Hammerstein had long careers in the musical theater already behind them when they agreed to work together in the early 1940s. Oscar Hammerstein II was born into a theatrical family and in the early 1920s worked with the veteran book writer Otto Harbach. In the middle of the decade he scored successes with Sigmund Romberg and Jerome Kern. After *Show Boat*, he continued to work with Kern intermittently. Their next hit was *Music in the Air* (1933). Hammerstein's career in the theater then entered upon a ten-year drought. He support-ed himself with lucrative Hollywood film contracts, but he had no com-mercial or artistic achievements in the theater until *Oklahoma!*

The years before had been much kinder to Rodgers. Working with the supremely talented but unstable Lorenz Hart from the early 1920s onward, he had composed an impressive number of successful shows including *A Connecticut Yankee* (1927), *Love Me Tonight* (1932), *On Your Toes* (1938), *The Boys from Syracuse* (1938), and *Pal Joey* (1940). This last play, concerning a rather dim but good-looking nightclub singer who is taken in by a wealthy but bored socialite, has been cited as an example of the musical theater's growing maturity in the late 1930s, and Lehman Engel, Geoffrey Block, and others believe it should be included in the top-drawer canon.[3] Although a large proportion of the score is given over to prop songs, other songs are integrated fairly well into the plot. Rodgers and Hart did not compromise its seamy setting and distasteful characters. The composer commented on the occasion of its successful 1952 revival, "While Joey himself may have been fairly adolescent in his thinking and his morality, the show bearing his name certainly wore long pants and in many respects forced the entire musi-cal-comedy theatre to wear long pants for the first time."[4]

Rodgers would have been quite content to continue his partnership with Hart if the writer's alcoholism had not made working conditions impossible. Even when Rodgers told him that he had been approached by the Theatre Guild to convert Lynn Riggs's *Green Grow the Lilacs* into a musical and that he might approach Oscar Hammerstein, Hart could not reform. Instead, he declined rapidly and died at the age of forty-eight in November 1943, eight months after *Oklahoma!* opened.

Lorenz Hart told Rodgers that he did not think the cowboy play would make a good musical, and indeed, in view of Hart's particular tal-ents, he was probably right in sensing that the deep sentimentality of the Riggs play was not for him. Ironically, the very dramatic qualities that put him off were beautifully suited to the subtle talents of Oscar Hammerstein II.

The lyricist's and the librettist's art has always placed a distant second to the composer's in opera criticism, and this book is no exception, even though the words that are sung in a piece are essential to its dramatic expression. Moreover, the phrase structure and rhyme scheme of a lyric influence decisively the important articulations in the music, since they must match if the sense of the words is to be conveyed. Because of this important function of rhyme, the most famous of Broadway's lyricists—Hart, Cole Porter, Alan Jay Lerner, Stephen Sondheim—have been virtuoso wordsmiths, masters of the internal rhyme, the feminine rhyme, the half-phrase. Such devices call attention to themselves and impress the listener with their difficulty. This sensation can be advantageous when the situation is comic. When W. S. Gilbert's Pirates of Penzance surprise the unsuspecting maidens and threaten to carry them off immediately to be married, the speech is as funny as the situation is outrageous:

> Here's a first-rate opportunity
> To get married with impunity;
> And indulge in the felicity
> of unbounded domesticity.
> You shall quickly be parsonified,
> Conjugally matrimonified,
> By a doctor of divinity,
> Who resides in this vicinity.

The audience is regaled not only by the image of twenty pirates threatening to marry off twenty maidens at a crack, but by their impudence in their successful attempt to rhyme with "opportunity," "domesticity," "parsonified," and "divinity."

But while comedy, satire, and cynicism may call for such lyrics, romance and other sincerities cannot really abide them. When constructing a situation of serious dramatic intent, the last thing one wants is a lyric that calls attention to its technique rather than to the drama. It is here that Hammerstein separates himself from his virtuoso forebears, Gilbert and Hart:

> While I, on occasion, place a timid, encroaching foot on the territory of these two masters, I never carry my invasion very far. I would not stand a chance with either of them in the field of brilliant light verse. I admire them and envy them their fluidity and humor, but I refuse to compete with them. Aside from my shortcomings as a wit and rhymester—or, perhaps, because of them—my inclinations lead me to a more primitive type of lyric.[5]

This gives the listener an entirely different impression of lyric technique. With Porter or Sondheim the reaction is, "I could never do that."

With Hammerstein it is more likely to be, "Anyone could do that." The apparent simplicity of the Hammerstein lyric hides an exceptionally appropriate and often penetrating characterization of the dramatic situation at hand. He is perfectly capable of comedy, and even of wordplay; listen to the comic juxtapositions in "June Is Bustin' Out All Over" from *Carousel*. But most often the comedy in his lyric derives from the comedy of the dramatic situation in the play. That is why the punch line in Ado Annie's verse of "All er Nuthin" and the ironic refrain from "Kansas City," both from *Oklahoma!*, work so well.

Hammerstein is best when he describes a complex emotion or experience in the simplest language. In *The King and I*, Anna Leonowens, a middle-aged widow, sings "Hello, Young Lovers," in which she assures everyone around that she knows what it is like to be young and in love. The lyric's release section is as follows:

> I know how it feels to have wings on your heels,
> And to fly down the street in a trance.
> You fly down a street on the chance that you'll meet,
> And you meet—not really by chance.

Nothing about this lyric seems complex; even the internal rhyme in the first line appears plain. And those repeated strong words "street" and "meet" seem to impoverish the song, that is, until it is realized that their repetition creates a most subtle acceleration in articulation that mirrors the action of flying down the street. The second "meet" is indeed a surprise, not only because it is a repetition, but because it occurs so early on in the first foot of the line. But most stunning of all is the last short phrase which completes the overall rhyme, because by insisting on the second "chance" it goes quickly to the heart of young lovers' experience, the pretense of spontaneity and surprise at a chance meeting when chance has nothing to do with it.

This "primitive type" of lyric has the most to gain from a sensitive musical setting. It seems so plain on the page, in contrast to the entertaining verbal gymnastics of the virtuoso lyric, and cries out for a musical expression to mine its hidden worth. In this regard, Hammerstein was immeasurably fortunate to work with Richard Rodgers, who was gifted with just this sort of musical sensibility. He begins the setting of the lyric from "Hello, Young Lovers" with a syncopated dotted rhythm that might suggest a tensed hurrying, and in a foreign key common in his release sections, the subdominant. This leads the listener to expect a return to the home, or tonic, key sooner or later. With the third line (m. 53), the key becomes more unstable and on the second "meet" the melody moves up climactically to the original tonic note, suggesting

Ex. 4-1 Rodgers and Hammerstein, *The King and I*,
"Hello, Young Lovers," (No. 3), mm. 44–60.

with a cadential gesture the sudden meeting that takes place in Anna's mind. But this is no final climax, for Rodgers has harmonized that decisive melodic motion with a deceptive cadence that must move on. The final word, "chance," is given special treatment, harmonized with the minor ii chord over V, a dissonance that seems the perfect expression for Anna's bittersweet reminiscence, but which then moves into the clear dominant under her sustained note, finally defining the home key of D for which the listener has been waiting. Thus, Hammerstein's imagined meeting is rendered with an equivalent musical metaphor: the cadence in mid phrase doubles for the unexpected encounter while its deceptive quality mirrors the lovers themselves and allows the phrase its normal period.

Rodgers was one of the most fluent melodists of the American musical theater, composing masterful songs with breathtaking speed. Numerous accounts support this appraisal: "Soliloquy" in two hours, "It Might As Well Be Spring" in one hour, "Oh, What a Beautiful Mornin'" in ten minutes. Hammerstein himself wrote:

> This is the annoying part of our collaboration. It takes me a week, and sometimes three weeks, to write the words of a song. After I give them to him, it takes him an hour or two and his work is over.[6]

Despite this remarkable facility, Rodgers's melodies are characterized by an expressive logic of development that seems so calculated and planned. "People Will Say We're in Love," the principal love duet of *Oklahoma!*, has a refrain melody composed almost entirely of fifths and step motion. As the melody progresses, however, these elements gradually

Ex. 4-2 Rodgers and Hammerstein, *Oklahoma!*,
"People Will Say We're in Love" (No. 12), mm. 19–34.

Ex. 4-3 Rodgers and Hammerstein, *Oklahoma!*,
"People Will Say We're In Love" (No. 12), mm. 47–54.

acquire more and more musical tension. The first fifth moves from steps
1 to 5 on the scale; the second from the comparatively more tense leading
tone (7) down to 3 (m. 21). The second phrase changes the descending
fifth from perfect to diminished (G to C-sharp setting "folks too much"),
yet remaining strictly in the key of D major. The third phrase introduces
another diminished fifth, now chromatic (D to G-sharp setting "jokes too
much"), increasing the tension again. This makes the explicit chromaticism of the next phrase seem well prepared and logical. The next section
is identical to the first, except that the end is changed so that it is no less
chromatic but more conclusive because it moves up to the tonic. The
release (Ex. 4-3) continues the development by using the more daring
lowered fifth step ("collecting"). The final phrase creates a melodic climax by rising to its highest notes yet, but cleverly adapting the chromatic motive once more so that it begins a perfect fifth higher than the
original (Ex. 4-4):

LAUREY

Peo - ple will say we're in love.

mf espr. rit.

Ex. 4-4 Rodgers and Hammerstein, *Oklahoma!*,
"People Will Say We're In Love" (No. 12), mm. 63–66.

Rodgers's style is an untainted adaptation of nineteenth-century
Romanticism. Chromaticism not only creates expressive effects and
emphatic gestures on certain choice lyrics, but by weakening the sense
of key delays the need for a structural cadence. It is true that he does not
always take advantage of this structural chromaticism—"People Will
Say," for example, has a strong cadence at the end of its second section—
but more often than not Rodgers's songs are examples of the "endless
melody" in miniature. What is remarkable in *Oklahoma!* is that he succeeds in retaining a folk song flavor in many of the numbers while refusing the frequent cadences that such a flavor might suggest. In the verse
of "Oh, What a Beautiful Mornin'" the melody makes a strong cadence
at the end of its consequent phrase (m. 55), just as a real folk song
might. Any firm sense of conclusion, however, is dispelled by the harmony and descending bass line; the chord at that point is vi, not I, and
the cadence is deceptive. The tension in the song is therefore main-

CURLY

All the cat - tle are stand-in' like sta - tues,

8va-

Ex. 4-5 Rodgers and Hammerstein, *Oklahoma!*,
"Oh, What a Beautiful Morning" (No. 1), mm. 48–64.

tained, and thereafter increased as the bass line becomes chromatic, and
as the last phrase sustains a prolonged dominant harmony under the
repeated Bs of the melody. There is no strong cadence at all until the very
end of the refrain. This sort of melodic tension, created by consistent
delay of cadence, is the strategem of the Romantic composer.

Such a technique naturally places great weight on the end of a piece, where strong cadences finally do occur. One of Rodgers's greatest gifts as a songwriter is his gift for ending, perhaps the most treacherous spot in a composition. His endings not only exploit the accumulated tensions beautifully but often have a way of summing up the content of the song at the same time. There are two salient features of this melody from "The Surrey with the Fringe on Top": the repeated low E and the leap upward, which Rodgers took to represent the flat country road and the scurrying fowl.[7] The successive leaps, however, are not identical and create in themselves a higher-level pattern. The leaps makes an overall line of A–B–C-sharp quite stable (Fig. 4-1). The next note would be D if the pattern continued, but instead the melody begins again for the second section of the song. After the release, the tune is heard for a third time, now changed in order to effect one of Rodgers's inimitable conclusions (Ex. 4–7).

Ex. 4-6 Rodgers and Hammerstein, *Oklahoma!*,
"The Surrey With The Fringe On Top" (No. 3), mm. 18–25.

Fig. 4-1 Diagram of high-level melodic pattern in "Surrey."

Ex. 4-7 Rodgers and Hammerstein, *Oklahoma!*,
"The Surrey With The Fringe On Top (No. 3), mm. 42–53.

This time, after the leap to C-sharp the melody progresses smoothly and slowly upward and does give the awaited D, emphasized by its strong position in the measure and the preceding secondary diminished chord (V09/ii). But most deft of all is the little three-measure tag (mm. 50–52), in which the pattering low E and the direct leap up to the D seem to remind the listener that this was what the melody was about all along, just at the moment when the first strong cadence of the whole refrain arrives.

The essential Romanticism of Rodgers's style and Hammerstein's affinity for the lyrical expression of sentiment were perfectly suited for the task of dramatic characterization. The main purpose of the songs in *Oklahoma!* is to reveal in detail the characters who sing them.

This is why the play's opening has been so often cited as such an effective beginning, revolutionary for its time. With no one but Aunt Eller on stage churning butter, Curly sings offstage the verse to "Oh, What A Beautiful Mornin'," which, unlike the second verse quoted above, is unaccompanied. Upon his appearance, he sings the famous refrain. The melody, once again folklike in its apparent simplicity, hides deep-seated emotion of the character about his subject. The lowered seventh ("mornin'") is the first sign of such emotion. When this phrase begins again ("I got a beautiful feelin' "), the expected D is replaced by the D-sharp leading tone in the very same spot, increasing the tension powerfully. The leading tone's resolution is false, harmonized with a diminished seventh (V09/V), yet another expressive delay of cadence. Only at the conclusion of the next phrase is this leading tone resolved, and even that somewhat obliquely, as the lower tonic is substituted for the higher, so that the melody must descend from the leading tone. The last refrain of this number, however, does end on the high E, resolving the melody at last.

Both perceptions of the melody, the impression of folklike simplicity and the impression of something deeper, are essential, and together they establish Curly as a real folk hero in the most economical way. A less often cited but equally important characterization occurs with Jud's song, "Lonely Room" (Ex. 4-9). The only song in *Oklahoma!* in the minor mode, it is the necessary explanation of Jud's villiany, the motivation for all the action in the second act.

The song begins with a quarter-note ostinato sounding an F-sharp/G clash which becomes the most characteristic sonority of the piece.

Ex. 4-8 Rodgers and Hammerstein, *Oklahoma!*,
"Oh, What a Beautiful Morning" (No. 1), mm. 29–44.

When the voice enters, the accompaniment is filled out, but with a chord that is functionally ambiguous, especially along with the ostinato. The melody that Jud sings for the most part is little more than a recitative-like expansion of the ostinato, mostly F-sharps and Gs. Only

with the arrival of the F-sharp major chord (m. 10) does the B minor
key become clear. By employing fairly nonfunctional harmony to that
point, Rodgers not only highlights the important lyric ("By myself in a
lonely room") but establishes a singular musical idiom in this song that
is different from all the other music in the play, a musical symbol, in
effect, for Jud's isolation from the community.

Ex. 4-9 Rodgers and Hammerstein, *Oklahoma!*,
"Lonely Room" (No. 15), mm. 1–12.

Jud's melody does not change much as it moves on (mm. 11–12), but the accompaniment begins running notes to effect Jud's "dream." When his dream reaches its climax in his imagination, his melody finally breaks out of the straitjacket that has confined it.

Ex. 4-10 Rodgers and Hammerstein, *Oklahoma!*,
"Lonely Room" (No. 15), mm. 22–34.

Given the melody's limited range thus far, Jud's twice rising to the tonic
B (mm. 31–32) seems dramatic enough, but the subsequent span of a
major seventh from D to the triumphant C-sharp (m. 34), harmonized
with a major triad, seems a liberation. That chord, however, leads quite

logically back to the ostinato and a recapitulation of the opening ten measures. The slow progression to the hymnodic F-sharp chord is heard once again, more painful this time as Jud sings "And the sun flicks my eyes/ It was all a pack o' lies/ I'm awake in a lonely room."

Ex. 4-11 Rodgers and Hammerstein, *Oklahoma!*,
"Lonely Room" (No. 15), mm. 43–53.

The coda (Ex. 4-11) reiterates what Jud has already told the Peddler, that he is through with pictures, that he wants "real things." The identity of the melody setting this resolution with the climax of the dream makes it perfectly clear exactly what things he wants. The final measures, which pit Jud's high C-sharp against the resolving B minor harmony, symbolize Jud's intended liberation and its precise terms more strongly than anything he could say.

"Lonely Room" transforms Jud from a formless villian into a motivated and credible agent of dramatic action.

> Jud is no longer only a sniveling, frightening, hideous, threatening misfit, but a pathetic human being. We recognize his dream, and we pity him even as we fear him.[8]

Rodgers's singular harmonic and melodic idiom in this song is more complex than in any other in the play, for Jud, the psychotic, is the most complex character. The depth of its characterization perhaps explains why this song has had such little popularity, and why it is sometimes—incredibly—omitted in performance. It makes little sense outside its dramatic context, and, like much of Sondheim's music, cannot be popular on the radio.

The "dream" ballet which ends the first act and which is one of the most famous features of *Oklahoma!*, is yet another crucial characterization. At this point in the story, Laurey cannot decide whether to go to the box social dance with Jud, whom she fears but promised anyway to spite Curly, or with Curly, whom she really loves. She sniffs some "Elixir of Egypt" which the peddler has sold her to help her think more clearly. She falls into a dream state which the ballet acts out.

The ballet, in brief, runs as follows:

Ballet Sequence

Action	Music
Laurey and Curly figures dance ecstatically	"Out Of My Dreams"
"Laurey" and "Curly" continue. Other figures, girls and cowboys, enter and exit. "Curly" kisses "Laurey" and walks off.	"Beautiful Morning"
Girls arrive and embrace "Laurey"	"Kansas City"

Bridal veil floats down and is placed on "Laurey"	"Beautiful Morning"
"Curly" and cowboys enter, astride horses	"Surrey"
A wedding procession is formed	"Surrey"
"Jud" enters and removes veil	"Surrey" (chromatic)
"French postcard" girls enter	"Pore Jud" and "I Cain't Say No"
"Postcard" girls dance with "Jud"	"I Cain't Say No"
"Curly" fires at "Jud" with pistol	"Pore Jud"
Fight	"Lonely Room" "Pore Jud" motives
"Jud" strangles "Curly"	"Surrey" (chromatic)
Jud awakens Laurey and she goes with him	"People" (chromatic)
Curly watches them depart with puzzlement	

Agnes De Mille, the famous choreographer of ballet, was quite conscious of the particular requirements of dance that was to be incorporated into a musical, and also well aware of what it revealed of Laurey's character:

> The ballet . . . showed what was going on in her mind and heart, her terrors, her fears, her hopes; so in fact the happiness of her life, her life itself, depended on the choice. And the first act, which normally would have ended with a bland and ordinary musical comedy finale, ended starkly with the murder of the hero. The audience was caught on the suspense of the girl's terror.[9]

The ballet is disappointing in only one respect: its music. As indicated in the above plan, the dance is set with only a loose ordering of songs that recalls medley overture. The tunes are mostly presented whole, without much adaptation or motivic development, and the relationship between them and the dancing action is tenuous at best. Indeed, there is no apparent reason at all why "Kansas City" is used the way it is, or why "The Surrey with the Fringe on Top" should set a wedding processional. Worse, the original meanings of some songs are distorted when their relationship to the dancing is plausible but superficial. Using "I Cain't Say No" for the pinup girls is just such a falsification, since the song has nothing to do with promiscuous behavior. Rather, it is a delightful expression of an adolescent girl's first feeble struggles to rein in her own instincts in the face of a universal social code.

Such adaptation of the tunes as does occur consists only of substituting chromatic for conventional harmony, but since the tunes are used whole, and the entire ballet is but a string of them, there is no thoroughgoing rationale behind such development. The musical effect is quite naive, as is the device itself.

It is difficult to assess Rodgers's role in this design. The music for dance routines in musical plays back then was usually thrown together from existing songs after the routine had been choreographed, often by a talented rehearsal pianist. In any case, a serious ballet demands a serious composition, through-composed, based, perhaps, on motives from earlier songs, but motives that can develop new ideas that might advance the psychological action. The ballet in *Carousel* that occurs when Billy, up in "heaven," watches his daughter being spurned by her community is also weakened by the use of whole themes of questionable choice and by music accompanying her final rejection that has no commensurate weight, but at least in one or two spots there is significant motivic development reflecting the action of the dancers. It is puzzling that Rodgers, who had composed a couple of pure ballet scores before 1943,[10] was not more careful with the dance music for *Oklahoma!*

Still, the ballet must be performed because it clarifies the most important dramatic issue. "Could anyone give a damn about a story whose burning issue was who takes whom to a box social?" Rodgers asked himself when trying to raise money to produce *Oklahoma!*[11] Indeed, the audience must. But the issue itself is not the problem; it is one of Eric Bentley's "little dramas," which "to the imagination, are big, and are cast in the likeness of precisely the big dramas described in the newspaper."[12] The problem is making the box social seem big, and this is precisely what the ballet does. It is an expression of Laurey's view of the world at that moment, and in that world the box social means all.

The depth of characterization in song and dance, then, is the outstanding achievement of *Oklahoma!* Because the music is directed to this end so exclusively, its dramatic quality is static rather than active. In *Show Boat's* "Make Believe," there is dramatic action between the beginning of the song and the end: Magnolia and Ravenal fall in love, or at least the audience is made aware of it. The songs in *Oklahoma!* tell much more about the characters who sing them, but the dramatic situation is little different after the song than before, unless one considers definition of character itself to be a dramatic act.

To compensate for this, Rodgers and Hammerstein developed a method of integration that, while not really new, revolutionized thinking about the placement of songs in a musical play. It meant actually decreasing the number of songs, but arranging them within the play more skillfully:

> The score of *Show Boat* contains twenty musical numbers, all different—a feast of lovely tunes that punctuate the action without necessarily advancing it. It is almost *too* tuneful. The score of *Oklahoma!* comprises just twelve basic musical numbers. But these twelve are not just . . . reprised. They are woven in and out of the story, sometimes under dialogue, sometimes quoted briefly, at others repeated in various guises. . . .[13]

Consider how the play's opening scene, an extraordinarily lengthy one, is designed.

Synopsis—*Oklahoma!*, Act I, scene 1

"Oh, What a Beautiful Mornin'" (Curly)   E major

> *Dialogue:* Curly makes clear to Aunt Eller that he has come to ask Laurey to the box social.

"Oh, What a Beautiful Mornin'" (Laurey)   E major

> *Dialogue:* Laurey enters and exchanges taunts with Curly. She asks how they would travel to the social.

"The Surrey with the Fringe on Top" (Curly)   A major

> *Melodrama:* Laurey teases him that he has hired the rig without anyone to go with him. Curly retorts that he made the whole thing up.

"The Surrey with the Fringe on Top" (Curly)   A major

> *Dialogue:* Laurey, thinking she has been tricked, flounces out. Cowboys enter. Will Parker intends to marry Ado Annie, now that he has won fifty dollars in Kansas City.

"Kansas City" (Will)   A-flat major

> *Dance:* Cowboys and Aunt Eller
> *Dialogue:* Aunt Eller tells Curly that Jud is infatuated with Laurey.

Jud appears and tells Aunt Eller that Laurey has agreed to go with him to the social. Curly then asks Aunt Eller to go with him in his surrey, which he has indeed hired after all.

"The Surrey with the Fringe" (half ref.) (Curly)   A major

Dialogue: Laurey reveals to Aunt Eller that she is afraid to go with Jud, that she asked him merely to spite Curly. Ado Annie enters. When Laurey tells her that Will has returned, Ado Annie confesses that she has trouble being faithful to just one "feller."

"I Cain't Say No!" (Ado Annie)   F major

Dialogue: Peddler enters. Ado Annie asks him if he is serious about marrying her. Will enters and woos Annie.

"I Cain't Say No!" (trio only) (Will)   D major

"Oh, What a Beautiful Mornin'" (Crowd, Curley)   E major

Dialogue: Girls notice that Curly is not paying attention to Laurey.

"Many a New Day" (Laurie, girls)   D major

Dance: Laurey, girls
Dialogue: Ado Annie, Peddler, and Annie's father enter. Annie's father forces Peddler to become engaged to Annie because of certain indiscretions.

"It's a Scandal" (Peddler, cowboys)   D major

Dialogue: Laurey tells Curly that people are gossiping about them, expecting them to be together.

"People Will Say We're in Love" (Curley, Laurie)   D major

Melodrama: Curly asks Laurey to tell Jud that she would rather go with him. She refuses.

"People Will Say" (half ref.) (Laurie)   D major

Melodrama: Aunt Eller comforts Laurey.
Change of scene.

The convention that is completely reformed in this scene is the reprise. Formerly, a song would be introduced into the play and, if it were a crowd-pleaser, would be sung again in the second act, usually for the sake of filler or applause. To hear the songs repeated almost immediately after short dialogue was unknown; even *Porgy and Bess*, which is rich with wonderful reprises, does not repeat them immediately.

The effect of these frequent reprises is to integrate song and spoken word much more closely, but just as important, to create another level of dramatic action. When Laurey enters by singing "Oh, What A Beautiful Mornin'," an affinity between her and Curly is established even before she has spoken a single word, an affinity which stands up to the contradictory dialogue that follows. Similarly, Will's ironic reprise of "I Cain't Say No" confirms his match with Ado Annie. Curly's short half refrain of "Surrey" is in effect a most appropriate parting taunt to Laurey, who set herself up for it.

This sort of integration, where it seems as if the dialogue interrupts the song as much as the song interrupts the dialogue, creates the dramatic action that the character songs alone would lack. The dramatic continuity takes place across the numbers, rather than within them. This continuity can have great range. One fine moment in the play occurs in the second act, when Curly and Laurey finally become engaged. After they kiss, "People Will Say We're in Love" begins in the orchestra. The first three phrases are instrumental, over which Curly shouts with foolish joy that Laurey is to marry him. When she warns him that he will be heard "all the way to Catoosie!" he replies:

Ex. 4-12 Rodgers and Hammerstein, *Oklahoma!*,
"People Will Say We're In Love" (No. 24), mm. 13–16.

By a change of a few lyrics, the song, referring far back to the end of the first scene, has been transformed from a pretense of propriety that concealed love into an honest expression of it. The reprise reveals all at once how far the two lovers have come.

This kind of dramaturgy, however, has a distinct disadvantage: because its musical elements are small and dramatically static, the method is quite incapable of expressing in music passages that have rapid dramatic action, even if this action is crucial to the plot. In *Oklahoma!*, the tense moments of the auction scene, the subsequent quarrel between Jud and Laurey, and the killing have no musical setting. Since these events all occur toward the end of the play, it makes the problem especially tricky, and Rodgers seems to have been aware of it. "Let's get to the curtain quickly after the killing," he told Hammerstein during the planning stages. "If we start developing anything new the play will go downhill."[14] This throws the whole conception out of balance in one respect, since in music drama everything that is sung automatically has greater significance than the spoken parts, and so one would like to have all the most important dramatic acts sung. That they are not is perhaps *Oklahoma!*'s only significant failing.

Oklahoma! is one of those art phenomena that seemed revolutionary from the outset. There were enormous difficulties in raising the production money; the usual Broadway backers were wary of investing in a show that broke so many rules. After the premiere, the critics praised such daring and were grateful that it "opened new vistas in musical plays."[15] The rush of composers and writers to conform to the new standard after *Oklahoma!* is quite amusing in retrospect. Rodgers recalls:

> Everyone suddenly became "integration"-conscious, as if the idea of welding together song, story and dance had never been thought of before. There were also a number of costume musicals, and no self-respecting production dared open without at least one "serious" ballet.[16]

Historian Abe Laufe fills in for Rodgers' discretion:

> Ballets were considered so essential that they were injected into musical comedies whether they fit the plot or not. In fact, ballet became so common in the theater that within a few years the same critics who had praised the dance routines in *Oklahoma!* became

almost ecstatic when leading players or a chorus line would break into an old, familiar tap routine.[17]

It is easy to see why this happened. The critic of *Dance Magazine* accorded *Oklahoma!*'s dream ballet a historic significance:

> These dances are Miss de Mille's greatest contribution to theatre dance; they popularized the ballet and concert idioms of Martha Graham, Doris Humphrey, Charles Weidman, Eugene Loring and Agnes de Mille herself.[18]

Other hindsights seem to suggest that some of the innovations are illusory. It is quite clear, for example, that the creators of *Oklahoma!* did not set out to revolutionize the theater; they were as reluctant to throw out convention as anyone. "Dick and I, for several days, sought ways and means of logically introducing a group of girls into the early action of the play," admits Hammerstein.[19] It was their faithfulness to dramatic logic that forced them to change.

But even the touted changes—the ballet, the setting, the killing—had strong precedents. Rodgers's own *Pal Joey* and *I Married an Angel* have dream ballets, and Hammerstein's *Rose Marie* has a killing, not to mention *Porgy and Bess*'s tally of two murders and two drownings. No, it is not the introduction of this or that element or technique that gives *Oklahoma!* its historical position and its artistic status among musicals. Explaining why it must be regarded as a milestone of the musical theater, another giant of that theater, Alan Jay Lerner, points to its synthesis of these techniques and elements:

> For what "Oklahoma!" had done was to unify and give form to trends that had been growing disparately in the music theater and, in doing so, provide a marker for the next mile into the future.[20]

In other words, *Oklahoma!* stands as a summation as well as a beginning. Its innovation is in its maturity.

Chapter 5

Morality Play as Musical

One of the most frequent questions I am asked is: "What is your favorite of all your musicals?" My answer is *Carousel*.[1]

Richard Rodgers

In the fall of 1944, Paul Whiteman, the famous band leader, convinced the Blue Radio Network (later the American Broadcasting Company) to fund a series of commissions of new instrumental compositions to be played on his radio program. The series, called *Music Out of the Blue*, gave composers advances on royalties in exchange for performance rights for one year. The original thirteen commissioned composers included Aaron Copland, Leonard Bernstein, Igor Stravinsky, and Richard Rodgers, who "worked on a concert waltz called *Tales Of Central Park*."[2] Curiously, Rodgers and Hammerstein's new musical play *Carousel* opened the following April with "The Carousel Waltz" in place of a medley overture, a concert waltz in several sections of roughly the length that Whiteman had been seeking. Are the two waltzes the same piece?

David Ewen believes so. He reports in his biography of Rodgers that although Whiteman commissioned the waltz he never used it, and that "its mood and movement so happily caught the gay and colorful feeling of the opening *Carousel* scene that Hammerstein persuaded Rodgers to use it for the play."[3] Indeed, the Paul Whiteman archives at Williams College list the title "Tales of Central Park" but contain no recording or arrangement. Rodgers himself, however, refers to no Whiteman commission in his autobiography:

> For the overture to *Carousel* I decided not to have an overture. I had become weary—I still am, in fact—of the sound that comes out of an orchestra pit during an overture. All that is ever heard is the brass because the orchestra never has a sufficient number of strings, and the audience must make a concerted effort to pick up any melody that is not blasted. Instead I tried to avoid this problem by making the audience pay attention, which I did simply by opening on a pantomime scene, with the orchestra playing a single piece, the "Carousel Waltz," rather than the usual medley. In this way we also gave the audience an emotional feeling for the characters in the story and helped to establish the mood for the entire play.[4]

Why all the history? What does it matter? It matters because "The Carousel Waltz" has an extraordinary relationship with the songs in the musical play. Like a classical overture, it sets the musical terms of the entire composition and is the main source of musical material, not tunes so much as basic musical elements and procedures. If Ewen's story is correct (unfortunately, no reference is given), then Hammerstein's suggestion is a better testament to his untrained yet profound musical sensitivity than perhaps any other episode, for the waltz establishes a musical idiom that belongs to this play alone. But the Whiteman commission challenges the very idea that Rodgers was a composer concerned with musical drama, for how could he take a piece composed for a completely unrelated purpose and stand it at the head of a serious musical play?

As it happens, Rodgers is in quite good company in the matter of adapting previously composed material for dramatic purposes. Handel's ability to do this is legendary, of course, but it was also a fairly common practice of early nineteenth century Italians. George Gershwin did it in *Of Thee I Sing.* Furthermore, this is hardly a case of dredging up some long forgotten movement. The precise chronology may never be known, but it is certain that Rodgers was deeply involved in *Carousel* when and if he accepted the commission. Even if he originally intended the waltz to be given to Whiteman, it is easy to imagine that salient musical elements of *Carousel* songs—motives, progressions, harmonic procedures—would be at the forefront of his composing mind. A strong relationship between those songs and the waltz might be the most natural outcome of such a situation. Indeed, the coincidence suggests the following chronology: (1) Rodgers and Hammerstein begin work on *Carousel* in 1944, composing "Soliloquy" first; (2) Rodgers accepts a Whiteman commission to compose a concert waltz called "Tales of Central Park"; (3) He composes the waltz while continuing to work on *Carousel*; (4) When the waltz is finished, Rodgers and Hammerstein see that it would be the perfect accompaniment for the pantomime; (5) Rodgers decides not to submit the waltz to Whiteman because he would yield performance rights just as the play opened.

In the end, of course, the dramatic effect of the music must stand or fall on its own terms in the context of the play, not on the facts of its origin. If a composer can make a successful adaptation, so much the better for him. In this case, the musical relationships between "The Carousel Waltz" and many of the other songs in the play are so compelling that it is difficult to believe that the waltz was not composed just for this purpose. Its unique tone, its vocabulary specific to this play, is established on the opening page.

The three most important musical elements are heard in the first long phrase (mm. 1–10). The tonic key of D major is established simply by strumming the chord, but the ear is soon surprised by a motive that seems to be in a different key. Then the short phrase is entirely transposed down a perfect fourth (m. 5–6) to make a dominant version of the first. The idea is repeated and the upper melody breaks the sequence, articulating the first long phrase (m. 10). So what has been heard? First, a slow and simple harmonic progression in the lower register accompanied by a much faster, chromatic one in the high register: a multilevel texture of harmonic rhythm. Second, chromatic juxtapositions that establish unusual pitch combinations as expressive norms for this play, above all the augmented triad, which is heard in measures 4 (D–F♮–A♮), 6 (A–C♮–E♮), 8 and 10 at the peaks of all the short phrases. Third, modal degrees of the scale, F-sharp (third degree) and B (sixth degree), are emphasized by melodic contour and the chromatics which give a hint of those keys. All these elements are strengthened anew in the next long phrase (mm. 11–17). The high-level underlying

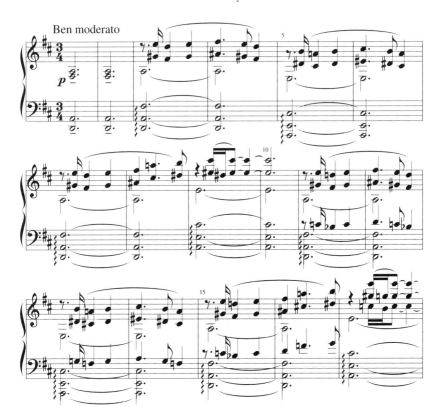

Ex. 5-1 Rodgers and Hammerstein, *Carousel*, "The Carousel Waltz,"
(No. 1), mm. 1–17.

progression in D is as firm as ever, while the low-level chromatic harmony becomes more biting still, now formed entirely of *parallel augmented chords.*

The power of the multilevel harmonic rhythm is unleashed as
Rodgers moves from introduction to waltz proper. The lower-level progressions are easily discerned as four-bar phrases, but under it all is a
steady dominant whose tension grows as it is prolonged. In Example
5-2, the high register moves from subdominant to tonic for each phrase,
while the dominant A is maintained below. The prolonged dominant
builds to a grand climax, with a final iii chord (F♯ minor, Ex. 5-3, m.
50) superimposed onto a V, which leads into the waltz proper. The
waltz tune is a transformation of the opening motive, now reconciled to
its key, and yet there is the same harmonic procedure. There are three
quick tiny chords for every measure in the upper parts, all subsumed in

a slower and more fundamental bass progression. The end of the first phrase shows once again an emphasis on the modal steps, in the F-sharp of the melody and in the Bs which color the tonic and dominant harmony below.

Ex. 5-2 Rodgers and Hammerstein, *Carousel*, "The Carousel Waltz" (No. 1), mm. 27–34.

Ex. 5-3 Rodgers and Hammerstein, *Carousel*, "The Carousel Waltz (No. 1), mm. 47–57.

It might seem as though this harmonic procedure would sound too sophisticated or learned for a play that takes place among the simple folk of a New England mill town, but its actual effect is quite the opposite. The slow and simple bass line gives the waltz tune the oom-pah-pah quality of a town band, especially when reinforced by the tuba, which Rodgers insisted on for the pit orchestra. Meanwhile the other benefits of such harmonic control are many. It creates the sense of climax just before the waltz tune because the high-level dominant chord has been stretched out for so long, awaiting resolution. The juxtaposition of two harmonic rhythms generates and justifies unusual chords and harmonic colorings, such as the augmented triad, which would be out of the question in a simpler context. In sum, this two-level harmonic movement, in conjunction with these augmented chords and the emphasis on the modal degrees, is responsible for a tone and ambience so peculiar to *Carousel* that it seems impossible to mistake any of its music for that of another play. As Rodgers himself states, it is "The Carousel Waltz" that establishes this tone, right from the opening bars.

The relationship of the waltz with the rest of the play is made dramatic by the activity that occurs on stage while it is being played: a pantomime in which most of the major characters are introduced in a carnival setting, with a carousel at center stage. It is this scene that establishes the main romantic interest between Billy Bigelow and Julie Jordan, quite abstractly, so that the audience knows almost nothing about them except that they have fallen in love. This is the basis for one of the central dramatic themes; their love has not been explained, and is indeed inexplicable, yet remains to be expressed.

Although the motion on stage is not balletic, it is coordinated with the waltz, originally by Rouben Mamoulian. He remarked on the originality of the concept of the mute prologue:

> The highest compliment I could get as a director is that no one has seemed to notice anything very unusual about the prelude, but there it is—seventy people onstage for five and a half minutes, and not a word spoken. In a straight play you couldn't think of getting away with that. But here it is so stylized that within its own framework it is perfectly logical and right.[5]

Mamoulian is quite wrong about its legitimacy in a straight play, for Ferenc Molnar did get away with the very same prologue concept in *Liliom*, the source play for *Carousel*. Indeed it is the successful adaptation of Molnar's prologue idea that is the basis for the transformation of *Liliom*, a complex drama, into a musical play of comparable depth.

The principal source of *Liliom's* complexity is its cast of characters, and translating these characters into operatic terms was Rodgers and Hammerstein's greatest difficulty and most admirable achievement. Indeed, in comparison with Curley and Laurey, the protagonists in *Liliom* are bundles of subtle contradictions that music could hardly hope to project:

> The dualistic hero, Andreas Zavoczki, is not a villian, only a maladjusted creature who ends up doing the wrong things in spite of all the possible good intentions. This braggart dreamer is an obstinate nonconformist, a primitive person with a vicious temper, yet a noble man full of compassion.
>
> Julie . . . emerges as the eternal female ideal. She loves unselfishly, with undemanding devotion and endurance. With almost supernatural insight and common sense, she grasps the realities of life and the true nature of her man. . . . She is taciturn and inarticulate . . .[6]

Furthermore, dramatic action occurs not just between characters, as in *Oklahoma!*, but within them, and this action is the more important one. That is why *Carousel* can justifiably be termed a morality play as well as fantasy (as it and *Liliom* are usually called), because the struggle between good and evil that defines a morality play takes place within Billy Bigelow.

Such complexity demands an equivalent complexity of musical expression, and Rodgers and Hammerstein respond to that demand with a number of musical resources. There is much more use of melodrama, which means that characters speak over music from the orchestra. There is also a large amount of sung music which has the freedom of organization, the absence of repetition, and the melodic and rhythmic flexibility of recitative, although the sense of meter never quite disappears. These techniques make transitions from spoken dialogue to song much more gradual and smooth. The musical play therefore seems more serious because one is much less aware of the seams of operatic convention.

The same variety of musical textures allows the construction of extended musical scenes of a type quite different and more sophisticated than those in *Oklahoma!* In that play, the musical unity of a scene depends on frequent reprises of a central song, but in *Carousel* there is true musical as well as dramatic progression. The first musical number after the prologue begins with dialogue that is rhythmically coordinated with the underplaying of the orchestra: Carrie asks Julie how she feels about Billy Bigelow. As the dialogue continues, it begins to be sung ("You're a Queer One, Julie Jordan"). The texture is close to song; the phrasing is regular and the dialogue rhymed. Next, Carrie describes how strangely Julie has been acting lately, singing monotonic lines to an orchestral accompaniment that represents the whirring of mill machinery. There is a brief return of "You're a Queer One," followed by yet another texture, pure melodrama. This leads into the first real song, "His Name is Mister Snow," but conventional form does not hold here either, for when Carrie describes Mr. Snow's proposal of marriage, her melody becomes again a *parlando* with chromatic harmony, another pseudorecitative. It does not conclude, but sets up dominant harmony which leads into the only completely closed song of the scene, "When I Marry Mister Snow."

The musical unity of this scene derives from the consistent key of G major, but also from the consistent usage of musical materials taken from the waltz. The multilevel harmony of "His Name Is Mister Snow" not only provides that song with the waltz's sophisticated yet folklike harmonic coloring, but allows Rodgers to construct the song on a very static alternation of high-level tonic and dominant harmony. Because the high-level harmony is so static, there is almost no sense of progression until a modulation to B minor (another modal emphasis) which begins the recitative-like proposal sequence. From this point on the listener

home ev-'ry night in his round bot-tomed boat With a net full of her-ring from the sea.

Ex. 5-4 Rodgers and Hammerstein, *Carousel*, "Mister Snow" (No. 4), mm. 67–75, with harmonic analysis.

awaits a clear return to the key of G, but this is delayed by the chromaticism, so that this piece sounds much more like a prelude to "When I Marry Mister Snow" than a song in its own right, and the more active harmony of the latter song is welcome relief to what has gone before.

When I mar-ry Mis-ter Snow, The

flow-ers 'll be buz-zin' with the hum of bees, The birds 'll make a rack-et in the

Ex. 5-5 Rodgers and Hammerstein, *Carousel*, "Mister Snow" (No. 4), mm. 115–125.

Here again the musical material for this apparently simple piece is drawn from the waltz. The first phrase begins and ends on modal scale degrees, and the repeated B note in the melody is intensified by the harmony of an augmented tonic triad. The two-level progressions return in the second and third phrases, and include chromatic juxtapositions—the G-sharp against the G, and C proceeding to C-sharp on "churchyard trees"—that recall the beginning of the waltz.

Carousel has a number of such scenes that, in their musical continuity and dramatic progression, are much more ambitious than anything in *Oklahoma!* Their flexibility of design allows the music to speak at length for the laconic New England characters, and the complexity of the musical idiom on all levels meets the demands of the drama.

Lavishing such attention on the likes of Carrie Pipperidge calls into question the nature of the subplot in *Carousel*. Once more *Oklahoma!* provides an instructive contrast because its own usage is so typical. In that play, the triangle of Ado Annie, Will Parker, and the Peddler form a symmetrical and essentially comic counterplot to the triangle of Curley, Laurey, and Jud. Their story is cleverly interwoven into the main story and its purpose is comic relief. The role of Carrie Pipperidge and Enoch Snow is hardly so simple; the musical setting of "When I Marry Mister Snow" reveals a seriousness that belies the naive comedy of some of her lines. This is especially apparent at the end, when the main tune returns to be elaborated by Rodgers's favorite device, the extension. The rise to the F-natural is the song's climax, a fresh contrast to the chromatic harmony derived from the sharp side of G major that characterizes the song to that point, and the phrase reiterates that F two measures later before moving inconclusively down to the A. Here the augmented triad reappears expressively (m. 157) and quite explicitly in that it does not arise from chromatic voice leading, only to be used again on "bold and darin'." The sentiment overcomes the humorous

Ex. 5-6 Rodgers and Hammerstein, *Carousel*, "Mister Snow (No. 5), mm. 147–166.

epithets of the final lyric, since the next clear triad and progression in G, as well as the peak of melody, come with "darlin' Mister Snow!"

The depth of feeling in Carrie is brought home only when it is fully realized what she has been singing about. This is no schoolgirl's idealized image of love here, but rather a simple and real-life wedding, and married life, certainly very unusual topics for any romantic character, let alone one that is, according to form, supposed to be comic. The song is reprised most appropriately when Carrie announces the engagement to her friends just before the clambake that concludes the first act. Its rendition is identical to the first (except for its key, now F major), until the final section, when Mr. Snow makes his surprise entrance and sings the conclusion in A major. This device shows that Mr. Snow's feelings are as deep as Carrie's, and it also provides a smooth transition to another extended musical scene between the two of them.

After a short scene, the two are left alone on stage and begin talking about their future together. Like the first scene of the play, it begins with a mélange of arioso and melodrama textures before the song proper, "When the Children Are Asleep," finally arrives, and again, Mr. Snow's participation in a scene of such design makes the audience take him seriously. The new song continues to develop the sentiments of "When I Marry Mr. Snow," for its subject is a domestic tranquility that rarely finds expression on any stage. The apparently simple melody is given expressive depth by its harmonization. The first phrase (mm. 87–90) is heard three times in the song, and its concluding note is treated differently, with increasing harmonic tension each time. In measure 89 it is set with a plain tonic chord, with the descending inner voice immediately moving to connect to the next phrase. The second instance (m. 97) finds it the goal of a temporary modulation to D major, an emphasis on the sixth scale degree of F that comes from the waltz. The

When the child-ren are a - sleep and lights are low. If I still love you The way I love you to - day, You'll par - don my say - ing: "I told you so!" When the child-ren are a - sleep I'll dream with you. We'll think, what

Ex. 5-7 Rodgers and Hammerstein, *Carousel*, "Carrie and Mr. Snow Sequence" (No. 12), mm. 87–114.

reference to the waltz is confirmed when the third occurrence (m. 109) is harmonized with an F augmented triad that demands in the strongest terms a continuation on to the conclusion.

The harmonization of this song is not the only agent of its expression, for it also has a subtlety of melodic phrasing that shows yet another advance from *Oklahoma!*, whose tunes are built on clear four-bar phrases through and through. In "When the Children Are Asleep" this easy symmetry is just slightly disturbed even at the beginning: the first phrase barely carries over into the fourth bar, while the second phrase is nearly five bars long. The implications of this slight imbalance are shortly realized. The third phrase is identical to the first, clearly setting up a consequent phrase to the original antecedent. Yet, the fourth one does not conclude, but instead breaks what should be a longer phrase into two subphrases ("If I still love you the way / I love you today"), and ends in the wrong key (D minor). The rhythm of the fifth phrase is clearly parallel with the fourth one, as are the lyrics, but this time the two sub-phrases are bound into a smooth continuous one. This magic transformation occurs in measure 104, where two half notes are substituted for the dotted half and quarter of the parallel spot (m. 100). The evenness of the rhythm, and Hammerstein's lyric, prevent the ear from perceiving a phrase break here where it is expected. Instead, the smooth continuation of the phrase seems the perfect reflection of an upwelling of emotion so strong that the force of its momentum carries through.

The consummation of this love song comes when it is sung as a duet, and Rodgers applies his considerable powers of extension to its conclusion. Now that odd emphasis on the offbeats in the accompaniment of the last phrase ("We'll think what fun we hev had/ And be glad that it all came true") is used to generate a rhapsodic extension of the last phrase. The climactic power of the moment depends upon the delay of the final cadence for eight more measures beyond its usual place, and upon Rodgers's withholding the texture of the two characters singing in parallel, for the first time, until the last moments.

The enhancement of the subplot that this musical treatment produces is really twofold. Most obviously, it represents a much deeper treatment of subplot characters than in almost any Broadway musical,

Ex. 5-8 Rodgers and Hammerstein, *Carousel*, "Carrie and Mr. Snow Sequence" (No. 12), mm. 155–167.

but it also is an enormous expansion of the original characters in *Liliom*. In that play, Wolf and Marie Beifeld are representatives of conventional society, and therein is the clue to the reason why the roles of Carrie and Enoch Snow had to be different. In Molnar's play, conventional society in the persons of the Beifelds is quite indifferent to Liliom's fate, and therefore the loss of this society after his suicide means nothing to him. In revising the conclusion of *Liliom*, Rodgers and Hammerstein created a ballet which reveals Billy's daughter, Louise, excluded from the New England community because of him. Thus, in order for this exclusion to mean something, in order for it to motivate Billy to descend once again to the world, the community must be important. So we have the loving, and lovable, Carrie and Enoch, who sing in earnest about weddings, married life, and a romance of a quiet evening after the children have been taken care of. Their music does what is quite rare on the stage: it idealizes conventionality, and thereby makes it valuable.

This portrayal of the comic couple causes a dramatic inconsistency in the second act, when Mr. Snow and some of his children, in snubbing Louise, are shown to be not only conventional in their behavior but uncharitable as well. This does not square well with the image of Snow that is constructed through the music of the first act, but by this time, the virtues of the New England community have been pretty well established.

To establish such virtues is the principal justification for adding a chorus to Molnar's *Liliom*. The chorus, of course, was virtually required by the Broadway tradition and was the principal reason why Rodgers and Hammerstein chose New England as an appropriate setting: the coastal mill town idea offered mill workers and fishermen. Yet the need to make the community itself a value allowed them to integrate the chorus into the dramatic scheme, and it imbues the chorus music with a seriousness of idiom consistent with the rest of the play. Unlike the unseen society of *Liliom*, the community in *Carousel* must have true value, its ways and traditions sacred. That is why "A Real Nice Clambake," ostensibly a light chorus number that opens the second act, is really a celebration of a community ritual. The connotation is made quite explicit when the last course of the holy meal, the steamed clams, is recalled.

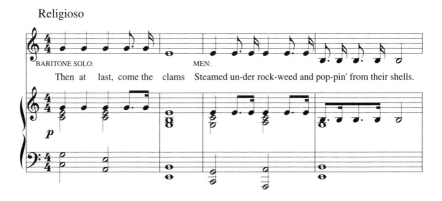

Ex. 5-9 Rodgers and Hammerstein, *Carousel*, "A Real Nice Clambake" (No. 19), mm. 131–134.

The processional rhythm, the preponderance of minor chords and modal progressions, and Rodgers's tempo mark require no further comment.

The serious tone that is special to the music of *Carousel*, then, dominates the musical-dramatic techniques of melodrama and quasi-recitative, and pervades the "comic" subplot characters and the chorus. Its characteristic progressions, harmonies, and subtleties of phrasing are heard everywhere. The result is an intensely dramatic integration, for all these distinct parts have bearing upon the central dramatic issue: how Billy Bigelow, the insecure braggart who sees himself as a strong man who can get along without the slightest help or dependency, will cope with his inexplicable love for Julie.

The struggle between good and evil in this morality play is within Billy himself. It is the struggle to free himself from the evil of his own mostly false self-image, which will not let him love Julie honestly. Music has little role in painting the dark side of his character, for that is mostly superficial, and music does not do well with pretense, falseness, and disingenuity. That is the task of the libretto. Rather, it is the role of music to illuminate Billy's goodness.

This illumination is concentrated in just three numbers which include the extended "Bench Scene," Billy's famous "Soliloquy," and a brief reprise late in the play. The "Bench Scene," early in the first act, finds Billy philosophizing about the nature of the world and his own place in it, responding through Rodgers's pseudorecitative to the impressive forces of sea and sky. This is the scene that makes explicit the love match between Billy and Julie so strongly implied in the opening pantomime. They share the same music in this scene, although they never sing together. The scene ends with Billy singing the love song which Julie had sung to him moments earlier.

The love song, "If I Loved You," has a lyric that even in its title seems conditional, but which is prescient in a very specific way and in fact announces one of the main dramatic themes: the couple's inability to express their love. The music, as in "People Will Say We're in Love," instantly banishes any impression that what they say in the lyrics might be true, and through *Carousel*'s characteristic harmonies, progressions, and phrasing brings the attention to the dramatic theme.

Ex. 5-10 Rodgers and Hammerstein, *Carousel*, "Billy and Julie Scene" (No. 5), mm. 236–271.

The phasing of the melody is, strictly speaking, in four-bar periods, but is not symmetrical. The last note of the first phrase is not heard until the end of the fourth measure; the second phrase, much more stable, reaches its conclusion on the strong third measure. The first phrase subdivides into two short phrases because of the long note in the second measure and because of the syntax of the lyric; the second phrase changes that rhythm just slightly and so remains a single articulation. The implications of this pattern change are realized in the release (m. 253: "Longin' to tell you . . ."), where the four-bar phrases are now inexorable, emphasizing the all-important lyric by removing a seam where the listener expects one.

The dramatic importance of the release section is brought out in other ways. The modulation to B-flat minor is the first strong chord change since the song's beginning. Indeed, all the others are tonic chords or tonic derivatives, with the exception of the harmonies that begin the second and fourth phrases, and these are in weak inversions that could be considered the result of voice leading from the surrounding tonic chords. The B-flat minor is the first new chord in root position. This harmonic goal is prepared by the opening melodic motive, an outlined B-flat minor triad ("If I loved you"), and its arrival is made inevitable by the introduction of a D-flat *augmented* triad (m. 252), with the A-natural moving smoothly to B-flat in the alto voice.

The release itself (mm. 252–259) is characterized by a remarkable harmonization that includes a D dominant seventh under the leading tone C (mm. 254–255, a reference to the key of the waltz?) and an increased harmonic rhythm that sets up the last dominant chord (mm. 258–259) and thereby emphasizes the most crucial lyric with the greatest structural tension.

The musical idiom of the waltz has its greatest impact at this moment of the play. It is the slow high-level harmonic rhythm that sets up the significance of the B-flat minor passage as the only harmonically active section and thereby justifies the tremendous climax when the music returns to D-flat (m. 260) for the close. It is the augmented triad which initiates this activity. Even the static tonic harmony of the opening section is colored in a way that recalls the waltz. An augmented chord is introduced by the fourth measure, and the long note at the end of the second phrase (mm. 242–243) is harmonized by a I^6 that turns into a iii chord for the end of the phrase, an unusual emphasis on a modal degree. This harmonic color is recalled even more decisively when, at the song's end, the melody soars to a high F (mm. 266–267), and the same two harmonies are used again, now alternating twice as fast.

"If I Loved You" is the first insight into the complexity of Billy's character and the course that this relationship will take. It is his first confession of weakness and dependency, a confession given only by the music, not by the words, and therefore not by his conscious self. While this song presages the conflict between self and self-image, the best musical expression of that conflict comes in "Soliloquy," which Billy sings at the very end of Act I when he finds out that he is about to be a father.

"Soliloquy" has long been renowned for its elaborate form, changing textures, and its ability to reflect a number of emotional changes. Actually, this is true of any of the extended scenes in *Carousel*. "Soliloquy" is exceptional only in that it is for a single character. It is constructed on just two passages that could be detached as separate songs, surrounded by a variety of connective pseudorecitative. It is the juxtaposition of the two songs that illustrates the conflict most clearly.

"My Boy, Bill" seems to be missing most of those characteristics peculiar to the sound of *Carousel*. The harmonic rhythm is fast and takes place on a single structural level.[7] There are no augmented chords and little chromaticism. The rhythm of the melody emphasizes the

Ex. 5-11 Rodgers and Hammerstein, *Carousel*, "Soliloquy" (No. 15), mm. 37–55.

strong beats and the voice leading is either a rather obvious step motion or an equally pedestrian arpeggiation toward the end. The trumpet fanfares in the blank measures add to the bombast.

The lyrics show why the music is this way:

> Like a tree he'll grow,
> With his head held high
> And his feet planted firm on the ground,
> And you won't see nobody dare to try
> To boss him or toss him around!
> No pot-bellied, baggy eyed bully'll boss him around!

Billy, in describing his imaginary son, is really describing his own image of himself, what he imagines himself to be. The music is no more substantial than the picture that he creates. Moments later, when he considers the sobering prospect of a baby girl who would need his help, he sings in a much different manner.

Now Billy is no longer talking about himself, and so reveals his capacity for sentiment, part of his true self. The setting of this song returns to the *Carousel* sound: an augmented triad in the second measure, chromatic melody and voice leading later on. The tune must be one of Rodgers's most remarkable in all his songs, for its wandering through several keys (mm. 215–220) makes it sound original and new at every moment and yet it all springs from just two motivic ideas. The second measure, for example, has exactly the same notes as the first, simply cast in a different rhythmic pattern. The only other motive occurs when the melody leaps upward by a major seventh (mm. 209–210), only to fall downward from the leading tone, against its tendency, in an exquisite chromatic decoration. This "chromatic-dotted" motive is then slowed in the next measure to rest on a half cadence. It is no wonder that Rodgers repeated this gesture for the end of his song.

The evil side of Billy's inner struggle wins, temporarily, when his admirable resolve to provide for his daughter is perverted into a

Ex. 5-12 Rodgers and Hammerstein, *Carousel*, "Soliloquy" (No. 15), mm. 205–228.

robbery attempt. Even when, after his suicide, he returns to help Louise, whose unhappiness he has caused, his inability to express love defeats him. He slaps her. But Julie has glimpsed him, and they are left alone as the orchestra plays "If I Loved You" under the action. He breaks in at the release:

Longing to tell you,
But afraid and shy,
I let my golden chances pass me by.
Now I've lost you;
Soon I will go in the mist of day,
And you never will know
How I loved you,
How I loved you.

This is one of the greatest and most sentimental reprises of the Broadway stage. It recalls the precise cause and best musical expression of the tragic action at a moment late in the play when the consequences of Billy's character struggle are most evident, and when time is running out. It is a tribute to Oscar Hammerstein's craft to note how little change the lyric requires to create this effect, and that the simplest change—the repetition of the penultimate line, removing all pretense and condition—is the most moving. For Rodgers's part, it shows a fine instinct to have Billy enter mid-song, and the careful harmonic preparation of that middle section has its greatest benefits here.

Rodgers recounted that this reprise was added during tryouts:

Our New Haven opening in March 1945 went well except for the scene in which we depicted a "Mr. and Mrs. God" as a New England minister and his wife. Oscar rewrote the scene and substituted the Starkeeper. The other major change was to add a reprise of "If I Loved You" in the second act because we felt it needed more music.[8]

If this statement is true, then it is one of the best pieces of evidence that composers create by instinct and not by calculation, often quite unaware of the audible effects of their actions. The reprise, including the orchestral underplaying, is about sixty measures, perhaps two minutes of music. The American musical theater can only be grateful that such a small addition was, somehow, deemed necessary, if not significant. It is difficult to imagine *Carousel* without it.

Rodgers writes in his autobiography that he was often asked which of his musicals was his favorite:

My answer is *Carousel*. Oscar never wrote more meaningful or more moving lyrics, and to me, my score is more satisfying than any I've ever written. But it's not just the songs; it's the whole play. Beautifully written, tender without being mawkish, it affects me deeply every time I see it performed.[9]

Ironically, it is exactly that charge of being overly sentimental that is occasionally leveled at the play. *Carousel*'s first London production was a popular success, but not a critical one; review after review denounced its shallow portrayal of human feeling.

If any single source can be found for such reactions, it must be in the play's ending, the only significant plot change introduced by Rodgers and Hammerstein. The original *Liliom* ends with the title character's final failure to put things right by Julie; the stark conclusion is a logical outcome of the hero's nature. Even though the play had been a hit on Broadway in the 1921 season, the creators of *Carousel* believed that neither the musical audience of the 1940s nor the genre itself was ready for such an overtly unhappy end. So they added the graduation scene, in which Billy, continuing his invisible visit to earth, encourages Louise to believe in herself, as the graduation speaker advises, and tells Julie at last that he did love her after all. This is accomplished in two brief lines: "Believe him, darling! Believe."; and "I loved you, Julie. Know that I loved you!"

For many, this dramatic solution to the moral struggle that the play has portrayed is just too pat, too easy. This impression, however, dawns upon the listener retrospectively, not in the immediate experience of the moment, but only after the play is over. While the scene is played out, the audience is caught up in the power of the musical accompaniment, the graduates singing the hymn about human spirit, "You'll Never Walk Alone." The spiritual dazes the critical sensibilities. But what happens after it is all over? Why has the music lost its power of lasting conviction, a power so evident at so many other points of the play?

Because, for once, the musical idiom is inconsistent, not quite true to itself. The compromises required of Rodgers in his attempt to compose a dramatic piece in the manner of a hymn were simply too great. The simple rhythms and step motion of the melody do indeed recall the hymns with which most Americans would be familiar, but it is not matched with a typical fast harmonic rhythm and simple cadences. Instead, Rodgers engineers a long delay of cadence by chromatic progression, which betrays the simplicity of the melody by making out of it something more than it appears to be. The contrast is most evident in the climactic phrase itself, with the repeated notes C and E reflecting the steadfastness of resolution while harmonies alter chromatically below. And yet, the attempt comes close to success, for the generous use of augmented triads, which in other cases might well be considered an overdose of schmaltz, are here perfectly consistent with the sound of *Carousel*.

The line between true sentiment and sentimentalism can be fine indeed, and perhaps it is crossed in the finale. It is noteworthy, however, that although the British critics took strong exception to this

Ex. 5-13 Rodgers and Hammerstein, *Carousel*, "Graduation Scene"
(No. 31), mm. 24–37.

flavor, the American critics never did, through revival after revival. It might be worth asking whether the unsubtle, unabashed sentiment—not sentimentalism—with which *Carousel* concludes is an Americanism, a characteristic of a number of important American musicals that does not translate well into other languages or cultures. If so, then it was well indeed that *Carousel* was one of two musical plays, along with Leonard Bernstein's *Wonderful Town*, sent to the Brussels World's Fair in 1959 to be part of the American exhibit. Certainly no play other than this musical adaptation of a Hungarian stage classic could better show the finest and most American qualities of its native theater tradition.

Chapter 6

Shakespeare as Musical

I have no book sense.[1]

Cole Porter

The ideal of an integrated musical play that Rodgers and Hammerstein's *Oklahoma!* made so convincing in March 1943 was no boon to the composers who had made successful careers not on the strength of dramatic instincts but simply on the superior quality of their songs as songs. Chief among these composers was Cole Porter, who from the late 1920s through the early 1940s had written show after show that charmed theatergoers with sophisticated and witty lyrics and tunes that have since become standards.

Porter was just not interested in the craft of a libretto, nor in the dramatic issues of characterization and development. His method of composition indicates his real priorities:

First I think of an idea for a song and then I fit it to a title. Then I go to work on a melody, spotting the title at certain moments in the melody. Then I write the lyric—the end first—that way it has a strong finish. It's terribly important for a song to have a strong finish. I do the lyrics the way I'd do a crossword puzzle. I try to give myself a meter which will make the lyric as easy as possible to write, but without being banal. . . . I try to pick for my rhyme words of which there is a long list with the same ending.[2]

It is telling that the song's creation centers on Porter's own idea, and that of all the ancillary considerations, none is dramatic. There is nothing said about character, how the song will fit into the scene, or how it will lead into the next. The composition of a single song seems a closed process, unrelated to anything else the show might involve. Porter worked with a comprehensive outline of the show, so that he was certainly aware of what type of song was required for a given spot, but he did not have a script, and rarely made suggestions about the book for which he composed. As he once remarked, "I have no book sense."[3]

The result was a series of vacuous plays which cannot stand revival spiced up with songs which have been sung and played as standards the world over. There is perhaps no better example of this curious situation than *Anything Goes* (1934), Porter's most famous and successful musical of the 1930s. It originally contained such hits as "You're the Top," "I Get a Kick Out of You," and the title song, but the book is so weak that the producers of the 1965 revival had to prop it up by ransacking several other Porter shows for "It's Delovely" (from *Red, Hot, and Blue*, 1936), "Friendship" (from *DuBarry Was a Lady*, 1939), and "Take Me Back to Manhattan" (from *The New Yorkers*, 1930). It is no wonder. The original story was written by veteran bookwriters P. G. Wodehouse and Guy Bolton on the subject of a shipwreck. Then the S. S. *Morro Castle* actually sank off New Jersey with a loss of 125 lives, and producer Vinton Freedley saw the comedy in his plot premise disappear just two months before the scheduled opening. Because Wodehouse and Bolton were in Europe, he quickly hired Howard Lindsay and Russel Crouse to rewrite the story, now set on a very safe ocean liner. But the book was not finished until two days before the Boston opening, and revisions were made even in the last rehearsals.

Such is not the recommended method for composing an integrated musical play, and in performance today *Anything Goes* shows quite plainly its unusual history. Yet it survived over 400 performances in the early thirties, and Porter's successful streak continued well into the next decade, finishing with a series of five shows each of which were box office smashes: *DuBarry Was a Lady* (1939), 408 performances; *Panama*

Hattie (1940), 501 performances; *Let's Face It* (1941), 547 performances; *Something for the Boys* (1942), 422 performances; and *Mexican Hayride* (1943), 481 performances. Then, suddenly, the Porter charm seemed to vanish. There were two flops, *Seven Lively Arts* (1944) and *Around the World in Eighty Days* (1946), film offers declined, and rumor had it that Porter was finished. It seems too easy to point to *Oklahoma!* and *Carousel* as the reason, if only because public standards are rarely altered so dramatically, but the integration of those plays was so explicit that it produced an awareness of it amounting to self-consciousness, and even Porter noticed the change wrought by Rodgers and Hammerstein. "The librettos are much better and the scores are much closer to the librettos than they used to be. Those two made it harder for everybody else."[4]

In view of his natural predilection for fusing melody and lyric into closed song forms, his working habits, and his recent history of failure against a background of dramatic reform, it is not surprising that Porter was reluctant to tackle as apparently complex a task as the musical adaptation of *The Taming of the Shrew*. Other factors too seemed to portend failure. Porter's health, never very good since a terrible riding accident in 1937 robbed him of the full use of his legs, was especially poor just when librettist Bella Spewack approached him with the proposal. Spewack, along with her husband Sam, although successful Broadway playwrights, had done only one libretto for a musical, Porter's *Leave It to Me* (1938). The director, John C. Wilson, and producers, Arnold Saint Subber and Lemuel Ayres, were similarly inexperienced in their particular roles, although well familiar with Broadway. The proposed cast included Alfred Drake but no other box office draws. But it was the idea of translating Shakespeare into a musical play that seemed to scare Porter most of all, despite Rodgers and Hart's popular precedent, *The Boys from Syracuse* (1938).

Once Bella Spewack convinced him, however, the score came from Porter's pen "like an avalanche,"[5] and he completed most of the score between February and May 1948. Although he collaborated closely with his librettists, it is fairly clear that he worked as he always had, from an outline, for the Spewacks report, "By the time of the Philadelphia tryout the parts of Lois and Bill contained only the essentials for plot and song cues."[6] What saved the play from the same sort of confusion that sank *Anything Goes* was the central dramatic conception of a play within a play, and credit for that must go to Bella Spewack. Ironically, she was rather reluctant to adapt *The Taming of the Shrew* herself, but "Then I came up with the story idea and it was exactly the show as it was."[7] It is the idea of a play within a play, and the skillful arrangement of scenes around that idea, that allowed Porter to succeed as a dramatic composer without changing his working methods or song style.

The plot of *Kiss Me, Kate* centers on a theater troupe in Baltimore putting on a musical version of *The Taming of the Shrew*. The whole, then, is an admixture of brilliantly contrasting scenes, some in Baltimore that show the backstage "reality" of the actors' lives and relationships, and others in Padua which portray various scenes from the "unreal" Shakespearean play. One can perhaps imagine why Bella Spewack saw this construction as an inspired solution to the problem of treating Shakespeare in the musical theater. By making *Shrew* the play within the framework of another play, the Shakespeare is made into a dramatic object rather than a vehicle. In a sense the issue of adapting Shakespeare is ducked altogether, since whatever of *Shrew* remains is not "the real play." The necessity of translating into music the complex Shakespearean characters and dramatic themes is eliminated, while allowing some of them to come out in correspondences between the two plays. It is just these correspondences that create the one serious dramatic issue and climax of *Kiss Me, Kate*. Fred Graham and his ex-wife Lilli Vanessi, the principals of the acting troupe, are Petrucchio and Katherine in the flesh.

There is a second advantage to the play within a play. Porter's lyrics, always dependent upon irony for much of their wit, live off the outrageous yet logical rhyme suited to an unusual situation. The juxtaposition of the two plays, so different in setting and style, provide a number of sources for the irony in the lyrics of *Kiss Me, Kate*.

One such source is the sixteenth-century Italian setting, with all its typical images of learning and courtly manners. Porter condenses Shakespeare's rather involved courting of Bianca by the three suitors into a single quartet that plays on the contrasts, real and apparent, between Padua and Baltimore (Ex. 6-1). The humor here comes from a collage of American and fake Renaissance idioms, poetic devices, and clever rhymes. The tone is set right from the start with an explicit Americanism, a gangster idiom. This is followed by a line containing another Americanism, an internal rhyming of "which" and "rich," and a triple alliteration, all within the space of three words. "Rip-roaring rich" is one of the cleverest phrases in the show, because it is not only

Ex. 6-1 Porter, *Kiss Me, Kate*, "Tom, Dick or Harry" (No. 6), mm. 4–19.

the linchpin of these effects, it also creates a posture of delightful brava-do for the suitor. The third line has the one concession to the sixteenth-century setting ("thou woulds't") followed by a reference to the American tax system. What makes it all work, of course, is that, taken together, this verbal virtuosity presents a credible, if uproarious, picture of the mythical Renaissance merchant making his suit.

Hortensio's suit continues the contrast of imagery:

I come to thee, a thoroughbred patrician,
Still spraying my decaying family tree.
To give a social lift to thy position,
Marry me, marry me, marry me . . .

Once more, Porter succeeds in evoking a classical flavor at the same time that he makes fun of classical symbols. "Patrician" recalls ancient noble status, but its nobility is immediately undermined by comparison to racehorses, and the metaphor of preventing tree rot is of course as modern as can be.

The musical setting is another source of ironic play between the Renaissance and modern settings, although its effect in this song takes place over whole sections and therefore is less intense, but nevertheless significant. The passage in Example 6-1 has its first phrase in A-flat minor (mm. 4–8), the next in G-flat minor (mm. 8–12), and the last two in A-flat major (mm. 12–19). While the use of parallel modes is an important feature of all the "Shakespeare" songs in *Kiss Me, Kate* save one, the use of G-flat minor, the minor mode on the seventh degree, is rare in any Western style. Clearly this is Porter's attempt to communicate a vestige, or a stereotype, of a modal Renaissance idiom. This attempt becomes obvious when Bianca joins the three suitors for the first time (Ex. 6-2). The four-voice a cappella texture here is certainly meant to recall the Italian madrigal, and the execution of such a characteristic timbre in barbershop harmony is yet another example of Porter's ironical imagination at work. Now the humor comes from a juxtaposition of musical styles.

A subtler exploitation of this musical source of irony occurs in Katherine's principal number, "I Hate Men" (Ex. 6-3). Its essential character is that of a pattersong, which presents a steady stream of humorous lyrics on a rather monotonous, fast-moving melody. But the end of each half verse breaks the patter into a startling melisma on the title (mm. 12–14), accompanied by suddenly faster harmonic rhythm and effecting a most classical modulation to the dominant, and there is the ironic moment. What was once a song in the most frivolous of styles has been instantly transformed into a hymn. The craft of this transformation takes its root from the song's beginning. The listener

Ex. 6-2 Porter, *Kiss Me, Kate*, "Tom, Dick or Harry" (No. 6), mm. 94-102.

Ex. 6-3 Porter, *Kiss Me, Kate*, "I Hate Men" (No. 9), mm. 1–14.

first hears a somewhat impressionistic progression by the harp, which establishes a rather solemn air. This solemnity is confirmed, if somewhat humorously, by Katherine, who presents the title in long notes. The next phrase (mm. 4–6) is nothing more than a variation of Katherine's first three notes, but it establishes the rhythm of the patter, so that the transition from introduction to pattersong is seamless. The near religious quotation of the refrain in measure 13 simply realizes the implications of the beginning, the same process reversed.

The Shakespearean motif of *Kiss Me, Kate*, of course, is itself a rich source of ironic amusement. The melismatic singing in "I Hate Men" makes ironic sense in the context of a pattersong because, after all, this is a Shakespearean character. In other words, Porter and the Spewacks take full advantage of the snob appeal of Shakespeare, a fully American sentiment to be sure. Nowhere is this clearer than in the hilarious exit number for the two gangsters who are forced to take tacit parts of their own design in the musical *Shrew*.

Porter added "Brush Up Your Shakespeare" at the last moment because he felt that the gangsters deserved an exit song. If one can forgive the rather obvious contrivance of its presentation, there is a wealth of comic juxtaposition to be savored. First there is the spectacle of two criminal ignoramuses quoting various Shakespearean titles and terms, an improbability made credible by a number of scenes like the following:

FRED: Quiet, dammit!

HOWELL: Look here, Graham!

FIRST GUNMAN: He said quiet, dammit.

SECOND GUNMAN: Shhh . . .

FIRST GUNMAN: (softly) Ain't you got no appreciation

of the finer things of life?

SECOND GUNMAN: (softly) Man cannot live by bread alone.

HOWELL: What?

FRED: (to GUNMEN, very quietly) Be tolerant, gentlemen. Remember Mr. Howell didn't have your advantages—eight years in the prison library in Atlanta!

So they are not quite ignoramuses after all. That they propose in their singing that familiarity with Shakespeare will help any man with his love life is clearly a contrivance, but the irony remains.

Next there is the "Bowery Waltz tempo" which Porter chooses for his gangsters. This is a texture common to popular songs from Tin Pan Alley around the turn of the century, and Porter wants it to conjure up images of middle-class gentility and sentiment. The perfection of the imitation of the old waltz style turns small harmonic details into humorous gestures. Every time a typical secondary dominant (mm. 62, 63, 73, etc.) comes along, the sense of the genteel style is reinforced and one cannot help but smile to see gangsters singing it.[8]

The most obvious source of ironic humor, however, is in the outrageous rhyming and increasingly bawdy imagery that Porter derives from Shakespeare's titles. The Porter trademark of the forced rhyme works here better than ever, because it is yet another play on the ignorant gangsters singing about Shakespeare.

Ex. 6-4 Porter, *Kiss Me, Kate*, "Brush Up Your Shakespeare"
(No. 20), mm. 61–83.

The play within a play construction is what allows all these many
sorts of juxtapositions, far more than a more straightforward adaptation
of *The Taming of the Shrew* would have afforded. And yet since the playing of *Shrew* within the framework of the larger play does occupy a

large portion of the stage time, it cannot simply be the butt of all the jokes. There must be a deeper dramatic reason for devoting as much music to it, for playing out as much of the Shakespearean dialogue as is presented. Because both plays receive equal emphasis, there must be a unification of their two sets of action.

Once source of this unity is in the arrangement of scenes and especially in the ordering of the musical numbers. This ordering in the first act results in two separate blocks of music which, in effect, are two small "subacts" (see figure). The first block, the "Baltimore songs" are those sung in the context of the larger framework play, and the second block, the "Padua songs," are those sung as part of the musical *Shrew* that the troupe is presenting.

Order of Music in *Kiss Me, Kate,* Act I

Action in Baltimore	*The Taming of the Shrew*
Overture	
1. Another Op'nin, Another Show (Hattie and company)	
2. Why Can't You Behave (Lois and Bill)	
3. Wunderbar (Fred and Lilli)	
4. So in Love (Lilli)	
	5. We Open in Venice (Ensemble)
	6. Tom, Dick or Harry (Gremio, Lucentio, Hortensio, Bianca)
	7. Rose Dance
	8. I've Come to Wive It Wealthily in Padua (Petruchio and ensemble)
	9. I Hate Men (Katherine)
	10. Were Thine That Special Face (Petruchio)

11. (Change of Scene—I Hate
    Men)
12. I Sing of Love
    (Chorus)
13. Finale—Act I
    (Petruchio, Katherine,
    Company)
14. Entr'acte

The two plays become distinct through their music as well as through the deployment of songs in the first act. The "Padua" songs all have a characteristic alternation of the parallel mode. The excerpt from "Tom, Dick or Harry" (Ex. 6-1, mm. 3–6) is as good an example as any. It begins in A-flat minor, then moves to the rather unusual G-flat minor, using that key as a substitute dominant. But the setting of the third phrase in A-flat major makes an obvious and startling contrast to the second phrase, since so many flats have now been removed. This special flavor, moving from a minor mode to the parallel major, is heard in all the Padua songs of the first act with the exception of "I've Come to Wive It Wealthily in Padua," in which the alternation is reversed. Clearly this contrast of modes is Porter's strategem for imbuing those songs with a Renaissance ethos, and the variety of ways in which this simple idea is put to use is remarkable: in "Tom, Dick or Harry" the contrast is within individual phrases; in "I Hate Men" only the introduction to each verse is in minor (Ex. 6-3, mm. 3–6); and "Were Thine That Special Face" is entirely in minor except for the last climactic phrase. To be sure, Porter takes advantage of a number of other musical stereotypes of early music—the pavane rhythm in "I've Come to Wive It Wealthily in Padua," the madrigal texture in "Tom, Dick or Harry"— but the alternation of minor and major modes is by far his most consistent and subtle means of distinguishing the *Shrew* part of *Kiss Me, Kate* from its frame.

The Baltimore songs have no such structural consistency, and show instead Porter's vaunted and bewildering eclecticism. The four songs in the first act are examples of four different stylistic effects: an old-fashioned musical chorus number, a blues song, a parody of a Viennese waltz song, and a very serious, almost operatic, soliloquy. Among the songs of comic intention, which means all of them except "So in Love" and "I Am Ashamed That Women Are So Simple," the only common characteristic is Porter's virtuoso lyric.

> In *Kiss Me, Kate* there is an effortless merger of high and low cultural references. Having had the advantage of a classical education with its emphasis on Latin and Greek—to say nothing of his later mastery of French, German, Italian and Spanish—Cole produced metaphors of a unique nature in popular music. Equally unexpected are the allusions to chemistry and biology which blend (seemingly with ease, but actually through hard work) with fashionable personalities, fads and foibles of modern society, in the larger sense.[9]

Indeed, catching all the inside jokes of *Kiss Me, Kate* poses quite a stiff challenge to the listener's erudition. One needs at least a smattering of Italian, German, and French, and passing familiarity with Italian cities and landmarks, Shakespearean titles and expressions, classical poets, the Kinsey report, the Theatre Guild, the "Jungfrau," the "Back Bay," L. B. Mayer, and Lassie.

Once the first act, in its ordering and use of stylistic references, has given the two plays palpable identities, the second act can begin to unite them.

Order of Musical Numbers in *Kiss Me, Kate*, Act II

Action in Baltimore	*The Taming of the Shrew*
15. Too Darn Hot (Paul and Boys)	
	16. Where Is the Life That Late I Led? (Petruchio)
17. Always True to You in My Fashion (Lois)	
18. Bianca (Bill)	
19. So in Love (Fred)	
20. Brush Up Your Shakespeare (Gunmen)	

21. Pavana (Why Can't You
Behave)
22. I Am Ashamed That Women
Are So Simple
(Katherine)
23. Finale—Act II
(Petruchio, Katherine, and
Company)

The distinctions made in the first act begin to blur in the second, as the two sets of action begin to merge. Gone is the blocklike arrangement of numbers for Baltimore and Padua; they are now intermingled. In addition, there are curious cross-references within the songs that are supposed to be contained in one play or the other. Bill Calhoun's romantic trifle to his lover Lois uses her character name, "Bianca," and the music for the pavane in the last scene of *The Taming of the Shrew* is a stately version of "Why Can't You Behave?"

A second unifying device of *Kiss Me, Kate* is the perhaps more obvious one of constructing a parallel plot between the two plays. Fred Graham, the rather overbearing leading actor and director, and Lilli Vanessi, the leading lady, are Petruchio and Katherine. Or are they? Their conflict and reconciliation at the play's end clearly mirrors that of their Shakespearean counterparts, but this is surely a superficial parallel. Do the complex motivations of Petruchio and Katherine bear upon the actions of Fred and Lilli?

> On the stage . . . Petruchio comes over far less as an aggressive male out to bully a refractory wife into total submission than he does as a man who genuinely prizes Katherina and, by exploiting an age-old and basic antagonism between the sexes, manoeuvres her into an understanding of his nature and also her own.[10]

There is no such subtlety in Fred's actions, not in the least. He is still in love with Lilli, and wants her, and that is that. A cynical listener might not be so generous: he wants her so that his play can continue its run. The parallel of Lilli and Katherine is not really much closer.

> Heartily sick of a single life . . . she is really more than ready to give herself to a man but, imprisoned within a set of aggressive

attitudes which have become habitual, has not the faintest idea how to do so.[11]

Lilli's aggressions are not habitual; each one has a perfectly obvious cause, usually some attention paid by Fred to Lois. There is a faint echo of boredom with the single life, not with the one she currently leads, but ironically with the married life she intends to begin with her new suitor Harrison, a married life which, according to Fred's malicious depiction, would in effect be single.

In short, any effort to make a parallel plot between the principals must be considered a partial success. However, there is a stronger parallel between the plays in terms of dramatic focus, their concentration on a single romantic relationship:

> Alone of the comedies, and virtually alone in the canon, *The Taming of the Shrew* concerns itself with such relationship. If we set aside *Antony and Cleopatra* and perhaps *Romeo and Juliet*, no other play of Shakespeare's concentrates on a single relationship. This play is about Katherina and Petruchio, and the rest of the dramatis personae compose the backdrop to their relationship.[12]

The comic couple of Bill Calhoun and Lois Lane seem to fill the Broadway form of the secondary plot, but there is really nothing to give substance to the form. There is no progression to their story, no resolution, and not a single serious musical number is sung by them. There is but one dramatic theme of *Kiss Me, Kate* and that is the reconciliation of Fred and Lilli.

The remarkable aspect of the treatment of this theme is that it is so simple and yet so long-range, occupying the entire stage time. The simplicity lies in its singularity of action. The causes of the conflict and divorce are never shown, only alluded to, so that the whole play could be described as an action of reconciliation. The range of this apparently simple action is brought about, again, by the ordering of scenes and musical numbers within the two-play scheme. The action begins when Lilli and Fred, alone in her dressing room, reminisce about the old days in the song "Wunderbar." This song has attracted a good deal of notice because of its brilliant parody of the sentimental Viennese waltz, but the important point about it is that by the end, it is clear that Fred and Lilli are still in love. This perception is utterly confirmed on Lilli's part when she sings "So in Love" upon Fred's departure.

Now the action is interrupted, first by the large block of music devoted to *Shrew*, then by some comic numbers that begin the second act, not to be resumed until late in the second act when Lilli walks out on the troupe for the last time. Fred sings "So in Love," and this reprise has an unusual double function, for it not only confirms that Fred loves as well as Lilli, but makes a structural link with the main action begun early in the first act. Porter seems to have appreciated the dramatic weight this song would have to bear, for it is one of only two serious songs of the show, and its melody shows all the learning of his remarkable musical training.

The first two phrases present the two most salient aspects of the melody, the half-step motion and the upward leap of a perfect fifth. The rising half-step ("Strange, dear" and "true dear") seems startling at first because the D makes a dissonant minor ninth over the bass, but

Ex. 6-5 Porter, *Kiss Me, Kate*, "So In Love" (No. 4), mm. 5–12.

Ex. 6-6 Porter, *Kiss Me, Kate*, "So In Love" (No. 4), mm. 12–20.

because the key is F-sharp minor, the melody is diatonic. The next phrases reach a peak and then descend. The upward leap to the high point is not the expected fifth, but only a minor third (mm. 13–14). When Porter begins the tune again and reaches the corresponding peak the second time, he stretches the leap to a fourth, to the high E (Ex. 6-7, mm. 29–30), before descending to a cadence in A major. This high E becomes the focal point of the release melody. The third phrase of the release melody, moving smoothly by step up the A scale as did the first two phrases, suddenly skips the E and climaxes on F natural, which shocks the ear because it is foreign to the key and especially since the previous phrase had ended on a low F-sharp, recalling the original key. And yet, the shock is quickly apprehended as a deeply expressive but eminently logical gesture, a new realization of the half-step motion so emphasized at the beginning. And yet, the most expressive peak is still

Ex. 6-7 Porter, *Kiss Me, Kate*, "So In Love" (No. 4), mm. 28–36.

to come. The return to the main melody is once again a literal repetition of the beginning, but the third and fourth phrases develop still more Porter's opening motives. The great leap to the high F-sharp at once restores the perfect fifth interval and completes the high-level half-step motion implied when the high E changes to high F natural (Fig. 6-1).[13] But the exploitation of expressive semitones is not over, for the last phrase is extended from its original four and one-half measure length to ten and one-half measures by interpolating every chromatic half-step from D down to B. This is of course the typical Romantic device of

Fig. 6-1 An implication-realization graph of "So in Love," main melody.

Ex. 6-8 Porter, *Kiss Me, Kate*, "So In Love" (No. 4), mm. 36–51.

delaying the cadence for expressive purposes, but in this case the chromatic extension has particular justification and musical logic.

In the context of the whole of *Kiss Me, Kate*, "So in Love" is the chief dramatic number. It confirms the love of both Fred and Lilli and establishes them as the only two serious characters. Further, the depth of its

Ex. 6-9 Porter, *Kiss Me, Kate*, "So In Love" (No. 4), mm. 60–73.

craft and musical expression qualify it as the only number with sufficient dramatic weight to resume by its reprise late in the second act the serious action that was suspended in the first.

The masterstroke of unifying the play within a play construction is the combination of both plot resolutions, and therefore the dual structure, in a single number, "I Am Ashamed That Women Are So Simple." When Fred sings his reprise of "So In Love," it is in reaction to Lilli's decision to walk out on the production, and on him. Because *Shrew* is now without a Katherine, Fred tries to improvise the wager scene:

> PETRUCHIO: I know she will not come. The fouler fortune mine and there an end.
>
> (Enter KATHERINE. *Startled sighs from guests, also relief.*)
>
> KATHERINE: (*going right into part as if she'd never quit the show*) What is your will, sir?
>
> PETRUCHIO: (*really moved, forgetting Shakespeare*) Darling— (*Then, as actor, picking up play again*) Katherine, that cap of yours becomes you not; Off with that bauble, throw it underfoot. (*She does so.*)
>
> BIANCA: Fie! What foolish duty call you this?
>
> PETRUCHIO: Kate, I charge thee, tell these headstrong women what duty they do owe their lords and husbands.[14]

The musical setting of Shakespeare's text that follows must be considered to be a resolution not only of the *Shrew* story, but also as a lasting reconciliation between Fred and Lilli. The Spewacks' clever device of having Lilli quit only to return with her entrance on stage makes this interpretation inevitable; it remains for Porter to make it credible.

He does so by drawing once more on his immense musical experience and composes a brief arietta in eighteenth-century style, a style that because of its revered status in Western culture has the necessary weight for the dramatic purpose at hand, and at the same time because of its anachronism recalls again a flavor of the past appropriate, to Porter's mind, for Shakespeare.

The evidence of the classical style is not only in the clear and periodic phrasing and fast harmonic rhythm, but in the overall form of the song. It is a tiny sonata form. The first two phrases firmly establish the key of E-flat major with a melody and accompaniment that makes two small cadences (m. 3 and m. 5). The third phrase makes a clear modulation to the dominant key, B-flat major, but an important point is not that Porter uses the same key relationships as are found in Mozart arias,

are our bod-ies soft and weak and smooth, Un - apt to toil and trou- ble in the

world. But that our soft con-di-tions and our hearts Should well a -

gree with our ex-ter - nal parts? So wife, hold your tem-per and

(Broader, with great emphasis)

Ex. 6-10 Porter, *Kiss Me, Kate*, "I Am Ashamed That
Women Are So Simple" (No. 22).

but that the modulation is so authentically classical in method. The
end of the first phrase in measure 3 is accompanied by a moving plagal
bass line; the end of the second is accompanied by the same bass line,
but accelerated so that the fast harmonic rhythm seems to propel the
modulation.

The development part of the song begins in G-flat major, a subdominant key which along with the delicate orchestration and high register of the accompaniment reflects the words at that point (mm. 10–12). Another reason for choosing that key becomes apparent at the end of the sixth phrase, when E-flat minor is touched upon (mm. 12–13), a last reminiscence of the contrast of parallel modes that has characterized all the Shakespearean numbers. Another two phrases that move through B-flat major set up the recapitulation, with the key of B-flat acting as a prolonged dominant chord here. This makes the recapitulation ("So wife, hold your temper . . .") as emphatic as the style demands, and it is again a credit to Porter as a lyricist that he is able to coordinate this central musical gesture of the sonata style with the definitive answer to Katherine's rhetorical queries. After that, the mimicry of the style falters—with the chromatic chord in measure 23, and in the asymmetrical delay of the last cadence—in favor of a more intuitive expression. In the main, however, it is apparent that Porter understood not only the form of the eighteenth-century aria but also its structural procedure.

The text for "I Am Ashamed," of course, is a direct adaptation, almost word for word, of about one-third of Katherine's long climactic speech in the last act of *The Taming of the Shrew*. One literary interpretation of this speech claims that Katherine is not saying what she means:

> In this most recent reading of the play, Petruchio, far from "taming" or subtly having a beneficent influence on a woman, is in reality tamed by her. While having the illusion of conquering, he is conquered by her; when she says what he wants to hear, she is being ironic, and undermining him with a show of acquiescence and virtually a wink to the audience.[15]

Because Porter makes such a near-perfect imitation of eighteenth- century classicism in the music, however, any such ambiguity is blasted, simply because the seriousness of the effort and the effect cannot admit of irony here. Porter, finally the dramatist, has clarified his text through his music.

It is furthermore ironic that the dramatically satisfying and musically logical conclusion which is missing from *Show Boat*, *Porgy and Bess*, *Oklahoma!*, and perhaps even from *Carousel* is the glory of *Kiss Me, Kate*, if only because the bulk of the show seems such lightweight stuff. There is so much that reminds the audience of the old Broadway shenanigans, such as the collapse of the madrigal singing into a silly foxtrot in "Tom, Dick or Harry" or the entertaining but dramatically vapid "Too Darn Hot" which begins the second act. And if it is too harsh to criticize the lack of any substantial deep parallelism between Fred-Lilli and Petruchio-Katherine, it can certainly be termed a missed opportunity. Yet, by focusing his most sophisticated and expressive musical resources on a single couple, on a simple dramatic action, in the end Porter has managed to succeed where many have failed at the end.

The irony points up the vexing problem of how to approach this musical among its contemporaries. Its popular success was enormous, both here and abroad, and it holds a secure place in the repertoire of the American musical theater and other popular theaters around the globe, and yet Brooks Atkinson was forced to ask himself:

> Does it rank with the immortal trio of "Show Boat," "Porgy and Bess," and "Oklahoma!," as some of its idolaters believe, or with "Annie Get Your Gun," which is perfection in the more modest field of book-and-song entertainment? In my opinion that is where it belongs.[16]

The matter of evaluating artistic success in terms of artistic aspiration comes again to the fore. *Kiss Me, Kate* is no *Carousel*, either in its characterizations, its portrayal of action through music, or its consistency of musical idiom, but Cole Porter is not Rodgers and Hammerstein, and there is certainly no discernible attempt to make *Kiss Me, Kate* like *Carousel*. It does not aim so high, but it does hit its own more modest mark. "Its only profundity is its skill, which is enormous"[17] is a remark that may be too stern in view of Porter's marvelous finale, but it is essentially true. *Kiss Me, Kate* is a musical which takes a complex production idea, the Shakespeare play within a play, and with it tells a simple story, and the skill required to turn that trick is quite enough to admire.

Chapter 7

The Pure Love Story

I can never forget a man who says: 'I saw a girl and I love her.'[1]

Frank Loesser

I f any distinction can be made between the musical plays of Broadway's golden age of the 1940s and 1950s and those of recent years, it is that the traditional musicals are always love stories of one sort or another. After the cynicism of *Evita* and *A Chorus Line*, after the bleak humor of *Sweeney Todd*, a popular nostalgia for the simpler stories might be understandable. Yet, the old formula was never quite as simple as it seemed. While most traditional musicals have the romantic love of a leading couple as its central musical-dramatic construct, it is almost always elaborated and complicated by other elements of the plot. In *Oklahoma!* the listener is never allowed to forget the ominous threat of Jud; in *Kiss Me, Kate* it is a pair of comic gangsters, an utterly improbable beau, and the pressure of making a successful play that divert the action; and in *Brigadoon* there is the mysterious miracle. Furthermore, these plays and most others like them have important comic subplots, which add another measure of romantic interest, to be sure, but which divert attention from the main dramatic action yet again. The truth is that, despite appearances, falling in love is not the action of a traditional musical; indeed, the fact that the leading couple are in love is never seriously in doubt. Rather, the action is concerned with surmounting obstacles to their living happily ever after, in the tradition of classic comedy.

Such a formula offers a clear design of dramatic conflict and resolution. With the attraction of the lovers taken for granted, their separation becomes the source of dramatic tension, and getting them together becomes the generating action. The obstacles may take a variety of forms, of course: another person, such as Jud, or Crown in *Porgy and Bess*; a peculiar situation, such as the ethos of tradition in *Fiddler on the Roof*, or the distinction in social rank in *The King and I*; or, perhaps best of all, flaws in the characters themselves, as in *Carousel*'s Billy. Why then the complications, the subplots? They lend necessary articulation to what is essentially a very simple action. The comic scenes and surprise twists in the story articulate the immediate stage activity so that the main tension can be prolonged for two acts. In addition, each turn of the elaborated story allows the principal characters to express their feelings for one another in a variety of ways.

None of this is very easy, of course, which is why only a comparatively small number of musicals succeed. What seems to be simple in theory turns out to be murderously difficult to execute, perhaps because in art it is the small details that become as essential as the form, that distinguish perfection from run-of-the-mill. A musical play that coordinates the complexities of plot so that the essential action, so simple in form, is extended but not obscured, and all the while convincingly carried by music, is an impressive thing. How much more impressive, then, is a musical which succeeds without all the necessary complications, without the elaborate form! Such a work is *The Most Happy Fella* of Frank Loesser.

The difference in *The Most Happy Fella* is that the love story is not just the essential action, it is the only action. There is really no other plot, and nothing else of significance happens. There are other events and even dramatic themes which affect the course of the love story, but these do not complicate the plot by diversion, but rather by enrichment. How is that possible? Why doesn't the audience fall asleep? Loesser, who is composer, lyricist, and librettist for this, his most ambitious work, enriches the action by taking away one of the fundamental assumptions of the traditional musical, the love of the leading couple.

By making the question of whether Rosabella will fall in love with Tony a real question, Loesser creates a new source of dramatic tension. In effect, the plot allows the audience a rare chance to watch a romance grow slowly and beautifully over the course of two acts.

When one recalls that a number of expert Broadway teams, including Rodgers and Hammerstein, and Lerner and Loewe on the first go round, gave up the idea of setting Shaw's *Pygmalion* simply because there was no subplot, the difficulties of composing *The Most Happy Fella*, which seems to have hardly any plot at all, can be appreciated. Without diversions from the main plot, Loesser somehow had to slow down the action without loss of interest. He had to develop the traditional sort of conflict and resolution, without overshadowing the main action of this play, the action of falling in love. It is extraordinary then, but not surprising, that Loesser took four years to finish the project.[2] He first considered the idea of setting Sidney Howard's *They Knew What They Wanted* in 1952, and *The Most Happy Fella* opened on May 3, 1956, at the Imperial Theater.

Well may Loesser have taken the time. His previous effort, *Guys and Dolls*, had opened in November 1950 and would run 1,200 performances, a tremendous popular and critical success in the mature strain of musical comedies descending directly from *Oklahoma!*, including *Kiss Me, Kate*, and continuing into the 1950s. It is mature in the sense that the techniques of musical-dramatic integration, so new and almost mysterious in *Oklahoma!*, are by now completely mastered and seem almost easy.

Guys and Dolls is a typical example of the embellished love story tradition against which *The Most Happy Fella* stands out so clearly. The libretto of Abe Burrows makes a double plot of "The Idylls of Sarah Brown," a short story of Damon Runyon, by adding a number of characters from Runyon's other stories.[3] That Nathan Detroit and Adelaide are in love, as are Sky Masterson and Sarah Brown, is an accepted fact from early on in the play. The audience does witness the capitulation of Sarah, but it is not a slow process, and not a dramatic issue. At issue are the obstacles to true happiness. Nathan has a compulsion to run a floating dice game, and the unpredictable exigencies of this profession interrupt his relationship with Adelaide: their wedding has been postponed for fourteen years. On the other side, Sarah, a Salvation Army mission officer, is put off by Masterson's principal occupation of high-stakes betting.

There is no question that *Guys and Dolls* is a consummate example of the comic love story formula at its best. Perhaps its greatest virtue is the translation of Runyon's highly ironic language, with its curious insistence on the present tense and sophisticated vocabulary in the mouths of gangsters and gamblers, into musical numbers. At the very outset, after a brief medley overture, three gamblers on a busy New York street give conflicting advice on which horse to back in "Fugue for Tinhorns." The comedy tone of this piece comes from its juxtaposition of musical rightness and dramatic absurdity: the strict imitation is a perfect setting for three different opinions on the same subject, with each character trying to outtalk the other, but to have gamblers sing a musical texture reminiscent of Bach is a typically outrageous translation of the Runyon *personae*. A larger ensemble of gamblers later on sings "The Oldest Established," a paean to Nathan's floating dice game. With its close chromatic harmony and concluding ornamental suspensions, this song is part alma mater and part hymn, an irony which is amplified in the second act when these same gamblers are forced to attend a real prayer meeting. Finally there is "Adelaide's Lament," an amusing spoof of modern psychoanalysis, replete with jargon, but sung by a nightclub dancer, another absurd contrast which maintains the Runyon flavor of the whole work.

The high standards of musical integration are set in the opening scene when, after the "Fugue for Tinhorns," the Salvation Army troop marches onstage singing "Follow the Fold" to round up sinners, concluding a musical sequence which begins with the overture and manages to introduce the opposed groups of gamblers and city missionaries who will dominate the play. The dramatic integrity is flawed only where most musical plays are flawed, at the end. Although the conversion of Sky Masterson is subtly implied from the beginning by his humorous familiarity with the Gideon Bible, there is no explanation for the reformation of Nathan Detroit. The musical finale, a reprise of the title song by the full company, is completely without dramatic motivation.

For all its typical features, *Guys and Dolls* contains the seeds of things essential to the much more innovative and ambitious play *The Most Happy Fella*. The latter is heavily dependent upon various types of recitative texture, which attracted some critical fire. No one complained of such textures in *Guys and Dolls*, but what is one to make of Masterson's "My Time of Day"?

Ex. 7-1 Frank Loesser, *Guys and Dolls*, "My Time of Day" (No. 17), mm. 8–17.

This is no *secco* recitative, of course, but the sense of meter is so obscured as to make it into something akin to an arioso. The first clue is in Loesser's tempo marking, "Slowly and freely." Then there are changes of time signature and irregular subdivisions of the beat, both greatly weakening the sense of downbeat. Chromaticism in both the main melody and underlying harmony obscures the sense of key as well, so it is difficult for the ear to assign any important metric status to a tonic note. What sort of piece this might be becomes clear at the end.

Ex. 7-2 Frank Loesser, *Guys and Dolls*, "My Time of Day" (No. 17), mm. 27–34, and "I've Never Been In Love Before" (No. 17a), mm. 1–8.

Clearly, the function of "My Time of Day," musically and dramatically, is to lead into the much more stable music and consistent emotion of "I've Never Been in Love Before." Just as many opera composers precede set pieces with accompanied recitatives to clarify the dramatic situation and to give the set piece a greater musical weight by virtue of a significant prelude, so has Loesser done here. It is curious that, although the rhythm of the second piece is now quite regular, the chromaticism has not disappeared from the accompaniment. This harmonic coloring will become a regular feature of *The Most Happy Fella* and make possible more distant harmonic relationships than would be likely in more conventional material.

The musical eclecticism of *Guys and Dolls* is another aspect that carries over into the later show. The counterpoint of the "Fugue for Tinhorns" and the college-song style in "The Oldest Established" have already been mentioned, but the show also offers traditional hymnody in "Follow the Fold," blues in "Adelaide's Lament," and gospel music in "Sit Down, You're Rockin' the Boat." This variety derives from the superb sense of integration that characterizes most of the play: each style is called forth by the dramatic situation in which it occurs. For Loesser, the coordination of such various styles is an essential aspect of his dramatic art: "If a song sounds like Verdi, Berlin, or Scarlatti, it's entitled to. I don't invent languages. I make use of them."[4]

The eclecticism in *The Most Happy Fella* is once again suggested by an American setting which appears to bring out quite naturally a number of ethnic types. The main character Tony is an Italian immigrant, and his ethnic devotion to family, particularly his mother, becomes an important dramatic issue that allows for a number of Italian song textures, but Loesser is able to bring in other musical associations drawn from the American characters as well. That these borrowings seem drawn from the associations of the characters themselves rather than the plot situation is especially fitting, since critics have generally agreed that in the case of Sidney Howard,

> Undoubtedly his forte is character portrayal. His finest creations along this line are the simpler types—sterling, vivid, individual, and solidly human—which people our heterogenous American scene. Be they immigrants, like Tony in *They Knew What They Wanted*, or deeply rooted national stock . . . they have a raciness, a

quality of forthrightness, independence, and integrity which epitomizes what is best and most typical in our American tradition.[5]

The play tells the story of Tony, a California bootleg vintner of middle age, who at the curtain's rise is at home on his ranch awaiting the arrival by train of a San Francisco waitress who is to be his bride. He had fallen in love with her at first sight while on a trip, but, nervous about his age and appearance, he chose not to introduce himself but to court her by mail. Worse still, he has sent her a picture of his handsome foreman, letting her believe it is his own. He is now so upset over this deception that he leaves for the station late, has an accident, and breaks both legs. Meanwhile Amy arrives and finds Joe, the foreman, at the ranch. She is stunned, first in finding out that her fiance is not whom she expected, and then by Tony's serious injury. In urgency and confusion she decides to go through with the marriage to Tony. In the second act, Amy goes along with the celebrations but feels utterly abandoned and even mocked by the turn of events. She turns to Joe, and in comforting her he kisses her. He chases after her as the curtain falls. The third act reveals that Amy has indeed grown to love Tony, but carries Joe's baby. In the last scene, she bravely tells Tony, and he, through great struggle, forgives her and decides to adopt the child as his own.

The play also concerns itself with themes of workers' rights and religious conflicts, but to Loesser these ideas were only so much chaff.[6] "I figured take out all this political talk, the labor talk, and the religious talk. Get rid of all that stuff and you have a good love story."[7] By concentrating on the love story, and only that, Loesser solved the principal dramatic problem of *They Knew What They Wanted*, the conflict aroused by Amy's pregnancy:

> Because this revelation is placed so late in the play, and in the act itself, the dramatist is obliged to crowd the principal problem of his drama—the effect of Joe's and Amy's casual and fortuitous affair upon a lasting relationship between Amy and Tony—into one tightly written scene. A situation rich in implications and dramatic possibilities is broached, discussed, and resolved in one scene. The dramatic action of *They Knew What They Wanted* is confined to the first act, one scene in the second, and one in the third. The rest is padding.[8]

This problem disappears from *The Most Happy Fella* because the affair and its effects are no longer the central dramatic action. Rather, they merely test and temper and clarify the main action: how Rosabella (Tony's pet name for Amy) falls in.

The simplicity of the plot is compensated by the complexity and variety of musical idiom. The paucity of spoken dialogue and frequency of recitative texture have encouraged critics to call *The Most Happy Fella* an opera, but that term does not do justice to the diversity of styles, from the most serious aria to the lightest American dance number, from the deceptively simple "Somebody, Somewhere" in the first act to the ensemble quartet "How Beautiful the Days" in the second. Now it is dangerous to evoke a variety of styles for variety's sake, as some recent megamusicals have discovered; there must be dramatic reasons, usually deriving from the characters involved, for using a style, reasons that go beyond the simple formula of having the comic characters always sing light music and the romantic leads serious music. When Tony's three servants sing "Benvenuta"—recalling the cavatina-cabaletta tradition of Italian opera while parodying it—the music is not light, or even simple, and yet the effect is comic. However, such variety does allow Loesser to save the most sublime effects for the principal characters alone, without having the whole seem so ponderous.

Above all, it is the recitatives which allow the musical-dramatic focus on the love story. There are fourteen solo roles in the musical, but only the six most important characters—Rosabella and Tony, his sister Marie, Joe, and the added comic couple Herman and Cleo—may sing recitative. And, with a single exception in the third act, they sing it only in connection with the main love story. Its most important function is to act as a supporting prelude to an important lyric number, just as "My Time of Day" precedes "I've Never Been in Love Before" in *Guys and Dolls*.

The central musical-dramatic problem of *The Most Happy Fella* remains how to portray in music the action of falling in love in stages, as a dramatic progression. Loesser's first strategy is to compose a series of duets for Tony and Rosabella that create such a progression by withholding love's ultimate and irrepressible expression until the last.

Rosabella's first lyric arioso ("I don no noting about you") arises when she reads to herself the love letter that Tony has left in the San Francisco restaurant where she waits on table.

Ex. 7-3 Frank Loesser, *The Most Happy Fella*, Act I, scene 1,
"Ooh! My Feet," mm. 115–27.

The emphatic parallel fifths in the accompaniment, almost a cultural
symbol of some mysterious power, lend this piece a sound unique to
itself and can only express the depth of Tony's feeling. The chromaticism is now functional; it effects the modulation from F major to G

major (mm.119–120), heightening the expression of the repeated lyric, and is responsible for the wistfully inconclusive marriage proposal (mm.126–127). The little piece may be called a kind of "separate duet" because Tony sings the same music minutes later in answer to his sister's skepticism about his romance. In any case, the piece beautifully accomplishes its purpose: the establishment of a powerful, but one-sided, love interest.

The next song Tony and Rosabella sing together occurs right after the wedding, when he is just beginning to recover from his injury. He apologizes for sending the wrong picture, and says that they must "start all over." So he introduces himself, and "Happy to Make Your Acquaintance" is nothing more than Rosabella's instruction in the proper English phrases of a polite introduction. It reveals an essential compatability of spirit and the possibility of true friendship, but stops short of love. The teacher-pupil role is reversed for "How Beautiful the Days," which follows upon a lesson in the Italian names for the days of the week. Its expression of happiness is deeper, but it does not articulate the cause.

The climax of this slow progression begins with a passionate *accompagnato* for both characters (Act II, scene 5) in which Rosabella makes it clear that she indeed loves Tony and needs him "like a woman needs a man." He is overjoyed, for such a speech is the fulfillment of his dreams, and the recitative leads directly into the great "My Heart Is So Full of You." Here the recitative passage is absolutely required, both musically and dramatically. The duet proper begins with a solo voice and the simplest of rhythmic textures; its power would be utterly lost if not preceded by the unstable *accompagnato*, to which the song is a resolution. At the same time, the sentiments expressed in the preceding justify those in the duet.

Just as the progression of duets mirrors the growing relationship, so does the construction of the individual duets. "How Beautiful the Days" begins with Rosabella echoing fragments of Tony's melody as she repeats the Italian names for the days of the week. The echo is regular for four bars (mm. 10–13). By simply moving Rosabella's response ahead by two beats in measure 14, however, Loesser brings the voices into closer proximity and creates a high-level rhythmic acceleration which hurries the end of the next phrase so that it arrives after only two measures. In this way, joining of the two voices in parallel sixths in the concluding phrase seems to arise naturally from the previous texture.

Ex. 7-4 Frank Loesser, *The Most Happy Fella*, Act II, scene 2, "How Beautiful The Days," mm. 4–18.

"Happy to Make Your Acquaintance" is a more sophisticated example of the same idea. Once again, a contrapuntal duet is justified dramatically because she is teaching him lines, and he repeats after her. Although the phrase pattern is a typical one of four bars, Tony's mimicry blurs the ends of her phrases by extending over the beginning of her next one. This effect, rather like a syncopation at the rhythmic level of the phrase, maintains a clear structural distinction in the music of the two singers, even though their words are the same. With the onset of the third and fourth phrases (mm. 25–32), however, Loesser begins to alter this delicate rhythmic balance. Tony's interjections become much

Ex. 7-5 Frank Loesser, *The Most Happy Fella*,
"Happy To Make Your Acquaintance," mm. 17–32.

shorter, so that they no longer make up a phrase system on their own. At the same time, Rosabella adds an extended anacrusis ("And let me say the . . .") to the beginning of the fourth phrase, so that her own separate system is less apparent. Both changes blur the structural distinction so clear at the beginning, so that for the first time, the two singers can agree on the end of their phrase (m. 32).

The transformation of separate melodies into a more unified texture becomes more forceful and conclusive as the song begins its melody again. Now the entire third phrase is sung together; the transformation comes sooner in the song and lasts longer than before. The same musical logic applies to the fourth phrase, extending it into a humorous coda (Ex. 7-7). Just as in "How Beautiful the Days," Loesser begins with a regular imitation, and by simply decreasing the amount of time for the third answer, he creates a rhythmic acceleration that both drives to the cadence and expresses the lack of hesitation that accompanies Tony's mastering the pronunciation. The cadence, which expresses the pleasure of the achievement, is the only authentic one in the piece, and the singers make it together.

Ex. 7-6 Frank Loesser, *The Most Happy Fella*,
"Happy To Make Your Acquaintance," mm. 33–43.

The song is reprised twice almost immediately, after two short dia-
logues. The arrival of Rosabella's friend Cleo occasions the first reprise,
an opportunity for Tony to practice his new etiquette. The second,
however, comes after Rosabella confesses that she really isn't so lone-
some on the farm because Tony is such a "nice kind man." In this
reprise, Tony and Rosabella sing every phrase in unison (octaves, actually) until the little coda, which is as before. This is a complete reversal
of the normal handling of musical texture in an operatic ensemble,
where tension and intensity of emotion are created by complicating the
texture. Here the most intense emotion is caused by what is signified in
simplifying the texture into the unison. Exactly the same effect occurs
in "My Heart Is So Full of You," when the harmonically and texturally
complex middle section is followed by the couple singing in unison.

So it is not merely in the lyrics and in the placement of these duets
that Loesser paces his action, it is the construction of the individual
numbers themselves that reflects, in miniature, the direction and outcome of that action.

When Tony and Rosabella sing "My Heart Is So Full of You" near the
end of Act II, that action is essentially complete. Loesser now has the
pretty problem of how to work in the conflict and resolution of Rosabella's pregnancy. How does the third act attach to an action that is over?

Ex. 7-7 Frank Loesser, *The Most Happy Fella*,
"Happy to Make Your Acquaintance," mm. 44–52.

Loesser's entirely original solution is to make the conflict appear to be the result of flaws in the principal characters, flaws which remain understated and inarticulate in the first two acts, but whose effects become explosive in the third. Rosabella's sensuality, portrayed as sympathetically as anyone could imagine in a musical play by her prelude to "My Heart Is So Full of You," is yet the cause of her downfall, a source of weakness in a time of great stress. But her affair with Joe can be no great surprise, because of what Loesser has given her to say in the very first scene of the opera, in response to the advances of her employer:

ROSABELLA: . . . I guess I've helped a few fellows prove they were fellows, but they were guys I liked and they thought I was something special . . .

Tony's defect is much more serious: a lack of faith in himself. This, the reason for the photograph deception, is developed by Loesser into a full-blown dramatic theme ancillary to the main action, fleshed out by Tony's sister, who time and again reminds him of his age, his lack of wit, and what his mother might think. The resolution of this theme, which has its own set of musical numbers and musical development,[9] comes at the close of the second act, when Tony sings what must be one of the great baritone arias of the Broadway tradition, "Mamma, Mamma." The full power of this piece can only be touched on here, as any detailed analysis would require discussing all the related pieces, but some sense of the joy that Rosabella has given him might be heard in the following. The accompaniment to this exultant lyric is a metaphor for Tony's character. Its meter and phrase rubato are unabashedly Italian, and its characteristic rocking motive (mm. 50, 52, 54) accompanying Tony's long notes is related to motives from his song "Rosabella" in Act I and to the leitmotif for his mother. The maternal connection is most explicit when the mother leitmotif is exactly quoted by the strings during Tony's long B-flat in the tremendous final cadence, the only one in this Romantic style piece. The placement of this song at the curtain of the second act gives it a bittersweet irony to go with its triumph. Rosabella, and the audience, have just learned of her pregnancy. In this way, the moment when Tony's greatest wishes have been granted is tied into the impending blow of the third act.

As a consequence of these aspects of character, the action of the second act can be seen not only in terms of Rosabella's growing to love Tony, but also in terms of her forgiving him his shallow deception. This forgiveness is never made explicit; it is left for the listener to construe through songs and actions. In Act III, the tables are turned: now it is Tony who must forgive.

There are indeed a number of criticisms one might make about the final sequence of *The Most Happy Fella*. Loesser feels that he must reconcile Cleo and Herman in classic Broadway fashion, and the comic number "I Made a Fist" interrupts the continuity of the much more serious events that surround it. Tony's discovery of his ability to forgive and

Ex. 7-8 Frank Loesser, *The Most Happy Fella*,
"Mamma, Mamma" (mm. 45–55).

his realization that his love for Rosabella outweighs his own pride are
expressed by a recitative and aria ("She gonna come home wit' me") that
seem to lack the length and weight commensurate with such a dramatic

Ex. 7-9 Frank Loesser, *The Most Happy Fella*,
"Mamma, Mamma" (mm. 55–69).

moment. But at the very end, when Tony has to convince Rosabella that he really has forgiven her—and her greatest fear is that he cannot, ever—that is when Loesser shows his best dramatic imagination. It begins with Tony's longest and most important speech.

ROSABELLA: (*Guiltily, apprehensively*) You'll know . . . you'll know and you'll hate me, and you'll hate the baby. I'm . . . scared.

TONY: (*Very gently*) Nunja be scared, Carissima. It's-a bad to be scared. Me, Tony, I was-a scared one night last springtime. Omma scared to drive down da station to meet my Rosabella. Omma scared omma too old, an' omma talk funny. So omma drive da truck too fast an' have accidente. Maybe dat same night . . . dat same night last springtime you was-a be scared too an' you was have accidente. An' before dat, I was all da time scared. I was-a so scared omma send you wrong fella's pitch, pitch young handsome fella. First time omma see you in da ristorante in Frisco, I should-a no left a sneaky li'l note onna bill o' fare. I should-a knew what I want an' say what I want. Now, tonight, we start all over.[10]

And so the two replay the first scene in the restaurant. Tony's speech reveals a symmetry in the character flaws that were the dark side of the love story. His proposition that her affair was an "accidente" analogous to his own is not merely a comforting line to make her feel better, for in it he realizes that his own lack of faith in himself was the direct cause not only of the car accident but of Rosabella's unspoken infatuation with the image of Joe. In fact, his leg injury has become a symbol of this deeper infirmity: that is why Tony rises to his feet from his wheelchair when he sings "My Heart Is So Full of You" in the second act and at the end of the finale. His cure is Rosabella herself.

The first music after the speech, Tony's reprise of "I don no noting about you/ Where you ever go/ Wat you ever done" is moving not because it is reminiscent of his powerful first sight and feeling of her in the restaurant, but because it expresses that, after all that has happened, he recognizes the cost of loving blindly, and accepts it anyway. This is all Rosabella needs to hear. The symmetry of fault yields to a symmetry of forgiveness.

As a confirmation of the happy ending to this pure love story there are the middle and final sections of "My Heart Is So Full of You." Because it represents both the consummation of Rosabella's love of Tony in Act II and the reconciliation of this love in Act III, this song perhaps carries the greatest expressive weight of any number in the opera, and there is no better example of Loesser's handling of chromatic harmony, texture, and form.

An asymmetrical phrase design at the very beginning of the song generates its most expressive features.

Ex. 7-10 Frank Loesser, *The Most Happy Fella*,
"My Heart Is So Full Of You," mm. 1–11.

The first phrase (mm. 1–6) is characterized by a sequence in the vocal melody, but because it creates the sequence by adopting only measures 3 and 4 as the pattern (transposed down one step to yield measures 5 and 6), the whole phrase is asymmetrical. Instead of two balanced subphrases of four bars each, measures 3 and 4 complete the first subphrase and begin the second one, made articulate by the sequence, at the same time. It needn't have been this way; Loesser could easily have composed a symmetrical eight-measure phrase by making a sequence out of the whole. Indeed, he did something quite close to this in "I've Never Been In Love Before" from *Guys and Dolls*.

Fig. 7-1 Alternative opening phrase to "My Heart Is So Full Of You."

Ex. 7-11 Frank Loesser, *Guys and Dolls*,
"I've Never Been in Love Before" (No. 17a), mm. 1–8.

Here, the sense of phrase is complete and balanced, or, to use a more technical term, closed. In "My Heart," Loesser wants some sense of something missing. Its first phrase has, by virtue of its V-I cadence in D-flat, a closed harmony, but the asymmetry of the sequence and an ambiguity of the high-level meter argue for continuity.[11] The result of this conflict is that the six-measure phrase, unusual in popular style, is taken by the listener to be real while requiring some sort of structural resolution.

This structural ambiguity justifies the surprising A dominant seventh chord in the next measure: perhaps the tension arising from this harmony being foreign to the key as well as its dissonant structure will carry the phrase to a new, balanced resolution in the eighth measure. Instead, its tension generates the next phrase, and Loesser's particular usage of this chord here determines important effects later on. The beautifully expressive high F-flat that Tony sings in measure 10 seems to grow out of that earlier harmony, for three of its five accompanying pitches (G, F-flat=E , D-flat=C♮), two of them chromatic, had sounded in the A dominant seventh. Curiously, the melody leading up to this F-flat contains the pattern that was "missing" from Loesser's sequence in the first phrase (see Ex. 7-10). The second phrase therefore responds to some aspect of the structural ambiguity of the first. However, in doing so it adds another, stronger, higher-level structural asymmetry, sounding a five-measure phrase (mm. 7–11) against the original six.

The resolution of that A dominant seventh is quite irregular, slipping right back into the key of D-flat with a half-step descent. Such progressions, deriving from the music of Tony's love letter (see Ex. 7-3, mm. 123–124), power the release section of the song. The modulation from A-flat major to G-flat major (mm. 23–27, Ex. 7-12) is made through a G dominant seventh which demands a resolution in the same manner as above. This is at first denied (m. 25), then completed. Later on the bass line moves from D-flat to C, then E-natural to E-flat. The harmonic ambiguity of these progressions transforms the song's release into a

Ex. 7-12 Frank Loesser, *The Most Happy Fella,*
"My Heart Is So Full of You," mm. 23–31.

tiny development section. Rosabella's melody, clearly the prominent
one, consists of a two-measure phrase repeated twice. The second repetition increases the tension by transposing the figure so that it is now
the dissonant seventh factor of the chord instead of the third (m. 27).
Her highest note of the whole song, the G flat, is reserved for the precise moment when harmonic functions begin to be clarified and the
strong progression ii–V–I in D-flat begins the return to the opening
theme, turning it into a recapitulation in the classical sense.

As recapitulations are designed to resolve high-level tension, so is the last phrase of the song changed to resolve the asymmetry of the opening. By extending the F-flat, Loesser restores the symmetry of balanced six-measure phrases which seemed missing from the beginning.

The duet is the most ambitious and successful piece in the opera. It integrates a number of expressive features—the C-flat chord of the fourth measure, the chromatic A dominant seventh, the high F-flat, and the whole midsection—into a short piece in which these features are introduced with impeccable skill. Each seems to grow from music which precedes it, proceeding from the design of the very first phrase.

Ex. 7-13 Frank Loesser, *The Most Happy Fella*,
"My Heart Is So Full Of You," mm. 30–43.

As the central number, "My Heart Is So Full of You" deserves its place as the climax of the love story. Indeed, that its full version appears in the second act, with only its last two sections used as the reprise in the third act, shows that the dramatic climax of the opera is in the second act. The conflict of the third is an affirmation of this central action.

The rarity of making a pure love story the central action of a musical play may have caused the confusion and disagreement that has characterized the critical history of *The Most Happy Fella*. A sample of the critical problems noted:

> [The actors] don't really have flesh-and-blood characters to create, nor much of a plot to embody.[12]

> Having established the foreman as the third party in this combustible romantic triangle, Loesser simply forgets about him in the second act.[13]

> The rather tatty recitatives in "The Most Happy Fella," for example, gain nothing by being sung, except a certain grand pretense . . .[14]

In each case the critic has missed the central dramatic issue. To say that the recitatives in *The Most Happy Fella* gain nothing is to be unaware of how carefully the recitatives are reserved for certain characters in certain situations, how they can slow down the musical action while creating a varied musical texture. Loesser has not forgotten part of the romantic triangle because there is no triangle. And naturally, if one cannot appreciate the simple action of falling in love, then there will seem to be no plot and no characters.

Of course, there are the ecstatic defenders as well:

> Egad! the nerve of it! One may write *lots of music*, including some that narrates plot! One may compose duets, trios, *quartets*, that express individual intents within group agreements, or even a *conflict*! One may try using music to shift the level of reality, to voice private thoughts in a public milieu! One may create vocal settings that demand voices of professional range and quality, and allow them to sing damn near as long as in, say, *Madama Butterfly*![15]

In a sense, even this deeply felt indignation misses the point. Yes, Loesser's work has all these things, but having them is not its great achievement, but rather coordinating them into a sure dramatic vision. The irony is that the usual plan for an American musical invariably calls for a complicated love story, but Loesser, in stripping the old love story to its simplest essentials required all the complexities of the operatic tradition. The pity is that, because this complexity makes it so difficult to sing, *The Most Happy Fella* is not better known, for there are few musicals that show as well how far the American theater tradition can reach.

Chapter 8

Myth as Musical

What Shaw wanted us to know about Higgins was that he was passionate about the English language . . . and that he was a misogynist. Because they are the outstanding aspects of his character, it seemed to us they should be dramatized in music and lyrics.[1]

Alan Jay Lerner

From time to time composers, lyricists, and writers of the American theater have borrowed stories from mythology for the main plots of musical plays. Rodgers and Hart's *A Connecticut Yankee* (1927) translated Twain's Arthurian tale and *By Jupiter* (1942), their last original collaboration, retells Hercules's quest for the magic girdle of Hippolyta. Cole Porter based his *Out of This World* (1950) on the story of Amphitryon. E. Y. Harburg adapted music of Jacques Offenbach to transform the plot of Aristophanes *Lysistrata* into *The Happiest Girl in the World* (1961). And the operatic score and libretto by Jerome Moross and John Latouche presenting the return of Ulysses in *The Golden Apple* (1953) was deemed so clever that it captured the Drama Critics Award for best musical of the season. However, in the great majority of these musicals and others based on mythology, the borrowing ceases with the outline of the plot. There is little attempt to translate other, deeper mythic elements into dramatic terms.

The treatment of mythic elements in modern literature seems to be an enormously complex subject that sees little agreement about the purpose or effect of such borrowing in novels, poetry, and drama. For some, the myth is merely a commonly understood point of departure:

> You display your originality by exercising ingenuity in discovering new ways of writing about old myths. Operating within a network of shared allusions among educated readers, you can by-pass the explicit in order to explore the tacit and ironic.[2]

For others, the relationship of the new work to the old can be quite beside the point:

> Yet one must ask to what extent the design once seen gives an associative enrichment to the work as a whole. Do we look back to the Telemacheia and understand Joyce better? In one sense we obviously do in that we see a dimension of Joyce's intention expressed. But the actual light thrown on Joyce's novel by the associative echoes from the Homeric original seems academic and thin, and to think too closely on it is to look away from the richness of what Joyce has created.[3]

Neither of these viewpoints is very useful for musical theater. They assume a detailed knowledge of classical mythology which is almost sure to be lacking in the popular audience. Much more appropriate is the approach of Eric Gould, who believes that the essence of myth in modern culture is that it is a familiar story or teaching, the meaning of which is never quite fixed:

> . . . myth is both hypothesis and compromise. Its meaning is perpetually open and universal only because once the absence of a final meaning is recognized, the gap itself demands interpretation which, in turn, must go on and on, for language is nothing if it is not a system of open meaning.[4]

Closing the gap, fixing the interpretation is the moment on which a drama can turn.

The attempt to fix an interpretation of a myth through music is what sets the work of Alan Jay Lerner and Frederick Loewe apart from most other Broadway adaptations. *My Fair Lady* (1956) and *Camelot* (1960) are based on mythological plots, of course, but they are also explorations of mythic elements carried in those plots across the ages. No small part of these stories' power comes from their legendary status, their age-old themes and associations as a common property of western culture. That is why the interpretation of Gould's mythic gap in a given work can be such an important event, and in a drama, perhaps the most important moment. That is also why Lerner and Loewe's earlier and excellent musical, *Brigadoon* (1947), is not germane to a discussion of myth, for although its premise of a Scottish village that materializes but one day in a century seems mythical, the story is original with Lerner and cannot claim the cultural associations so essential to myth.[5]

My Fair Lady is a musical adaptation of George Bernard Shaw's *Pygmalion* (1912), which in turn is a dramatic adaptation of the classical myth about the sculptor who brings his own statue of a woman to life. One version of the story is told in Ovid's *Metamorphoses* 10, beginning with Pygmalion's disgust for the first prostitutes of Cyprus:

> Pygmalion saw these women leading a life of sin and was repelled by the many vices that nature had implanted in the feminine mind. And so he lived alone without a wife for a long time, doing without a woman to share his bed. Meanwhile he fashioned happily a statue of ivory, white as snow, and gave it a beauty surpassing that of any woman born; and he fell in love with what he had made. It looked like a real maiden who you would believe was alive and willing to move, had not modesty prevented her. To such an extent art concealed art; Pygmalion wondered at the body he had fashioned and the flames of passion burned in his breast. He often ran his hands over the creation to test whether it was real flesh and blood or ivory. And he would not go so far as to admit that it was ivory. He gave it kisses and thought that they were returned; he spoke to it and held it and believed that his fingers sank into the limbs that he touched and was afraid that a bruise might appear as he pressed her close. . . .
>
> The most celebrated feast day of Venus in the whole of Cyprus arrived; heifers, their crooked horns adorned with gold, were slaughtered by the blow of the axe on their snowy necks and incense smoked. When he had made his offering at the altar, Pygmalion stood and timidly prayed: "If you gods are able to grant everything, I desire for my wife . . . " He did not dare to say "my ivory maiden." Golden Venus herself was present at her festival

and understood what his prayers meant. As an omen of her kindly will a tongue of flame burned bright and flared up in the air. When he returned home Pygmalion grasped the image of his girl and lay beside her on the bed and showered her with kisses. She seemed to be warm. He touched her with his lips again and felt her breasts with his hands. At his touch the ivory grew soft, and its rigidity gave way to the pressure of his fingers; it yielded just as Hymettan wax when melted in the sun is fashioned into many shapes by the working of the hands and made pliable. He is stunned but dubious of his joy and fearful he is wrong. In his love he touches this answer to his prayers. It was a body; the veins throbbed as he felt them with his thumb. Then in truth Pygmalion was full of prayers in which he gave thanks to Venus. At last he presses his lips on lips that are real and the maiden feels the kisses she is given and as she raises her eyes to meet his she sees both her lover and the sky.[6]

Shaw turns Pygmalion into Henry Higgins, a dialectician and phonetics expert, who on a dare from a colleague takes a common girl, Eliza Doolittle, into his home, teaches her proper English, and turns her into a gentlewoman in all respects but birth. The interpretation of the myth fixed in the play, however, emphasizes Pygmalion's initial misogyny and eliminates the infatuation for his creation so prominent in Ovid. Although Higgins has strong feelings about Eliza, their true nature is left unclear, as is the destiny of the couple even at the play's conclusion:

> That famous unresolved ending of the play, teasing us forever with the question of whether Eliza will come back to Higgins after she has walked out on him, is of course far more than an effective theatrical finale. It reflects, as do the finest plots, aspects of character and theme. The ambiguity of the ending transposes into structure the ambiguities of feeling between Higgins and Eliza which date from their first encounter . . .[7]

Shaw added a prose postscript to the published play two years after its opening which explained why, contrary to popular will, Eliza had really married someone else. Arnold Silver attributes this postscript to Shaw's upset over actress Stella Campbell, for whom he had written the lead part and who had married just prior to the opening. Arguing that the ambiguous ending is truer to the themes of the play, Silver believes that the characters of Eliza and Higgins are completely spoiled in the postscript.[8] In any case, the ending has left a mythic gap to be closed by the musical drama in *My Fair Lady*.

> What Shaw wanted us to know about Higgins was that he was passionate about the English language, believed it to be the principal barrier separating class from class, and that he was a misogynist. Because they are the outstanding aspects of his character, it seemed to us they should be dramatized in music and lyrics.[9]

So recalls Alan Jay Lerner. Outstanding aspects they are, but only the misogyny is mythic, and so while "Why Can't the English?" is an important initial statement about Higgins's love of English, his second song, "I'm an Ordinary Man," is the one that establishes his character in a way that begins to interpret the myth.

The song is built on two contrasting sections which alternate for three hearings each. In the first (A) section Higgins describes himself.

Ex. 8-1 Lerner and Loewe, *My Fair Lady*, "I'm An Ordinary Man" (No. 5), mm. 1-8.

In the second (B) section Higgins describes what would happen to this sterling character if he ever allowed himself to become involved with a woman. The lyrics of all the B sections obviously establish Higgins as a misogynist, but equally important, the A sections reveal that he lives with a much idealized and warped image of himself. Though he has

Ex. 8-2 Lerner and Loewe, *My Fair Lady*, "I'm An Ordinary Man"
(No. 5), mm. 13–33.

been on stage but a few minutes, it is quite clear to the audience that Higgins is far from "ordinary," "average," or "of no eccentric whim." Subsequent action will give the lie to his further claims that he is "a very gentle man" or "a quiet living man." The accompanying music seems ill-matched to these weighty confessions; its quick dotted rhythms trip along more in the manner of the lightest intermezzo than of a soliloquy. But if this setting can be understood to suggest that all is not what Higgins claims it is, should not the music of the B second section be similarly considered? For here the increased tempo, pattersong rhythms, absolutely periodic phrasing, and brassy orchestration give over a vaudevillian superficiality. Funny, yes, but is it real? This is the first hint of Loewe's reinterpretation of the Pygmalion myth: if Higgins's self-image must be questioned, then so must his misogyny.

Eliza's opening song reveals a character that sharply contrasts with that of Higgins.

Ex. 8-3 Lerner and Loewe, *My Fair Lady*, "Wouldn't It Be Loverly?"
(No. 3), mm. 20–27.

Like Higgins, she fantasizes, but instead of imagining the worst that could happen to herself, she imagines the best. And the images of that best are simple images, not Higgins's high-minded contemplation of Keats and Milton. The music, again, is composed in a light Broadway texture, but its phrasing lends an impression of sincerity quite absent in Higgins's music. Chord changes establish a clear two-bar period at the beginning with strong metric accents on every downbeat. The third phrase, however, begins in measure 24 by eliminating the downbeat altogether, and this disruption of the established pattern, together with a chromatic intensification that makes every chord act like an upbeat, cause the next accent to be delayed until the highest note of the melody in measure 26. The coordination of the refrain lyric with this melodic climax makes the wistful sentiment credible.

By far the most important interpolation Lerner introduces into Shaw's script, which otherwise is followed quite faithfully, is the latter half of Act I, scene 5, which shows Pygmalion sculpting his statue.[10] It is a succession of vignettes, made distinct by stage lighting, showing the tedious, repetitive drilling Eliza has to endure under the watchful eye of her indefatigable taskmaster, a succession which develops Higgins's sardonic character rapidly and makes it quite clear that he does not really think of Eliza as a human person. Eliza makes no progress, and yet the torture continues, the atmosphere charged by looming defeat.

ELIZA: I can't. I'm so tired. I'm so tired.

PICKERING: (*Half asleep*) Oh, for God's sake, Higgins. It must be three o'clock in the morning. Do be reasonable.

HIGGINS: (*Rising*) I am always reasonable. Eliza, if I can go on with a blistering headache, you can.

ELIZA: I have a headache, too.

HIGGINS: Here. (*He plops the ice-bag on her head. She takes it off her head and buries her face in her hands, exhausted to the point of tears*)

(*With sudden gentleness*) Eliza, I know you're tired. I know your head aches. I know your nerves are as raw as meat in a butcher's window. But think what you're trying to accomplish. (*He sits next to her on the sofa*) Think what you're dealing with. The majesty and grandeur of the English language. It's the greatest possession we have. The noblest sentiments that ever flowed in the hearts of men are contained in its extraordinary, imaginative and musical mixtures of sounds. That's what you've set yourself to conquer, Eliza. And conquer it you will. (*He rises, goes to the chair behind his desk and seats himself heavily*) Now, try it again.

ELIZA: (*Slowly*) The rain in Spain stays mainly in the plain.[11]

The brilliant flash of insight is possible not because of the appeal to the language of Shakespeare and Milton, but because in the opening lines of the speech lie the first indications that Higgins recognizes the person in Eliza, and therein perhaps she catches the first glimpse of common humanity in Higgins himself.

The famous tango that follows Eliza's triumph is in the mold of the classic operatic set piece. "The Rain in Spain" has not a speck of dramatic intuition. Its sole function is to heighten the emotion far beyond the level of any speech, and to give the three main characters a chance to revel in the amazing turn of events. Yet, the song is so beautifully placed, just after the peak tension of the drilling scene, understated, comic, and yet deep, and just before listeners have had a chance to realize that victory has been won, that it can hardly fail to move despite its simplicity. It caps the joy of creation.

The creation scene ends with Eliza singing "I Could Have Danced All Night." This song has commonly been taken to express, through its lyric, Eliza's joy in her own achievement. That it well may do, but the music conveys another meaning. The melody of the refrain is sequential in typical Romantic style: the second phrase (mm. 21-28) is little more than a transposition of the first phrase (mm. 13-21) upward by one step. The release has two short phrases based on a variant of the main motive (contained in mm. 13-14), and then the climactic A section of the song arrives (Ex. 8-5). The climax is produced not only by the *tenuto* upbeat chords of measure 38, but by the melodic structure of the last phrase, for it is an accelerated combination of the first two phrases: the essen-

Ex. 8-4 Lerner and Loewe, *My Fair Lady*,
"I Could Have Danced All Night" (No. 10), mm.13–28.

tial notes C and B ("know when he") are then transposed up to become D and C ("dance with me"). This musical emphasis on a key lyric brings out the first hint of Eliza's almost paradoxical attraction to Higgins and makes it the song's primary statement.

In Act III of Shaw's *Pygmalion*, Mrs. Higgins, Henry's mother, points out to Higgins and Pickering that, in taking in Eliza, they have taken on a big problem:

PICKERING: Oh, I see. The problem of how to pass her off as a lady.

HIGGINS: I'll solve that problem. I've half solved it already.

MRS HIGGINS: No, you two infinitely stupid male creatures: the problem of what is to be done with her afterwards.[12]

In the original myth, the obstacle is the creation itself. In Shaw, it becomes the consequences of creation, and although *My Fair Lady*

Ex. 8-5 Lerner and Loewe, *My Fair Lady*,
"I Could Have Danced All Night" (No. 10), mm. 37–45.

touches on both, it is the latter that dominates the drama of the second
act. The second act therefore bears an unusual distinction among
American musical plays: it is more serious than the first.

The tone changes abruptly with the shouting match between Higgins
and Eliza that occurs just after their victory at the ball. Eliza, ignored
and hurt by Higgins, realizes that now that the ball is over, her sabbati-
cal is indeed through. A series of four musical numbers follows, with
remarkably little dialogue separating them. This is a reprise of Eliza's
escape fantasy that she permitted herself in the beginning of her language training (Ex. 8-6). At that point the song, although funny, had
the intensity and weight of a two-year old's tantrum. How changed in
effect it is here! The difference is that the lyrics no longer convey fantasy: Eliza now has the power to do what she says.

The next two numbers, a reprise of "On the Street Where You Live"
and "Show Me," introduce Freddy Eynesford-Hill as a half comic, half

Ex. 8-6 Lerner and Loewe, *My Fair Lady*,
"Reprise: Just You Wait" (No. 20), mm. 5–12.

serious suitor. Then there is a reprise of Eliza's very first song, "Loverly,"
as she attempts to return to her home environment at the flower market. The cockneys who sing it, her old friends, believe her to be a gentlewoman and do not recognize her, and in response to her growing
isolation, Eliza picks up this strain.

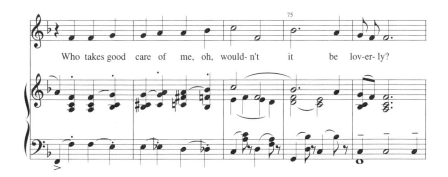

Ex. 8-7 Lerner and Loewe, *My Fair Lady*, "Loverly" (No. 21), mm. 68–76.

Once again the point of this emphasis on a particular phrase of lyric is unmistakable, though understated. It is remarkable how little altered are these two reprises and yet how much the new dramatic context alters their effect.

At the end, the nature and meaning of the mythic relationship between Eliza and Higgins, a relationship which has been tormenting Eliza since her "creation" while leaving Higgins apparently untouched, is crystallized in a single number, "I've Grown Accustomed To Her Face" (Ex. 8-8).

What is immediately arresting about this piece is how outstanding is its character in the context of the whole show. The lyric is still of a pattering sort, as all the lyrics for Higgins are, but for once the language is simple, direct, and honest, as a confession should be. The music is by far the most serious of the play. The harmonic functions of the accompaniment are often weakened by lack of clear identity—is the last chord of the second phrase (mm. 22–23) a dominant, subdominant, or tonic?—which gives the melody an impressionistic vagueness that seems curiously appropriate for the overt nostalgia that has engulfed Higgins. The rhythm within each phrase, a few quick notes ending with a very long note, adds to this musing quality by making each one appear to be spontaneous and independent, almost like talking to oneself, and yet the overall phrase structure is clearly designed for motion. The long notes all occur on the weak beat of the measure, so that the cadence of each phrase is effectively cancelled, and so demands yet another phrase. Only at the end, when the third hearing of "accustomed" is accompanied by a

na-ture to me now;   Like breath-ing out and breath-ing in.

I   was se - rene-ly in - de-pend-ent and con - tent be-fore we met;

Sure-ly I could al-ways be that way a- gain and yet   I've grown ac- cus-tomed to her looks; Ac-

Ex. 8-8 Lerner and Loewe, *My Fair Lady*,
"I've Grown Accustomed To Her Face" (No. 26), mm. 19–39.

deft slowing of rhythm (m. 38), is there a strong cadence on the downbeat. The accumulated power of this delayed cadence, with the lyric in
the last phrase emphasizing "her looks," "her voice," "her face," under-
lines the cause of Higgins's new wonder at himself.

Even if this song were set off by itself, alone, barely twenty measures
long, it would command attention, but when it is set amid other musical sections that clarify its dramatic function, "I've Grown Accum-
stomed to Her Face" becomes the capstone of the play.

The song is introduced with Higgins stomping across the stage in a
great rage, accompanied by what must be considered his leitmotif.

Ex. 8-9 Lerner and Loewe, *My Fair Lady*,
"I've Grown Accustomed To Her Face" (No. 26), mm. 1–7.

The quotation is actually a parody of the original because some beats are missing (see Ex. 8-2), which is just as well, since the intention of the introduction is ironical. Higgins is furious because he at last has let a woman into his life, as "I've Grown Accustomed" is about to make clear.

The first rendition of the main song (Ex. 8-8) is followed by an interlude in which Higgins imagines the consequences of Eliza's threat to marry Freddy. When this interlude turns to the minor mode, it takes on a curious but indubitable resemblance to an earlier song. The melody is a transformation of "Just You Wait," another fantasy song (Fig. 8-1). Does this turnabout on the revenge motive imply a mutual affinity between the two protagonists, who have been portrayed so differently throughout, or merely that Higgins's emotional maturity is at a stage comparable to Eliza's at the beginning of the play?

The course of Higgins's fantasy takes him to an image of Eliza coming to him in tears and beggging to be taken in once again. His reaction calls for another reprise (Ex. 8-11). At last, through the contradiction of his imagined rejection and his self-described nature, all the pretense of the

Ex. 8-10 Lerner and Loewe, *My Fair Lady*,
"I've Grown Accustomed To Her Face" (No. 26), (mm. 72-85).

Fig. 8-1 Comparison of melodies from "Just You Wait" and
"I've Grown Accustomed To Her Face," *Meno mosso.*

original "I'm an Ordinary Man" is revealed, and by Higgins himself.
What had been once only hinted at in the music becomes undeniable.
But the most revealing moment is still to come, for the motives of "Let a
woman in my life" lead directly to the second and final rendition of "I've
Grown Accustomed to Her Face" (Fig. 8-2). Now, because one leads

Ex. 8-11 Lerner and Loewe, *My Fair Lady*,
"I've Grown Accustomed To Her Face" (No. 26), mm. 119–133.

directly into the other, it is clear that the principal motive of "Accustomed" is a dramatic transformation of the motive of "Let a woman . . ."
The anacrusis beats and the entire melodic shape make the relationship
quite audible. The wonderfully ironic transformation of the motive mir-

Ex. 8-12 Lerner and Loewe, *My Fair Lady*,
"I've Grown Accustomed To Her Face" (No. 26), mm. 141–148.

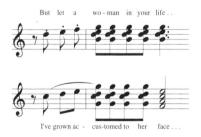

Fig. 8-2 Comparison of motives setting "Let a woman in your life"
and "I've grown accustomed to her face."

rors the transformation of Higgins, from a self-imagined misogynist to
someone who has become accustomed to love a woman.

Eric Bentley, somewhat predictably, objects to what he calls the
"utter sentimentalizing" of Shaw's ending:

> In *My Fair Lady*, what had been a hint stuck on at the end [of *Pygmalion*] becomes the main theme of the second half of the show and involves having Higgins turn into the standard leading man of musical comedy and at that as cornily love-lorn as they come.[13]

But as effective as Shaw's own ending is for his own play, so is the ending of *My Fair Lady* in its own terms. The relationship between Higgins and Eliza is developed with consistent subtlety—the word *love* never comes between them—through the music of the play, which is, of course, the principal addition to *Pygmalion*. The tone of even their music is so understated that it demands a compromise of style: Lerner and Loewe forswear all of the serious devices of romantic expression that the Broadway tradition makes available to them, so that even "I've Grown Accustomed to Her Face," the weightiest number of the play, is restrained in overt expression. Its dramatic impact derives only partly from its own musical resources, more from how its music interprets what has already happened.

"I've Grown Accustomed To Her Face" is the capstone of the play because it is in that moment that the mythic elements are fixed, and not just the love relationship, but its specific character. For the transformation of the principal motives in the song reveals that the principal characters have reversed roles. Eliza is the sculptor, after all, and Higgins the block. Such a theme is discernible in Shaw:

> Eliza, in the role reversal that occurs during the play, becomes the teacher and sculptor, and we want her to finish the job by bringing her wooden man to life. We want this particularly because the phonetics professor contains bits of ourselves, for who has not at times been more wooden than he would wish to admit?[14]

Lerner himself seems to have been aware of this interpretation:

> In a far less tangible way, Higgins goes through as much of a transformation as Eliza, the only difference being that Shaw would never allow the transformation to run its natural course.[15]

The achievement of *My Fair Lady* lies not in that it chose this particular interpretation of the myth, but in that it crystallized the mythic elements in its music with such subtlety.

• • •

How different is the case of *Camelot*. To point out that the adaptation of T. H. White's Arthurian tetralogy, *The Once and Future King*, for the musical stage was a much more imposing task than the adaptation of *Pygmalion* does not tarnish in the least the shining achievement of *My Fair Lady*; it simply underscores some rather obvious facts. First, there is enormous difference in the breadth of the two myths. The Pygmalion legend is a short story of a sculptor, a statue, and a goddess, requiring of Ovid only fifty-four lines for the telling. The legend of King Arthur is a vast tapestry of tales contributed by a variety of sources spanning several centuries. There are a good number of subplots set into the main story, and there are dozens of important characters. Second, George Bernard Shaw did Lerner and Loewe the enormous favor of translating Pygmalion directly to the stage, with a plot so ingenious and dialogue so witty that there was little to add but music. That, of course, is no trivial task, but it is a limited one. To fashion *Camelot*, Lerner had to boil down over six hundred pages of dense novel into a workable libretto that would play under three hours and still allow for music.

He helped himself by eliminating from consideration the book of Arthur's youth, *The Sword in the Stone*, and concentrating on material from the third book, *The Ill-Made Knight*, while working in some background from the second, *The Queen of Air and Darkness*, and the denouement from the fourth, *The Candle in the Wind*. Even so, he was still left with a tremendous saga filled with elements of satire, playful anachronism, and complex motivations and characters. Even the story of the love triangle among Arthur, Guenevere, and Lancelot is far from simple, as John K. Crane notes in his study of White:

> . . . it is a wonderful study of three human beings who are in conflict and in love with one another. More than this, White investigates three human beings who are in conflict with themselves when their developed noble ideals fight furiously to overcome their inbred selfishness and inadequacies.[16]

The causes of the final tragedy in the tetralogy are many, and its course occupies hundreds of pages as Arthur tries heroically, but in vain, to keep his dream alive by initiating quests and inventing legal systems that subvert the inclinations of his knights to war:

White is careful to avoid taxing the adultery of Lancelot and
Guinevere with responsiblity for the failure of Arthur and the fall
of Camelot. He blames the tragedy on the greed and selfishness
and violence in the heart of man.[17]

Making the fall of Camelot dependent upon the adultery, however, is
precisely Lerner's strategy. In this way he strips the Arthurian legend
down to two mythic elements upon which the drama should hang: the
triangle and the fate of the Round Table, which to Lerner seemed the
"universal dream."[18] The resolution of Lancelot's and Guinevere's affair
therefore takes on a mythical significance well beyond that of the typical love story.

Despite such a promising version of this vast legend, *Camelot* fails to
dramatize the mythic elements set in relief so clearly.

The book is fatally defective in several ways. Much of the dialogue,
though inspiring in theme, is badly overwritten. Consider Arthur's
soliloquy which concludes the first act:

ARTHUR: Proposition: If I could choose, from every woman
who breathes on this earth, the face I would most love, the smile,
the touch, the voice, the heart, the laugh, the soul itself, every
detail and feature to the smallest strand of hair—they would all be
Jenny's.

Proposition: If I could choose from every man who breathes
on this earth a man for my brother and a man for my son, a man for
my friend, they would all be Lance.

(*His bitterness mounts*)

Yes, I love them. I love them, and they answer me with pain and
torment. Be it sin or not sin, they betray me in their hearts, and
that's far sin enough. I see it in their eyes and feel it when they
speak, and they must pay for it and be punished. I shan't be
wounded and not return it in kind. I'm done with feeble hoping.
I demand a man's vengeance!

(*He moves violently, then tries to control himself*)

Proposition: I'm a king, not a man. And a civilized king. Could it
possibly be civilized to destroy what I love? Could it possibly be

civilized to love myself above all? What of their pain and their torment? Did they ask for this calamity? Can passion be selected?

(*His voice rising*)

Is there any doubt of their devotion . . . to me, or to our Table?

(*He raises high the sword in his hand*)

By God, Excalibur, I shall be a King! This is the time of King Arthur, and we reach for the stars! This is the time of King Arthur, and violence is not strength and compassion is not weakness. We are civilized! Resolved: We shall live through this together, Excalibur: They, you and I! And God have mercy on us all.[19]

It is a fair summary of the mythic elements of the play, but an academic, not a dramatic one. Why the formal propositions and resolutions, which clash sharply with Arthur's usual good humor and easy dismissal of court formality, and which lend the whole scene more an air of parliamentary debate than of an internal agony? And why the rehearsal of Arthurian ideals, by now well familiar to the audience, which turn the moment into an uncomfortable sermon?

A casualty of this kind of writing is the character of Lancelot, who is portrayed as a pretentious boor at best, a buffoon at worst. There is no precedence whatsoever for this kind of Lancelot in White. Indeed, it is difficult to account for such a transformation, for it threatens the very credibility of the triangle on which the drama is based. "Why was Guenevere disenchanted with Arthur, a kind, loving and attractive husband, and so carried away by Lancelot, a second-rate romantic superman?" asks Engel, and quite rightly.[20]

Then, too, much of the plot seems undermotivated. The tragic element of Arthur's soliloquy is hard to grasp because it is not yet clear that if Guenevere is unfaithful, the very existence of the Table is threatened. Evidence of Lerner's struggle with the sheer complexity of the original story shows through now and again. "Many of the crucial events—the invention of the Round Table, Guenevere's sudden infatuation with Lancelot, the appearance of the villianous Mordred—spring up almost arbitrarily."[21]

This is because these crucial events find hardly any musical expression, which must be the primary agent of motivation in a music drama.

The moment right after Lancelot's miracle of the tournament, when he and Guenevere look at one another in love for the first time, has no song to express this love. There is only an orchestral underscoring of "C'est Moi," which has only the most banal leitmotivic association with Lancelot and certainly adds nothing to the drama of the scene. Underscoring is again the best that Loewe can do for the finale of the first act, which contains Arthur's soliloquy quoted above; this time it is "How to Handle a Woman" for the first part (until "I demand a man's vengeance") and then, incredibly, "I Wonder What the King Is Doing Tonight," Arthur's self-mocking comedy song, for the second. The rescue of Guenevere, set as a sort of oratorio sung by the company of ladies and knights, has been universally condemned, and Lerner himself recognized the flaw in the very design of the scene:

> The one scene in the play that I knew was a breach in style was the penultimate scene involving the song "Guinevere" in which the story of Lancelot's rescue is told. . . . It was not only a stylistic change, but it was breaking a second major theatrical law: it was describing events that took place offstage.[22]

Strangely enough, the saving grace of *Camelot* occurs just where most shows are weakest, at the very end. The second act finale at last brings into dim focus one of the mythic elements with which composer and lyricist grappled:

> For me, the raison d'etre of *Camelot* was the end of the journey when Arthur has lost his love, his friend, and his Round Table and believes his life has been a failure. Then a small boy appears from behind a tent who doesn't know the Round Table is dead and who wishes to become a knight. Arthur realizes that as long as his vision is alive in some small heart he has not failed. Men die but an idea does not.[23]

The reality of the dream is expressed in one of those reprises characteristic of *My Fair Lady*, which dramatically changes the meaning of a song by a new context, and not by significant changes in the song itself. The last scene shows Arthur almost chanting the title song, which at the play's beginning was a whimsical account of Camelot's meterological perfection, but whose whimsy has by now become legend. The name "Camelot" is now synonymous with the dream, and it is the last word sung in the play, by Arthur and his full court, accompanied by the triadic fanfare which is its musical symbol.

Lerner's recognition of this central mythic element came to him during *Camelot*'s Boston tryout, after the Toronto opening, and too late for extensive rewriting that might have provided the focus that this stage version of the myth so desperately needed.[24] Yet, although it is a truism that the plot and book form the cornerstone of any traditional musical play, it is too easy to blame *Camelot*'s critical failure on the quality of the libretto alone. Why composer and lyricist did not provide original music for some of the play's most significant events remains a great mystery, for it amounts to an abdication on their part. Perhaps these moments were the victims of Broadway's three-hour rule, which in the case of *The Once and Future King* made a Herculean task of adaptation quite impossible. The limitations of time and space that help to define the American musical play did not allow the music its proper dramatic role.

That is indeed a pity, because the music composed for *Camelot*, taken as music alone, is perhaps Loewe's best score. The songs are more serious than those of *My Fair Lady* and have more ambitious designs. "Fie on Goodness," a choral number for the knights which was unfortunately cut early in the New York run, is a masterful synthesis of sardonic humor and chivalrous frustration that rises to an impressive musical climax and expresses an important mythic element of White's novel. The triadic "Camelot" motive is pervasive, so that its accumulated meaning is not lost on listeners in the finale. Indeed, *Camelot* is one of those sad cases where one enjoys listening to the original cast recording more than to a performance of the play itself.

It is curious that *Camelot* remains in the "repertoire" of the American musical theater; its unusual place is probably due to its unusual performance history. The opening of *Camelot* on December 3, 1960, at the Majestic Theater marked one of the very few times before 1980 that critical disdain did not doom a show's commercial success, for *Camelot* had already sold two years' worth of tickets on the strength of Lerner and Loewe's reputation as the creators of *Brigadoon*, the musical film *Gigi*, and above all *My Fair Lady*. Meanwhile, its cast recording was vigorously promoted by the exploding recording industry, so that the show was nationally famous, in a sense, before being seen. It created its own legend.[25]

It could be argued that such status is not entirely undeserved, that *Camelot*, in undertaking to interpret such a vast mythical tale, had aimed very high and just missed. It is the opposite number to *Kiss Me, Kate*. Yet, to dwell on the dimension of the original myth is to miss part of the point of a myth's adaptation. How comparatively simple is the legend of Pygmalion, and how powerful are the several revelations of "I've Grown Accustomed to Her Face." The musical interpretation of this simple and small mythical gap is found again and again to be more wonderful than what might have been with the manifold myth of *Camelot*.

Chapter 9

Tragedy as Musical

Street brawls, double death . . . it's all much less important
than the bigger idea of making a musical that tells a tragic
story in musical-comedy terms . . . . Can it succeed?[1]

—*Leonard Bernstein*

Tragedy has been the most elusive dramatic expression for the Broadway tradition. Though a number of its best plots have offered opportunities for tragic composition, Broadway music has generally failed those moments that come closest to tragedy. Gershwin could not find the means to set the despair of either Porgy or his beloved community after Bess's final departure. Jerry Bock's "Anatevka," more nostalgic than tragic, falls far short of conveying the shattered lives and the death of an ethnic tradition at the end of *Fiddler on the Roof*. And Sweeney Todd is given the tragic situation, but not the music that would express his comprehension of his own destruction. Often composers have simply given up the attempt and avoided the necessity of tragic music by leaving the matter in the hands of the librettist or by changing the plot. Thus Gershwin composes the uplifting "O Lawd, I'm on My Way" to transform the end of *Porgy and Bess*. Thus, Rodgers and Hammerstein rewrite the end of Molnar's *Liliom* for their *Carousel*, and leave no music at all for Julie's grief over Billy's suicide, only a song of consolation. The missed chances and unanswered challenges have ironically made tragic drama in the American musical theater into an Olympus, beckoning beyond reach. Indeed, that the Broadway tradition has been counted as a lightweight music drama is due in no small measure to its little success with the most serious genres: epic, sacred history, and tragedy.

To comprehend the brilliant creation of a tragic music drama within this tradition in Leonard Bernstein's *West Side Story* is to appreciate a beneficent set of circumstances that brought together four men who were or who would be major Broadway talents—Bernstein, director and choreographer Jerome Robbins, playwright Arthur Laurents, and lyricist Stephen Sondheim—at a time when gang wars in New York City encouraged faith in Robbins's original conception. But it is also to comprehend what tragedy demands.

It demands first of all a tragic plot. That means much more than a story in which the hero dies some terrible death at the end. "The tragic writer has generally been concerned with last things, with death, with the meaning of life as a whole, with 'destiny' or 'fate' . . . ."[2] The tragic circumstances are ordered so that they not only portray good and evil in characters, but make sense of them. "Observing that human beings suffer, go to pieces, or die prematurely, the tragic vision . . . will not permit these things to happen meaninglessly."[3] Rather, they are seen to occur as part of a higher order that in many plays is a moral order. So "tragedy, like many societies, decrees that a terrible death is evidence of terrible sin, and by this alchemy which is not the logic of philosophy or history as we know it, some meaning is drawn from human calamity."[4]

In its purest form, the sin or "tragic flaw" resides in the character around which the tragedy evolves: Oedipus the King, or Macbeth. But in Shakespeare's *Romeo and Juliet*, the model upon which playwright Arthur Laurents based the libretto for *West Side Story*, the sin is far removed from the principals. Indeed, there is not the slightest suggestion of malice in them. One could stretch the theory by arguing that the tragic flaw lies in Romeo's lack of self-control, so that he kills Tybalt in a frenzy after seeing him run Mercutio through, just as Tony stabs Bernardo after Riff's death, and so precipitates the banishment and all the rest, but such a view forgets the baseless hatred of the two families, which certainly must be considered to be the greater sin. Otherwise, what sense can be made of Prince Escalus's awful remonstrance to them?

See what a scourge is laid upon your hate,
That heaven finds means to kill your joys with love.
(V, iii, 192–193)

Not for its missing "terrible sin," but for some lack of "tragic necessity" has Romeo and Juliet been criticized. Because Friar John is prevented by a suspicion of plague from delivering to Romeo the message that Juliet is just asleep, not dead, in the Capulet tomb, critics have contended that Shakespeare "offends against his own criteria for tragedy by allowing mere chance to determine the destiny of the hero and heroine." For this, the play "has been admired for its pathetic rather than for its tragic power."[5]

West Side Story follows the plot of *Romeo and Juliet* even down to the transmutation of particular lines in spots, but Laurents introduces two changes toward the end, the first of which answers this very criticism and, in a tragic sense, improves the plot. After Anita, Maria's confidante and friend, reluctantly agrees to take Tony the message that will ensure the lovers' escape, she is prevented from delivering it by the Jets, who mock her story and begin to abuse her maliciously. They are stopped just short of rape by the appearance of Doc the drugstore owner. Anita, livid, cries out that Maria has been killed by her former fiance. "Chance, which Shakespeare uses to bring about the final disaster, is eliminated by Laurents. Instead, the social prejudice, the mutual suspicion and hate that motivate the gang warfare become, in Act II Scene 4, the causes for Anita's lie about Maria's death and thus of the disaster that follows."[6] This projects the tragic flaw much more directly onto society and makes *West Side Story* more of a social tragedy than *Romeo and Juliet*.

Laurents's other change is that Maria, unlike Juliet, lives at the end. Otherwise the story is much the same. The parallels of the lovers' meeting, the famous balcony scene, the wedding, the duel, were all noticed even in the first reviews. The parallels run deeper than plot, however. *West Side Story* has the same sense of fatefulness, of inevitability, that marks *Romeo and Juliet* from its opening chorus. Before entering the Capulet ball Romeo remarks

for my mind misgives
Some consequence, yet hanging in the stars,

Shall bitterly begin his fearful date
With this night's revels, and expire the term
Of a despised life closed in my breast,
By some vile forfeit of untimely death.
(I, iv, 106–111)

Likewise, Tony sings "Something's Coming" just before the dance at the gym where he will meet Maria.

For Bernstein, the tragic plot was a new challenge. Completely sympathetic to the Broadway tradition despite his status as a world-class conductor of Western art music, he had three successful Broadway shows already behind him in 1957, but none of them serious. *On The Town* (1944) was adapted from his own ballet *Fancy Free* about three sailors on a wild shore leave in New York City. *Wonderful Town* (1953) set a popular comic play, *My Sister Eileen*. Neither of these has a single moment of gravity comparable even to, say, any of the Sky and Sarah Brown scenes in *Guys and Dolls*. Ironically, his ambitious *Candide* (1956) does have such moments, but they work at cross purposes to the overall theme of Voltaire's classic satire and Lillian Hellman's libretto. The music for all of these shows was much acclaimed, and it deserves to be, but Bernstein seemed not to be very fussy about the sort of librettos he set. His talent was waiting for an idea and a libretto such as *West Side Story* to come along.

For what tragedy demands of a music drama, besides the tragic plot, is a music that is capable of the darker emotions, even of evil, that can yet relate them to utterly opposite human aspirations. That is because tragedy is itself a twofold dramatic expression:

> Tragedy cannot be extreme optimism, for that would be to underestimate the problem; it cannot be extreme pessimism, for that would be to lose faith in man. At the heart of tragedy is a tough dialectical struggle in which the victory of either side is credible.[7]

West Side Story demanded an accessible musical integration the like of which Broadway had never heard, and that is the challenge for which Bernstein's compositional imagination, with its peculiar brand of popular eclecticism and its thorough acquaintance with the Western art tradition, was ready.

Critics have occasionally noted clear motivic relationships in the music of *West Side Story*. In his essay for a recording conducted by Bernstein himself, David Stearns describes how the interval that Tony sings to begin "Something's Coming" is inverted to become the first interval in the main tune of "Maria," in effect a resolution of his feeling of expectancy.[8]

Ex. 9-1 Bernstein and Sondheim, *West Side Story*, "Something's Coming" (No. 3), mm. 8-9 and "Maria" (No. 5), mm. 8–9.

This is but the most famous example of a motivic and thematic integration so thorough that by it alone is *West Side Story* set apart from any preceding Broadway musical. The interval above is the tritone, a traditional dissonance of three whole steps, a favorite interval of Bernstein in his whole corpus. Its prominence in "Something's Coming" and "Maria" is important, but only the tip of the iceberg, for it is heard in every other musical number of the play. But even that understates the variety of dramatic and musical uses to which this characteristic sound is put. Between Tony's two songs, for instance, comes "The Dance at the Gym" which begins this way.

Ex. 9-2 Bernstein and Sondheim, *West Side Story*, "The Dance At The Gym" (No. 4), m. 1.

The scoring and orchestration of the octaves is such that the E-natural, the raised fourth step that makes the tritone, seems approached from above and below at the same time. So the inversion of Example 9-1 is not abrupt, but mediated just before the meeting that prompts Tony to sing "Maria."

The tritone is just the beginning. There are at least four other important elements of structure which characterize the music of *West Side
Story* and, as in *Carousel* and *Porgy and Bess*, lend it a sound so particular that it seems impossible to mistake any of its songs for those of
another play. One of these is the chromatically lowered seventh step of
the scale (Ex. 9-3). The A-flat in measure 32 is a lowered seventh in the
local context of B-flat major. The D-flat in measure 41 is a lowered seventh in the local context of E-flat major. In "Something's Coming" the
lowered seventh is introduced in Tony's melody at the end of the second
phrase (mm. 17–18), gradually becoming so prominent that it ends the
whole song, even though it is a dissonance (Ex. 9-4).

A third characteristic element is a tone cluster made up of a triad
with both major and minor third factors. Many of the chords harmo-
nizing the "Jet Song" are constructed in this way (Ex. 9-3, e.g. the first
two chords). Such a sound has a double effect for *West Side Story*. It
stamps the music with an American flavor appropriate to the story's setting, since the simultaneous major/minor third approximates pitch

Ex. 9-3 Bernstein and Sondheim, *West Side Story*,
"Jet Song" (No. 2), mm. 28–43.

shadings in jazz, particularly the blue third. The association is reinforced by the typical rhythmic texture of a solidly metric bass line
against which the upper parts are syncopated. The other effect concerns
structure. Along with the tritone, the half-step juxtapositions of this
cluster soon accustom the ear to an idiom of chromatic progressions
and modulations that are so important to the latter part of the play.

Indeed, the chromatic half-step develops into another element in its
own right. By establishing the tritone as a structural interval at the outset,
Bernstein makes easy a vocabulary of chromatic modulations that would
otherwise be distant (Fig. 9-1). To the Western ear, the leap of the perfect
fifth can establish a key, since it signals a cadence. By combining that interval with the chromatic tritone, tonal centers one half-step above and one
half-step below the original tonic become accessible. Theory becomes
practice in the interludes between the verses of "Tonight" (Ex. 9-5).

Finally, there is the hemiola, a characteristic rhythm that juxtaposes
a division of a beat (or a measure, itself a big beat) into three parts

Ex. 9-4 Bernstein and Sondheim, *West Side Story*,
"Something's Coming" (No. 3), mm. 138–148.
The last sung note is a lowered seventh in the key of this song, D major.

against a division into two. The most famous example from *West Side Story* is the alternation of 3/4 and 6/8 meters in the refrain of "America," famous perhaps because it is such a classic case, but there are many variants of the hemiola idea throughout the score. In the "Jet Song" (Ex. 9-3), the contrasting division of the measure by the vocal melody against that by the bass melody has the same effect, but it is complicated further because the accompaniment repeats its pattern every two bars, and its

Fig. 9-1 Modulation possibilities using the tritone.

Ex. 9-5 Bernstein and Sondheim, *West Side Story*, "Balcony Scene" (No. 6), mm. 81–90.

principal motive is a two-beat cell (one beat being a dotted quarter). One level of triple meter given by the singer competes with several levels of duple in the orchestra. Similarly, the bass line of "Something's Coming" (Ex. 9-4) pits a clear triple pattern against a duple division in the upper parts. This gentle sort of syncopation is what lends this song its effect of anticipation, almost breathlessness.

How striking these elements are, striking in the sense of being on the fringe of the Western tonal language. The normal procedure is to organize the rhythm with a steady simple meter and clear rhythmic groupings, not with complex hemiolas. The tritone, for centuries strictly controlled or avoided altogether, can be found in the diatonic scale, but not in the way Bernstein usually uses it, as an augmented fourth above the tonic. And the clash of third factors, regardless of any appeal to jazz idioms, is a very strong semitonal dissonance. Yet, these sounds emerge so naturally from the "Prologue" of the work that in the end the listener notices not how weird or unusual they are, but how well they work together.

Like *Carousel*, *West Side Story* dispenses with the medley overture and begins the play with a "Prologue" that accompanies silent action on stage. The scene is given as "The months before" and as the "Prologue" is played, the Jets and Sharks dance and mime their growing rivalry, until the Sharks leader Bernardo cuts the ear of one of the Jets in ritual fashion as the police whistle sounds. As the action on stage is the premise for the rest of the drama, so is the music of the "Prologue" the source of all Bernstein's important musical elements.

The very first chord introduces the first important element, the major/minor triad (Ex. 9-6). Again, its rhythmic disposition and the cultural setting justify this dissonance as "blues" sound. It quickly becomes a norm, since every chord is built the same way, save for alterations needed when the fifth is diminished (mm. 4, 8).[9] The first cadence comes at the end of measure 8, defined by the first simple pitch formation, the unison C.

Next, the tritone is heard, from the A to D-sharp in measure 12, arising from a theme that seems to be in the key of A. Then, when that theme repeats three bars later, its C-sharp clashes with a C-natural in the following measure (m. 17). Yet, what should be a disturbing chromaticism develops easily from the earlier material. The sustained D-sharp is a pitch that has already been heard, in the very first chord. In fact, all the notes of that A major theme have already been in the listener's ear from the first two bars. The relationship is made explicit when Bernstein sounds the opening chord progression to accompany the long D-sharp (mm. 13–15). Similarly, the theme which juxtaposes C-sharp /C-natural later on is nothing more than an arpeggiation of Bernstein's chord on the downbeat of measure 3 (A–B-sharp–C-sharp–E) with the added D-sharp.

After the second cadence in C (m. 18), the "Prologue" begins again with a fresh motive (Ex. 9-7). It sounds fresh because the prominent pitches, F in the high melody and F-sharp in the bass, are the only two of

Ex. 9-6 Leonard Bernstein, *West Side Story*, "Prologue" (No. 1), mm. 1–18.

the complete twelve-tone collection which have not been sounded. The upper melody is clearly derived from the opening bars both in rhythm and contour. The bass, however, introduces the hemiola idea, since it is an ostinato of three chords that moves across the duple measures; the upper melody counterpoises its two measure periods, as in the "Jet Song." The bass also raises the tritone to higher structural significance: it is in the key of F-sharp, a tritone distance from the original key of C, in which the upper melody can still be heard at the same time.

Ex. 9-7 Leonard Bernstein, *West Side Story*, "Prologue" (No. 1),
mm. 19–40.

When this melody is heard again two pages later, it is recomposed to
"fit in" with the harmony of this bass line (Ex. 9-8). The important feature here is that what should be the key-defining leading tone, E-sharp,
is missing. Finally, the melody rises to a peak and culminates with an E-
natural, so that the sound of the modal lowered seventh, perhaps the
least striking of all these elements, is made explicit (mm. 105–106).

Ex. 9-8 Leonard Bernstein, *West Side Story*, "Prologue" (No. 1), 101–9.

The more anomalous and dissonant harmonization of the "swing" melody is heard first, not second, because it is consistent with a harmonic procedure heard from the beginning. The music has polytonal aspects; that is, more than one key can be simultaneously implied or actually sounded. The opening phrase, for example (Ex. 9-6), begins with a colored C triad and a colored A triad, and ends on a G-sharp triad, also colored. Is the real key C, as the first bass note would suggest, or A, as the second and last would suggest? The issue is resolved by the first cadence, the unambiguous unison in measure 8, but meanwhile Bernstein has founded an important high-level feature, a harmonic polarity between C and A. It is immediately strengthened as the first theme is sounded in A major (mm. 11–13, 15–17), yet harmonized with exactly the same chords that began the piece, and rounded off with the same C cadence (m. 18). The next passage expands the idea yet again (Ex. 9-7). The C/A polarity continues in the upper melody, while the bass part moves in the key of F-sharp, which of course is the relative minor of A. Once more the structural predominance of C is emphasized as the section ends with the unison cadence (m. 40).

So the "Prologue" establishes not only the significant melodic and rhythmic elements for the play, but also significant harmonic procedures and pitches, C, A, and F-sharp, which will unify the musical numbers in a way that no other Broadway composer has attempted. *West Side Story* is the first American musical play to be organized around a central pitch.[10]

Such a deep and multifaceted musical integration is wholly admirable but should not be so astonishing, coming as it does from a composer who by 1957 had composed two full-length symphonies and several other important instrumental works, for such integration in instrumental music is essential. The easy alliance of jazz idioms and symphonic textures are as nothing to one who was a practicing jazzman and Koussevitzky protégé at the same time. To attribute the high achievement of *West Side Story* to its symphonic organization, however, is to underrate it seriously and miss its singular drama. Indeed, many of the same elements that characterize this play are also heard in abundance in *Candide,* particularly the tritone, the lowered seventh, and the hemiola.[11] Once the scheme of musical integration is apparent, what becomes important is its power to project tragic drama.

From the dramatic perspective, there is no surprise in Bernstein's choice of materials: they are dissonant, chromatic, syncopated—in other words, filled with musical tension, a roughness that matches the story and its setting. But if Eric Bentley's tragic dialectic is to be translated into music, these same materials must also project the other side. That is the basis for the tragedy within the music: not the collection of motives, keys, and musical ideas alone, but these together with their transformation. Consider the main tune of the famous balcony scene, "Tonight." There in the middle-voice accompaniment is the tone cluster as before, but the half-step dissonance has been exchanged in favor of the less dissonant whole-step so that the whole chord sounds like a mild tonic ninth. There is the E-natural sounding the tritone against the tonic B-flat, but now its harmonic context transforms it into an old-fashioned secondary dominant. There is the chromatic half-step in the bass moving from A-natural to A-flat (mm. 57–58) and in the vocal melody right after, but since the voice leading in all the other voices produces a concomitant change of chord, the effect is no more startling than in Wagner. More explicit chromaticism is limited to the modulation passages that separate each verse. Tragedy is made possible through Bernstein's design of a musical idiom capable of both sorts of expression, pessimism and optimism, evil and aspiration, which are thus related in musical terms. The motivic unity of the idiom is, of

Ex. 9-9 Bernstein and Sondheim, *West Side Story*, "Balcony Scene"
(No. 6), mm. 51–60.

course, essential, but so is its capacity for expressive range through transformations.

Thematic correspondences among the musical numbers are also resources for dramatic transformations, although by and large their role has more to do with structure and musical continuity. Bernstein does not use leitmotifs in the Wagnerian sense of symbolizing characters or emotions, but rather as a means to connect the musical parts in long chains. This is most evident in the opening scenes of the play. The music of the "Prologue" is so similar to the "Jet Song" that one leads directly into the other without any noticeable break. In the middle of the song (m. 100 ff.), the Jets sing the tune that will become the opening stage band melody in "The Dance at the Gym." Later in the gym sequence comes the delicate "Cha-Cha," which is a dance arrangement of "Maria." That song in turn is quoted to begin the "Balcony Scene."

Such relationships create a high-level continuity among the numbers that allows Bernstein to slow the action around Tony and Maria's meeting to a pace suitable for tragedy.

It is also possible, although difficult to demonstrate convincingly, that Bernstein's use of tonal centers has a dramatic symbolism attached. There is the central pitch of the musical, C. Certain keys on the sharp side seem reserved for the expressions of the lovers: "Something's Coming" in D, "Cha-Cha" in G, the wedding vows music in G, C, and E, "Somewhere" in E. Flat keys are related to themes of violence and hate: the chase music of the "Prologue" in B-flat, the first "Jet Song" in B-flat, "Cool" in C minor, "A Boy Like That" in B-flat minor. E-flat is the last pitch heard in the first act, sustained in tremolo as the curtain covers the dead bodies of Riff and Bernardo. That E-flat and E-natural create the first dissonance of the musical may have some connection with the choice of E-flat for the latter "Rumble" music and for the reservation of E major for "Somewhere." The one gross inconsistency is the setting of "Maria" in E-flat major, but a comment by Larry Kert, who created the part of Tony, indicates that Bernstein's original key may have been different:

> At the audition I sang 'Maria' in the original key. I cracked on the high note. Still they saw something they liked and had me do it again one note lower.[12]

Restoring the transposition would put "Maria" in E major, and since the introduction is set in the key a major third down, that would be C, which connects very nicely with the C of the last dance of the previous scene, the "Jump." Again, since "Maria" moves right into the "Balcony Scene," perhaps its original keys were B, B-flat, and A major.

To build his tragic idiom into the higher structural levels of *West Side Story*, Bernstein depends on two techniques which, although not new to Broadway, are in this play exploited as never before: the continuity of several musical numbers in succession, and the drama of dance.

Three times in the course of the play musical numbers follow in succession without appreciable break for dialogue, and each such succession occurs at a crucial point in the tragic plot. The first extends from the "Mambo" of the dance scene through the following "Cha-Cha" and "Jump" into "Maria," and finally ends with the "Balcony Scene." There are short conversations but music plays under all of them, and various musical connections leave no doubt that continuity is intended.

This music, of course, accompanies the dance scene where Tony and Maria meet, and the most immediate effect of the continuous sequence is to portray in music how their love arises miraculously from a battleground. The "Mambo" is a barely disguised show of force between the two gangs. After the lovers catch sight of one another, the lights dim and the crowd moves offstage as the music in the key of A begins to sound a sequence of I-VII progressions, using the major triad of the lowered seventh step to shift the key in a subdominant direction. Then the "Cha-Cha" begins in G, and Tony and Maria become lost in their intimate dance.

That they fall in love at first sight is a necessary economy of Shakespeare's plot. The circumstances and aftermath are so complex that no time is left to develop a love relationship; it must happen at once. And the audience must be fully convinced of the profundity of their love and their utter helplessness in giving themselves to it. Shakespeare carries it off with his great love poetry. "Did he wonder for a moment," asks Granville-Barker, "how to make this stand out from everything else in the play? They [the lovers] share a sonnet between them, and it is a charming device."[13] Bernstein relies on his music, its particular character and the succession of numbers that slow the action. The "Cha-Cha," for example, has such a different texture and orchestration from the preceding dances that the separate world in which Tony and Maria find themselves is immediately apparent. The many long rests which articulate phrase endings and the feminine cadences make it easy for Bernstein to fashion a transition into the "Meeting Scene" melodrama.

The first full expression of sentiment comes in Tony's song "Maria," a piece with an astonishing number of wonderful features for its short length. Bernstein captures Tony's dazed amazement with an introduction that is sung, beginning with a monotone on D-sharp (Ex. 9-10). The sense of bewilderment comes from the insecurity of key, nominally in B major but without any confirming cadence or rhythm. Only when the rhythm accelerates and the music erupts into the key of E-flat does the listener realize that Tony's monotone was the tonic after all. The "Cha-Cha" melody returns in full-blown lyricism over a bass line tango of mild Spanish character which at the same time recalls the jazz idiom through its tied notes in mid-measure. The high point comes with what should be the onset of the second verse and instead becomes a great rhapsodic singing counterpoint to the main tune in the orchestra, as if to suggest that Tony's sudden happiness is so boundless that he can do nothing but name its cause (Ex. 9-11).

The famous tritone setting Maria's name is already muted in its dissonant effect, since Bernstein allows the raised fourth step in the third bar of the melody (m. 11) to fulfill its traditional function as a secondary leading tone. As regards the tragic development, the downbeat upward appoggiatura associated with "Maria" becomes more important

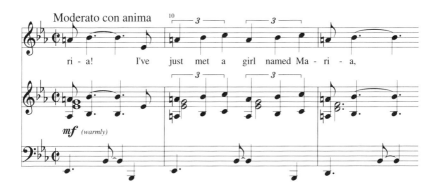

Ex. 9-10 Bernstein and Sondheim, *West Side Story*, "Maria"
(No. 5), mm. 1–11.

Ex. 9-11 Bernstein and Sondheim, *West Side Story*, "Maria"
(No. 5), mm. 27–33.

than its tritone setting, although the connections which that interval makes with previous numbers, especially the dance numbers, cannot be gainsaid. The coda of the song, whose harmony recalls the mysterious introduction, leaves this "Maria" motive as the last gesture in the listener's ear just before it is significantly developed in the following "Balcony Scene" (Ex. 9-12).

The dramatic function of the main tune "Tonight" from the "Balcony Scene" is to allow Maria the chance to express her own feelings as a balance to Tony's previous song, and then to deepen and make credible the relationship itself, as does Shakespeare's balcony scene. It is significant, therefore, that she sings the first verse alone. Otherwise, little more need be said, except that it is a beautiful song which makes its effect in traditional Romantic manner: every phrase is in a different key, so that the

Ex. 9-12 Bernstein and Sondheim, *West Side Story*, "Maria" (No. 5), mm. 46–53.

return to the original in the last phrase resolves a high-level tension in its single cadence. However, the melodrama surrounding the verses contains dialogue which begins to describe the particular quality of this love. As Juliet warns Romeo of the dangers her kinsmen pose, and he replies:

> Alack there lies more peril in thine eye
> Than twenty of their swords; look thou but sweet,
> And I am proof against their emnity.
> (II, ii, 71–73)

so does Maria warn Tony, who says, simply, "I'm not afraid." Their love is a fearless love, and this fearlessness will lead to Tony's hopeless attempt to stop the rumble. This first glimpse of looming tragedy, ironic in that such a disaster could spring from such a love, is turned into music at the very end of the scene (Ex. 9-13). For the first time, the singers do not sustain the fifth scale degree on the last "Tonight," as they have done in every verse till now, but rise to the tonic, making the strongest cadence of the whole piece. As they sing this high A-flat, a striking melody in the 'cellos decorates a plagal cadence, the first phrase from the song "Somewhere," a song not to be heard until well into the second act. The final gesture is the upward appoggiatura "Maria" motive less the chromatic half-step, now allied to another song to which it already belongs so well, since it will set the very word "Somewhere."

This curious practice of giving the listener advance notice of very important melodies to come, first in the "Cha-Cha" and now at the end of "Tonight," can have only a dramatic explanation. Of course the gestures must work on their own musical terms, whether one recognizes their connections or not; the "Cha-Cha" is a perfectly fine little dance whose different character makes its point immediately, and the last cadence of "Tonight" has a very nice bit of part writing which amplifies the cadential effect so that it can convincingly finish the scene. For the listener who already knows the musical, however, the forward direction of such references builds a sense of destiny that is so much a part of the original *Romeo and Juliet*. Who can fail to sense the implication of the "Somewhere" quotation at the very moment when Tony and Maria are celebrating their fearless love?

The second continuous musical sequence ends the first act and includes "One Hand, One Heart," the quintet "Tonight" and "The Rumble." Its purpose is quite different from the first one, for the depth and

Ex. 9-13 Bernstein and Sondheim, *West Side Story*, "Balcony Scene" (No. 6), mm. 144–54.

character of the love relationship are no longer at issue. The second sequence, coming at the end of the act, operates much more in the manner of a traditional classical finale, juxtaposing various dramatic themes and characters in order to accelerate the pace before the curtain falls. The order of the numbers makes this intention quite clear: the first song continues the love theme, the last presents the violence of hatred, and the middle number contrasts both at once in climactic fashion.

It is unfortunate that the bridal shop scene is often described as a "mock" wedding just because Tony and Maria playfully banter about

wedding plans and surround themselves with a wedding party of man-
nequins. This view neglects the profound change of mood brought
about by the "Somewhere" motive, heard just before they take their
vows. It also neglects the Catholic teaching, to which Tony, the Polish-
American, and Maria, the Puerto Rican immigrant, would presumably
be sympathetic, that the sacrament of marriage is conferred, not by a
priest, but by the man and woman on one another. For the tragedy to
have its greatest pathos, the love sacrificed at the end must be the greatest love possible, love for a lifetime. Thus Shakespeare includes the
brief sixth scene of the second act in which it is made clear that Romeo
and Juliet do marry. Even though it is rare for a Broadway musical play
to show a wedding, mostly because that is the presumed end of the plot,
here it is the subject of very moving music.

Barely have the final *pianissimo* chords of "One Hand, One Heart"
died away when the ear is jarred by the opening of the great ensemble
"Tonight." Here all the important elements that have been continually
transformed since their first occurrence in the "Prologue" return in
their harshest, most dissonant form. Most obvious is the hemiola
rhythm, the bass line proceeding in groups of three quarter notes
against duple meter in the upper parts. The texture is polytonal, not in
the sense of the key being ambiguous, but in the sense of two keys pit-
ted against one another, and the two keys are C and A, the two harmonic poles established on the opening page of the play. The rising bass
line E–F-sharp–G-sharp, heard against the upper part, gives the impression of A while the insistent G natural in the middle voice (mm. 2–3)
allows the upper parts to be heard in C. This harmonic design allows
other important motives to be embedded in the texture: the E
major/minor triad resulting from the simultaneous G-natural and G-
sharp; and G-natural acting as a lowered seventh in the context of A.
The tritone is used more circumspectly, in the contour of the melody
which emphasizes B and F (mm. 11–13) and F-sharp and C (mm.
15–18), but nevertheless colors the music.

So much for the symbols of tragedy. The dramatic purpose of the
quintet is to present the five principal characters anticipating the
coming evening in a way that summarizes their fated courses in
the drama. The construction is quite traditional: each principal gets a
solo in the first half (except Maria, who has the same music as Tony) in
order to present both words and music clearly, and then the intensify-

Ex. 9-14 Bernstein and Sondheim, *West Side Story*, "Tonight" (No. 10), mm. 1–13.

ing counterpoint on two musical themes can begin. Bernstein is bitterly ironic when he gives the Jets and Sharks the same music to sing
(although its use for Anita's part must be considered a musical economy). For the lovers' side, he reprises the "Tonight" song from the "Bal-

Ex. 9-15 Bernstein and Sondheim, *West Side Story*, "Tonight"
(No. 10), mm. 14–20.

cony Scene." The transition from the violent to the sublime is prepared
when the gangs anticipate the modulation to A major (Ex. 9-16). The
G-naturals in the vocal melody and the F-naturals in the bass part
maintain a certain connection to C, yet the sense of tonal center is
much closer to a real A than it was before. Anita's solo returns the music
to C/A, but the preceding interlude for Jets and Sharks effectively prepares Tony's change to an unambiguous A major (Ex. 9-17).

The reprise of "Tonight" supports the polytonal design of the beginning beautifully, since the modulation plan of the tune moves the music
from A major to C major with the second phrase. The danger in incor-
porating such a lyrical piece into the quintet is a loss of tension after the
dissonance of the opening. To avert it, Bernstein has the violins double

Ex. 9-16 Bernstein and Sondheim, *West Side Story*, "Tonight"
(No. 10), mm. 33–41.

Tony's singing in the second phrase. Then, for the third phrase, they continue to play his melody, but one measure later than his singing, as a canon (Ex. 9-18). This solution is so breathtakingly simple that it is hard to believe the original tune was not designed for it, for it gives up none of the lyricism that the situation demands while the counterpoint intensifies the texture without extreme dissonance.

Tony's song finishes without a firm cadence, and now the first music returns briefly in the key of E-flat/C. The reason for this transposition is purely structural, so that the second reprise of "Tonight" will occur in C major, not A major, and so end the quintet in C. It is important, though, that the return to the first Jet/Shark theme be brief, so that the immediate onset of Maria singing "Tonight" may quicken the pace. Thereafter the five parts are severally introduced, the chromatic notes of the first

Ex. 9-17 Bernstein and Sondheim, *West Side Story*, "Tonight" (No. 10), mm. 63–71.

theme coloring the predominant second theme, the structure of which governs the rest of the course. The greatest intensity of contrast occurs in its third phrase, where the key of C minor expresses at once the lovers' longing and the gangs' raging (Ex. 9-19). Even here, the tonal idiom is so flexible that the Jets can sing "They began it" on an E-flat minor triad (mm. 138–139), a considerable harmonic distance from C, without losing the continuity of the overall key. The end of the quintet, in one sense, has been prepared from the beginning, since there have been no strong cadences, and none at all since Anita's first solo (Ex. 9-20). The moment when the five parts come together, the topmost hitting the high C, is the most climactic musical moment in the play.

The last measures of the ensemble, filling out the powerful cadence, contain the E-natural/E-flat conflict and the F-sharp, all of which, in

Ex. 9-18 Bernstein and Sondheim, *West Side Story*, "Tonight"
(No. 10), mm. 83–93.

the context of C, recall the musical premises of the "Prologue." That, in short, is the secret of the entire ensemble. By dramatizing this inextricable intertwining of love and hate in consistent musical motives and symbols, the quintet summarizes the progress of the tragedy just before the fatal moment. It is the musical-dramatic climax of the first act and the greatest operatic ensemble ever composed for the Broadway stage.

A short dialogue precedes the rumble. Tony tries in vain to prevent the fight from starting. He endures Bernardo's insults, but his best friend Riff cannot, and when he punches Bernardo "The Rumble" music begins.

Ex. 9-19 Bernstein and Sondheim, *West Side Story*, "Tonight" (No. 10), mm. 133–40.

The opening measures continue the development of explicit "Prologue" material. The first chord in the bass is C–F-sharp–C, answered by an A major/minor cluster. Later on the keys of E-flat major and minor become important (the last note of the act is E-flat), having been

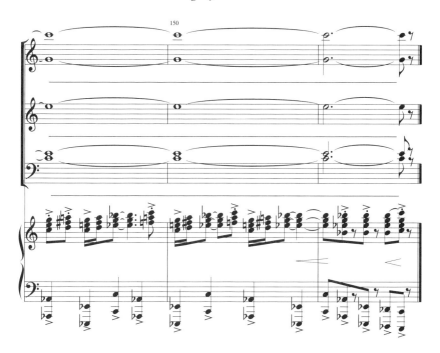

Ex. 9-20 Bernstein and Sondheim, *West Side Story*, "Tonight"
(No. 10), mm. 143–51.

prepared by the closing bars of the quintet and connected to the other material by the common G-flat/F-sharp of the minor mode. Much music from the "Prologue" is recapitulated with little change. The music surrounding the moment when Tony kills Bernardo is the same as that setting Bernardo's knifing the Jet A-Rab, a plausible symmetry.

A stronger element of symmetry between the beginning and the end of the first act is their choreography. They are dances. Dance, of course, has always been an essential part of the Broadway tradition, but *West Side Story* used it to such an extent that many critics named it the most outstanding element of the show, one calling the piece a "ballet-opera."[14] There are twelve choreographed pieces in the play. That Jerome Robbins, the original choreographer, was not only the show's director but the one who came up with the original conception for the play in the late 1940s certainly influenced the show's final shape.[15] By that time, his extremely fortunate match with Bernstein was years old, for it was Robbins who helped launch the composer's career when he asked Bernstein to compose a ballet in 1943, before the famous conducting debut with the New

York Philharmonic. This turned out to be *Fancy Free*, which was so popular in New York that the collaborators persuaded Betty Comden and Adolph Green to help them turn it into a Broadway musical, *On the Town*, also a hit.

So many dance numbers in a single musical play would be intolerable had they not a significant dramatic purpose. That is why *West Side Story* is the first musical for which the composer himself created significant and separate pieces of music for the dance sequences, rather than leave them for an arranger to patch together out of the song material. Serious music drama with serious dancing demands serious music.

The most important dance sequences—"Prologue," "Cha-Cha," "The Rumble," "Ballet Sequence," "Taunting Scene," "Finale"—narrate the story while abstracting it. They narrate in that they convey facts which need to be known. "There's hardly a divertissment. We tell everything, the dance hall incident, the killing of the men, the taunting of the girl in the drugstore, through dance."[16] The "Prologue" tells that the Jets and Sharks have been warring for months. "The Rumble" shows who is killed and how. The "Taunting Scene" reveals the assault on Anita when she tries to give Tony Maria's message. But narration alone is insufficient for the drama of dance; the dances must abstract the events that they portray. That allows the integration of the events themselves with accompanying emotional reactions that are carried in the accompanying music. But more than that, abstraction can make the event more frightening, triumphant, powerful than if it were seen true to life, because it allows the viewer's imagination to become an active participant, to blow what it has seen out of all proportion. Just as an actress's gesture or movement in cinema, sufficiently subtle, can be more erotic than a full-length love scene, so can the choreographed violence of a gang fight seem more horrible than any attempt at staging the real thing with fake punches and pratfalls.

The third continuous music sequence of *West Side Story*, the "Ballet Sequence," is dominated by such dancing. When Tony and Maria are together after the rumble, he sings the arioso "I'll Take You Away." The bass motives are developed into transition material based on the "Somewhere" motive. The dream ballet begins:

> . . . the two lovers begin to run, battering against the walls of the
> city, beginning to break through as chaotic figures of the gangs, of

violence, flail around them. But they do break through, and suddenly—they are in a world of space and air and sun. They stop,
looking at it, pleased, startled, as boys and girls from both sides
come on. . . . They begin to dance, to play: no sides, no hostility
no; just joy and pleasure and warmth.[17]

During this sequence, an off-stage voice sings "Somewhere." The dancers
on stage join in a brief reprise in the "Procession" before the "Nightmare"
recalls both the music and events of the rumble.

It is unfortunate that both choreography and stage directions paint
the lovers' dream as a sort of paradise, for this is quite untrue to the
tragic plot and denigrates the pathetic loss at the end. There is no reason why the lovers deserve such a paradise, and no audience would feel
pity at their failure to find one. The pity is rather that they are denied
the simplest joy, to be left alone in their love. The spirit of that longing
is caught by Shakespeare when Romeo bemoans his banishment:

> heaven is here
> Where Juliet lives; and every cat and dog,
> And little mouse, every unworthy thing,
> Live here in heaven and may look on her,
> But Romeo may not. (III, iii, 29–33)

Tony's dying words, "They won't let us be," express as a negative the
source of the pathos much better than the utopia of the ballet. And yet,
to express somehow in dance this simpler freedom for Tony and Maria
would also be insufficient, for that would leave the cause of this social
tragedy unchecked. It would mean an escape, not a resolution. The
gang characters must be included as an expiation of the tragic flaw, but
including them falsifies the lovers' role in the story. It truly is a dramatic
dilemma, which is perhaps why the ballet has not been well received by
critics. Even Robbins himself, reflecting on the ballet in 1980, doubted
its purpose.[18]

Despite such problems on stage, the music of the ballet is quite faithful to the tragic plot and so requires the performance of the whole
sequence. The central piece, the song "Somewhere," speaks nothing of
harmony between races or the perfect society but only "peace and quiet
and open air," "time together" to be left alone. It is the musical expression for Tony and Maria's simpler dream, woven into the tragic plot by

its use of all the important musical elements that characterize the whole play, although, as in the other lyric numbers for the lovers, their tensions are softened. The song begins with an upward leap of a minor seventh which, when imitated at the fourth, introduces the lowered seventh scale step.

Ex. 9-21 Bernstein and Sondheim, *West Side Story*, "Somewhere" (No. 13d), mm. 1–8.

The gentle triplet in measure 5 becomes a more explicit, although still gentle, hemiola effect later on when the harmony changes against it (mm. 19, 21). Other elements arise out of the harmonic design. The principal key of the song is E major, but the triumphant central section modulates to C, the central tone of the whole play (Ex. 9-22). It is no coincidence that the highest note of that phrase is an F-sharp, nor that the tritone relationship is further enhanced by a modulation to that key (m. 23). But again, it is the motivic development that carries tragedy forward. The choice of setting for "Someday! Somewhere . . ." seems so

Ex. 9-22 Bernstein and Sondheim, *West Side Story*, "Somewhere"
(No. 13d), mm. 13–24.

suited to the accent pattern of the words that the listener might miss its
clear derivation with the "Maria" motive that became an omen in the
"Balcony Scene." Now the upward appoggiatura has become a complete
harmony, but the identity of its rhythm and essential dissonance is

unmistakable. The lovers' longing for peace has become inseparable from love itself, for indeed, one causes the other.

Even though this climax is set in C major, Bernstein's motivic integration has power enough to recall this essential moment at the end of the song, which of course is in E (Ex. 9-23). The melody moves as before, toward C major, but the last measures interpret the D-natural as a lowered seventh in E, a melodic and harmonic progression which by now is so idiomatic in the play that the final cadence (VII-I, m. 35) is as convincing as any.

The "Procession" makes a march, a dirge really, out of this motive, until it is cut off by a recapitulation of "The Rumble" music. The rather too obvious message is that there can be no paradise, not even escape. Curiously, this does not spoil the final moment of the dream sequence, when a sustained note in the oboe leaps up a seventh to begin the "Somewhere" melody again, soon joined by the flute, a nice touch of orchestration. When Tony picks up with "Hold my hand and we're

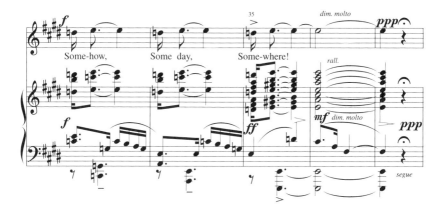

Ex. 9-23 Bernstein and Sondheim, *West Side Story*, "Somewhere"
(No. 13d), mm. 25–37.

halfway there," the fearless love triumphs again, and the lovers' faith in
it, however naive, is nonetheless moving.

The power of love against all odds must be considered one of the
important subthemes of *West Side Story*. Certainly it characterizes the
high-level articulations of its music. The harsh music of the "Prologue"
and "The Dance at the Gym" becomes transmuted into the "Cha-Cha,"
"Maria," and the "Balcony Scene." Here the memory of "The Rumble"
is subverted and soothed by a brief reprise of "Somewhere." The
denouement of the tragedy bleakly reverses this order, but not before
that contrast is prepared and heightened by one last fleeting triumph of
love over mindless hate.

"A Boy Like That," Anita's bitter rebuke of Maria for her relationship
with Tony, brings back in its opening measures the "Prologue" material
in its harshest form yet (Ex. 9-24). The texture is full of tone clusters,
tritones, and halting weak beat accents that all contribute to Anita's
venom. Most striking of all is how the D-natural D-flat semitone which
makes the difference between major and minor is emphasized by putting it right in the vocal melody, on "brother" (m. 4) and "find another"
(m. 6). The more dissonant harmonic minor ninths and major sev-
enths, introduced early in the "Prologue" when Bernstein wanted F-
naturals against F-sharps and E-naturals (see Ex. 9-7) return here with
both musical and textual accents: "*One* of your own *kind, stick* to your
own *kind*." The conversion of Anita's reproach to some kind of under-

Ex. 9-24 Bernstein and Sondheim, *West Side Story*, "A Boy Like That"
(No. 15), mm. 1–8.

standing of Maria's plight is reflected in Bernstein's handling of theme
and motive (discussed in Chapter 1), yet another instance of a consistent musical-dramatic conception that forms the whole play. Once
again the tone clusters in measure 68, the tritone in measure 69 which,
as in "Somewhere," prepares a modulation to the tritone key (here, D-
flat major, m. 90), the semitone progressions and the hemiola in measure 72, all are cut from the same material as Anita's singing, yet muted
in their tensions. When Bernstein pulls out the old trick of having the
two sing in parallel to show Anita's complete capitulation to Maria's

Ex. 9-25 Bernstein and Sondheim, *West Side Story*, "A Boy Like That" (No. 15), mm. 68–73.

conviction (mm. 105–116), it works beautifully, indeed it is a tremendous moment, because it confirms what the listener has already understood on a more fundamental level of musical discourse.

The most immediate apprehension of the tragic moment in *West Side Story*, as in *Romeo and Juliet*, is as a deeply pathetic one. "Somewhere," since it represents the lovers' simple hope, becomes the central piece of the play's denouement, which reveals the ultimate denial of that hope. But its reprise at the end is no simple quotation. After Tony's last spoken words, Maria begins, without any accompaniment, to sing the end of the song, picking it up at the precise spot where Tony did to rally her courage at the end of the nightmare sequence. Now it is for her to brace his failing faith, even if she cannot save his failing life. Bernstein's melody loses little of its power for the missing orchestra; the essential modulation from E to C is implied in its very notes. That Tony dies at

Ex. 9-26 Bernstein and Sondheim, *West Side Story*, "Finale" (No. 17), mm. 1–14.

its climax summarizes the awful juxtaposition of hope and hate that the play is about. The significance for the Broadway tradition is that he dies while he is singing. Tragedy is within reach at last.

And what of Maria? She cannot complete the melody, for she is broken by her loss; the orchestra must do it for her, and in so doing returns the music to E major, as before. But now comes Bernstein's greatest touch of imagination. That plagal cadence, which ended the "Balcony Scene" and the ballet, which has always been based on "Somewhere"'s opening phrase, now uses that phrase to begin the piece again in the subdominant key. The renewal is absolutely stunning, but nothing could be more appropriate musically, nor dramatically. This is Maria's moment of grief, when her intense sorrow is translated into musical terms of pathos, however brief.

To move from the pathetic to the truly tragic demands something beyond the loss of a couple in love, some meaning, some renewal of the wider world. Shakespeare has been criticized for making this movement a rather awkward conclusion:

> The story of a young and idealistic love thwarted is not enough to make it a great tragedy; but Shakespeare, trying to place it within a grander conception, has not been able to achieve a larger unity. . . . The awe that we should feel as well is not inherent in their story but is indicated (rather than effected) in what seems to us like an epilogue; it is something explained to us at the end rather than rendered immediately dramatic and compelling as the heart of the design.[19]

The epilogue, Friar Lawrence's recitation of the series of mischances, is necessary since "the action of the tragedy is not complete until the survivors have been influenced by the events, and the explanations are necessary that we may witness their effect,"[20] especially in *Romeo and Juliet* where the sin of tragedy lies outside the dead ones.

Arthur Laurents's design has two remedies that go far to achieve such larger unity. The first is that the gang members witness the disaster and the loss; the stage is full while "Somewhere" is sung. The second, more important remedy is that Maria survives, and cries out in anguish during a pause in the "Finale," confronting the sinners with the result: "WE ALL KILLED HIM; and my brother and Riff. I, too. I CAN KILL

NOW BECAUSE *I* HATE NOW." Bernstein was disappointed that he
could not find music to set this speech:

> My first thought was that this was to be her biggest aria. I can't tell
> you how many tries I made on that aria. I tried once to make it
> cynical and swift. Another time like a recitative. Another time like
> a Puccini aria. In every case, after five or six bars, I gave up. It was
> phony . . .[21]

His confession emphasizes once again the supreme difficulty of tragic
music drama, but the speech on its own terms does bring the tragic
meaning in close proximity to the pathetic loss:

> . . . her act of *not* killing herself or any of the gang members whom
> she threatens in the final scene, underlines the basic difference
> between this play and Shakespeare's: *West Side Story* is conceived
> as a social document, *Romeo and Juliet* as a *Liebestod*. Consequent-
> ly, it becomes important to the contemporary play's message that a
> resolution of the gang warfare be effected, not as a postscript, so
> to speak, but by the hand of one of the play's protagonists.[22]

Her speech ended, her last farewell to Tony spoken, Maria silently
begs various members of both gangs to carry the body away. The "Procession" music has no words, but perhaps that is most appropriate in a
play in which dance has become so much a part of the drama, at a
moment when the players are moving to the world's most solemn dance.
The dirge is more than a funeral march. Composed as it is of the "I Have
a Love" melody in the top voice, the "Somewhere" motive in the middle voice and a last reminiscence of its opening phrase toward the end,
the dirge crystallizes the meaning of the tragic loss. How fitting that the
last sound is a high C major triad over the doleful F-sharp in the bass.
The larger unity has been glimpsed with musical means.

Whether *West Side Story* is tragic music drama depends to an extent
on one's conception of tragedy. Although one could complain with some
justice that the plot, stolen from Shakespeare, must share the flaws of
Romeo and Juliet, or that Maria's last speech should indeed have been her
biggest aria, somehow such complaints seem petty in view of what has
been achieved, especially given the constraints of the Broadway tradition. Certainly they have been overlooked in the universal acclaim the

Ex. 9-27 Bernstein and Sondheim, *West Side Story*, "Finale" (No. 17), 15–28.

work has inspired, from its initial Broadway run of 732 performances at the Winter Garden Theater, to its wild receptions in London and inhospitable Paris, to its incorporation into the permanent repertory of the Vienna *Volksoper*. And the achievement is not only in the creation of a musical play whose numbers are all motivically related or that fits some grand theory of tragedy. The most precise understanding of tragedy and the most thorough musical integration will be for nothing if the individual pieces are not wonderful music besides. In art the details are as important as the design. When one realizes that "I Feel Pretty," which has little function in the tragic scheme other than to offer a comic relief at the opening of the second act, would have been hailed as a top song in almost any other show, one approaches the true excellence of the score. There are no dull numbers, and there is the sense of something grand among all of them. On this account, as on many others, *West Side Story* may be called not only tragedy, but masterpiece.

Chapter 10

The Ethnic Musical

I felt a sense of quiet confidence in being able to write this score . . . because I was able to draw on my own background, my own memories of music I grew up with. I never felt the urge to research the score; I felt it was inside me.[1]

—*Jerry Bock*

W hen librettist Joseph Stein was asked in 1967 to explain the stunning and rather unexpected commercial success of his *Fiddler on the Roof*, he remarked, "This isn't a play about Jewish people, it's a play about people who happen to be Jewish."[2] The comment points up the apparent paradox in the best musical plays based on an ethnic setting: the particular choice of ethnic quality is not supposed to matter, but it nevertheless seems essential.

Perhaps the exotic is an intrinsically attractive element in music drama. Certainly a large number of operas have settings foreign to the composer's home culture: *The Abduction from the Seraglio* (Mozart in Turkey), *Aida* (Verdi in Egypt), and *Turandot* (Puccini in China) come to mind immediately, and perhaps the entire Baroque tradition of *opera seria*, preoccupied with antiquity and myth, could be compared with these, although it does not use the foreign elements in the same way. In the American tradition, the melodramatic operettas of the 1910s and 1920s were so dominated by the exotic that it became the main attraction, at the expense of dramatic interest (see chapter 2). A wiser and

265

more restrained handling of the ethnic setting came about with the maturing of the American musical theater. Exotic places were just as common, if not more so, in the 1940s and 1950s as in the 1920s, but they ceased to be the play's dominating theme and instead formed a rather highly flavored background against which the real action was played out.

A typical example of this more mature ethnic setting is Lerner and Loewe's *Brigadoon*. The story is about two American hillwalkers on vacation in Scotland who lose their way and come upon a strange village that appears in the Highlands for one day each century. The songs are therefore filled with jig rhythms and melodies that emphasize the sixth step of the major scale in order to sound Scottish. The principal drama, however, has little to do with this setting, but instead asks whether the main character can give up everything he knows for a love that must be bound to this mysterious village. Such a theme could be set anywhere. A different locale would require different music, to be sure, but perhaps not as different as one might expect.

George Gershwin's *Porgy and Bess* is a more complicated case owing to its intensity of ethnic setting and expression. *Brigadoon* can offer an occasional "Almost Like Being in Love," which does not sound Scottish in the least, even in context, but Gershwin's effort to compose a folk opera that develops the community at large as a character required that the ethnic idiom permeate every moment. That he succeeded in cutting the whole out of one such piece without being overbearing or tiresome is indeed one of the opera's triumphs. The stature of the community is so important to the essence and impact of the opera that here the ethnic element very nearly becomes an inextricable part of the drama, and in fact does become part if one considers the formation of the community character as a legitimate dramatic issue. Otherwise, the main dramas of Porgy's loneliness and Bess's weakness are bigger than the Charleston setting in which they are framed, and so *Porgy and Bess* remains an extreme but typical case of ethnic usage.

The work of Richard Rodgers and Oscar Hammerstein depends more on ethnic settings than perhaps any other composer or librettist from the mature period. *Oklahoma!*, the "cowboy musical," and *South Pacific* are examples of fine shows in which the foreign setting remains in the background. The characters who sing in South Pacific have much more say about the varied style characteristics of the songs than do Polynesian islands. Thereafter, however, Rodgers and Hammerstein learned to take advantage of ethnic elements to give sharper articulation to dramatic problems, if not to actually form them. The clash of western and oriental values in *The King and I*, for example, arises quite naturally from the story of a Welsh schoolteacher who goes to work in the palace of the King of Siam. So Rodgers uses his "Siamese" music to help define the sides of the conflict. The King's "A Puzzlement," the slave lovers' two songs, and all the incidental music for marching and ceremonial officials have the open fifth chords, parallel fifth progressions, and pentatonic scales that create Rodgers' "Siamese" idiom, but Anna's music—"I Whistle a Happy Tune," "Hello, Young Lovers," "Getting to Know You," and "Shall We Dance"—concedes nothing to the setting, dominated instead by Western dance rhythms and harmony. *Flower Drum Song*, a musical of San Francisco's Chinatown, portrays two young Chinese couples who at first are confused about who is really the object of their mutual desires, but their true intentions are matched in the styles of the songs they sing even before the characters themselves realize them.

So Wang Ta, the traditional dutiful son who thinks he loves a night-club dancer, and Mei Li, the immigrant mail-order bride who is supposedly intended for the older nightclub owner, only sing "Chinese" songs: "You Are Beautiful," "Like a God," and "I Am Going to Like It Here." Meanwhile, the dancer Linda Low and the owner Sammy Fong, both quite acculturated to their new country, sing numbers that are nothing but American Broadway: "I Enjoy Being a Girl," "Don't Marry Me," and "Sunday."

But what are the musical sources of these ethnic idioms, however they are disposed in the play? How is the ethos of the setting carried in the music?

History has shown that composers have consistently paid scant attention to any ethnomusicology that might bear upon the musical setting of their ethnic operas. In the American tradition, Rodgers himself is not in the least apologetic about his refusal to be accurate in the ethnomusicological sense:

> If my melodies [in *Oklahoma!*] were going to be authentic, they'd have to be authentic in my own terms.
>
> This is the way I have always worked, no matter what the setting of the story. It was true of my "Chinese" music for *Chee-Chee*,

of my "French" music for *Love Me, Tonight*, and later of my "Siamese" music for *The King and I*. Had I attempted to duplicate the real thing, it would never have sounded genuine, for the obvious reason that I am neither Chinese, French, Siamese, nor from the Southwest. All a composer—any composer—can do is to make an audience believe it is hearing an authentic sound without losing his own musical identity.[3]

Such an attitude does not preclude familiarity with the real thing, of course, but suggests that it is seldom required and that in any case, authenticity will be subordinated to the needs of drama.

In short, projection of ethnic idioms in music drama depends on musical stereotypes, sets of musical commonplaces which the audience associates with a culture in which the play is set. The composer selects, by instinct or reason, characteristics that will work together to conjure an idiom that for the American audience seems to be typically Chinese, Scottish, or French without ever giving up the fundamental musical grammar of the West. More often than not, the results have some connection with the real thing: authentic oriental music does have pentatonic scales and open fifths; the modes typical of Scottish folk music often emphasize the sixth degree. George Gershwin took the trouble to spend some hot summer weeks on Folly Island to immerse himself in Gullah culture there, and the folk idiom of *Porgy and Bess* seemed so close to the real thing that he got into trouble over the ethnic issue (see Chapter 3). Fabricated idioms of the musical theater are stereotypical not as much in their inaccuracy as in their incompleteness. The line is fine but nevertheless real. There can be no excuse for demeaning musical stereotypes, yet an incomplete but otherwise sympathetic ethnic portrayal may be defended on the grounds of dramatic art itself. Musical plays and operas are dramatic works, and they must communicate with their audiences. The medium of such communication is the musical language of the culture viewing the drama. If intelligibility is compromised in the interest of ethnic authenticity, communication breaks down and so does the drama.

When composers think that they have no conception at all of a particular setting or style, they either refuse the project or take extraordinary measures. Even Rodgers felt compelled to do research when composing the "Catholic" chant for the opening scene of *The Sound of Music*:

> Writing "Western" songs for *Oklahoma!* or "Oriental" songs for *The King And I* had never fazed me, but the idea of composing a Catholic prayer made me apprehensive. Given my lack of familiarity with liturgical music, as well as the fact that I was of a different faith, I had to make sure that what I wrote would sound as authentic as possible.[4]

His apprehensiveness may have been rooted in the certainty that a significant number of viewers in an American audience would be quite familiar with real Catholic polyphony and chant compared with the number familiar with authentic Asian music. Hammerstein, too, occasionally drew on authentic ethnic forms, never for the sake of cultural accuracy, but only when he thought it would help him achieve some necessary dramatic effect. Thus he borrows a Malaysian poetic form, the pantoum, for the lyric of "I Am Going to Like It Here," sung by Mei Li, a Chinese character in *Flower Drum Song*.

In any case, theater composers, writing for their audiences, depend upon their own sensitivity to the musical preconceptions of their own cultures to choose the proper set of musical characteristics for an ethnic suggestion. Curiously, a particular commonplace may be used for remarkably differing and distant ethnic purposes. Stephen Sondheim discovered this when he tried to invent a texture that would approximate the flexibility of the Japanese scales for his *Pacific Overtures*:

> I was searching for a Western equivalent, and one day I hit on the correlation between the Japanese scale and the music of Manuel de Falla, a composer whose work I admire a lot. So I just started to imitate him. I took the pentatonic scale and bunched the chords together until they resembled that terrific guitar sound. And I was able to relate to it because suddenly it had a Spanish Western feeling and at the same time an Eastern feeling.[5]

Both *Brigadoon* and *Flower Drum Song* have melodies which emphasize the sixth scale step, sometimes as a false tonic. In the former case this is a significant aspect of the show's Scottish flavor; in the latter, it makes the music sound Chinese. Similarly, *Show Boat* uses the "gapped" pentatonic scale to characterize the black people in its opening scene, while *The King and I* uses it to portray the Siamese. What matters is not the presence or absence of a particular motive, but coordination in the whole set that constructs the idiom.

Specifying the idiom precisely depends on essential dramatic context, defined by the scenery, the time and place, and the foreknowledge that the audience brings with it to the theater. "People want to believe what they see on a stage, and they will gladly go along with whatever is done to achieve the desired effect. Ask them to accept Ezio Pinza as a Frenchman, Yul Brynner as a Siamese or a heterogeneous group of actors as Chinese, and they are prepared to meet you nine tenths of the way even before the curtain goes up."[6] In other words, the suspension of disbelief accounts for much of the effect of ethnic commonplaces in the music. A repeated emphasis on the sixth degree in the overture and opening song sounds a bit strange, but the stage setting is vaguely Asian and the singer Chinese, so that must be Chinese music. A different stage and a few men dressed in kilts will transform the same emphasis into something quite different.

Of all ethnic sources, perhaps Jewish folk music is most apt to adaptation since that tradition itself has borrowed from a great number of other ethnic traditions encountered during the period of worldwide wanderings of the Jewish people.

> The stylistic basis of hasidic tunes, as of eastern Jewish song in general, is a mixture of a variety of styles, including ancient formulae of oriental chanting and prayers; Russian, Ukranian, Romanian, Hungarian and German songs, instrumental pieces adapted to devotional vocalizing; and even marches and vaudevilles. All these elements are however to some extent unified by means of a tonal basis, mainly variants of the minor mode.[7]

This variety of characteristics, combined with the willingness of a theater audience to hear what it expects to hear, gave composer Jerry Bock a free hand to establish a pervasive and original ethnic idiom for *Fiddler on the Roof* without giving up the resources of Western functional harmony.

Bock had known success with such idioms in his previous work. *She Loves Me* (1963), which opened the year before *Fiddler on the Roof*, has a number of waltzes and gypsy songs to go along with its east European setting. His Pulitzer Prize–winning *Fiorello!* (1959) has one scene in which the main character, politician Fiorello LaGuardia, campaigns for Congress in a number of ethnic neighborhoods of New York. Bock dresses each verse of "The Name's LaGuardia" in music aimed at the group he addresses. Curiously, the last verse is addressed to hasidic Jews, and ends with a lively hora that could have been found just as easily in the wedding scene of his best known musical play, *Fiddler on the Roof.*

In that musical, Bock concentrates the greatest number of "Jewish" commonplaces in "If I Were A Rich Man." That the song offers such a strong dose of idiom early in the show is good for the overall unity, of course, but it also has an important dramatic function, for it introduces in music the character of Tevye, the rock on which *Fiddler on the Roof* is built.

The first suggestion of mode rather than major scale comes early on at an emphatic point in the melody, the high C-flat in measure 6. The

Ex. 10-1 *Bock* and Harnick, *Fiddler on the Roof*,
"If I Were a Rich Man" (No. 4), mm. 4–19.

second phrase builds on this suggestion, slipping easily into a chro-
maticized version of the minor mode. The alternation of parallel major
and minor modes within songs, sometimes within phrases, is an
extremely important and very audible characteristic of the show as a
whole, informing almost every song, and Bock's technique differs
essentially from Cole Porter's in *Kiss Me, Kate* (see chapter 6). In that

play, Porter alternates modes to suggest a Renaissance flavor for the "Shakespeare" scenes by changing the third scale step, usually after an intervening dominant chord. In *Fiddler on the Roof*, the modal change is almost always routed through the subdominant. It is the sixth degree (the B-double flat in measure 8) that announces the change, and the third simply follows suit. It is on such technical minutiae that ethnic idioms succeed or fail.

Ex. 10-2 Bock and Harnick, *Fiddler on the Roof*, "If I Were A Rich Man" (No. 4), mm. 19–26.

Thus, the final cadence of the section (m. 19) is a major triad, which can then act as a dominant to introduce the next section in the subdominant minor, already well prepared by the earlier phrases. By now, the mix of minor subdominant (mm. 20, 21, 24), minor tonic (m. 22, 23) and major tonic (m. 26) has been well established. How surprising it is, then, when the same tune is immediately repeated with the subdominant major chord substituted on its first downbeat.

Ex. 10-3 Bock and Harnick, *Fiddler on the Roof*,
"If I Were A Rich Man" (No. 4), mm. 35–42.

This harmony is actually closer to the original key of D-flat major than the more prominent minor subdominant, but Bock saves it until after it has been distanced by the idiom that he is trying to create. Perhaps that accounts for the perfectly appropriate wistful effect of the change.

After the half cadence of this section, the song goes back to the beginning strain and once again has the section based on the subdominant (like Ex. 10-2). This time, however, it is interrupted (Ex. 10-4). This passage, entirely in the subdominant minor key of G-flat, suggests chant with its unison texture, then moves unabashedly into a chant texture where Bock marks the music "Freely." Another important characteristic occurs in measure 83: the lowered second degree (E-double flat), an unusual but unmistakably modal reference suggesting the oriental roots of much Jewish music.[8] This altered scale step is so important to the sound of *Fiddler on the Roof* that it is introduced in the first music the audience hears, the famous "fiddler" tune (Ex. 10-5). When this lowered tone is conjoined with the normal third of the major scale, the melody takes on more Jewish flavor through the resulting augmented second interval. In "If I Were a Rich Man," this interval is the basis for the expressive ending of the chant section (m. 90).

Ex. 10-4 Bock and Harnick, *Fiddler on the Roof*,
"If I Were A Rich Man" (No. 4), mm. 83–92.

To dwell on the harmonic and melodic constructions does not necessarily mean that the more local effects—the nonsense syllables used throughout, the dance rhythms and instrumental ornaments in the accompaniment, even the pronounced use of the accordian as an ethnic sign—contribute but little to the ethnic character of the music. But chords and intervals must be the preeminent ethnic ingredients of *Fiddler on the Roof* because they can be integrated into a system which Bock can use to construct and unify the music of the whole play. The augmented second interval, for example, is very familiar to Western listeners through its prominent usage in compositions composed in the minor. In such pieces it occurs as the space between the lowered sixth step and raised seventh step (leading tone), and is therefore an important cue for the perception of key. Now when Bock introduces the same interval between steps 2 and 3, the same associations between the augmented second and the tonal center create in the western listener a bias toward the subdominant (Fig. 10-1).

Ex. 10-5 Bock and Harnick, *Fiddler on the Roof*,
"Prologue —Tradition" (No. 1), mm. 1–9.

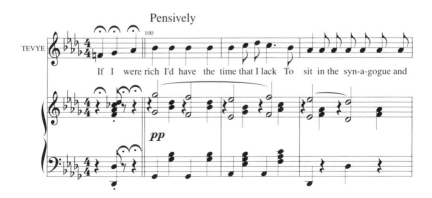

Fig. 10-1 The melodic augmented second interval in traditional minor scales and in Bock's modal scale for *Fiddler on the Roof*.

The third degree becomes a false leading tone, identified by the augmented second interval below it. The penchant to alternate major and minor modes through the subdominant chord, acting as a tiny key, is therefore justified by the characteristic intervals with which Bock constructs his "Jewish" idiom.

Despite this ingenuity of integration, the expressive qualities of the songs come not from these particular "Jewish" commonplaces but from Bock's manipulation of song forms. The chant section (Ex. 10-4) of "If I Were a Rich Man" interrupts the second section, which originally contained four phrases: two phrases based on the subdominant minor (Ex. 10-2), one on the subdominant major (Ex. 10-3), and a final one back in the minor which leads to a half cadence. Consistency of form would lead the listener to expect a return of the major form after the interruption, but the chant section instead moves into the minor form (Ex. 10-4, m. 92). Only after the next half cadence does the expected phrase in major arrive (Ex. 10-6). The recall of this formally delayed harmony at this point, with Harnick's telling lyric, completely reforms the dramatic function of the song. No longer the typical comic character piece, it quickly reveals Tevye's deep and traditional religious side, without which much of the later action would be incomprehensible. Even when the harmony

Ex. 10-6 Bock and Harnick, *Fiddler on the Roof*,
"If I Were A Rich Man" (No. 4), mm. 99–115.

returns to the minor mode, in an extension of Bock's pattern, the high
melody in the string parts accompanying the contemplation of Talmudic
scholarship (mm. 110–114) maintains the delicate force of this moment.

The credibility of the ethos in *Fiddler on the Roof* is most in debt to the
source of the play itself. Most Broadway musicals take ethnic models

written by authors who are not themselves members of the ethnic communities they attempt to describe. Gershwin depended on a white Southerner's image of the Gullah community for *Porgy and Bess*, and Richard Rodgers chose stories by James Michener for *South Pacific* and British novelist Margaret Landon for *The King and I*. But Sholem Aleichem is renowned the world over for his tragicomic portrayals of the Yiddish *shtetls* of the Ukraine, and there is no denying his authority to write about them, since he grew up among them. The plot of *Fiddler on the Roof* is drawn from Sholem Aleichem's eight stories about Tevye the Dairyman, which appeared separately between 1895 and 1914. Four of those stories—"Modern Children" (1899), "Hodel" (1904), "Chava" (1905), and "Get Thee Out" (1914)—supply the main plot for the play, but inspiration is not limited to them.

Here is a brief paragraph in "The Bubble Bursts" (1899) that describes one of Tevye's many daydreams:

> God in Heaven! If I had only a tenth of what all of this is worth! What more could I ask of God and who would be my equal? First of all, I would marry off my oldest daughter, give her a suitable dowry and still have enough left over for wedding expenses, gifts, and clothing for the bride. Then I would sell my horse and wagon and my cows and move into town. I would buy myself a Synagogue seat by the Eastern Wall, hang strings of pearls around my wife's neck, and hand out charity like the richest householders.[9]

Surely this was the beginning of "If I Were a Rich Man." Reforming the four separate stories into a continuous book was the task of librettist Joseph Stein, who was singularly equipped for the job. He could speak Yiddish and read the almost untranslatable Sholem Aleichem in the original. Even though he refrained from using even one word of Yiddish, he believed that "through the quality of the talk, the construction of sentences, there is a kind of ethnic rhythm without any Yiddishisms."[10]

The title of the musical, however, does not originate in Sholem Aleichem. That was inspired by an entirely different source, but one that shared the same time and culture with the Yiddish author: the Russian painter Marc Chagall. His large oil painting "The Green Violinist" of 1923–1924, "an oval-eyed violinist seemingly dangling in space over the roofs of a peasant village—inspired the title . . . as well as the whole

Credit: © 2002 Artists Rights Society (ARS), New York / ADAGP, Paris

decor of the production," according to assistant director Richard Altman.[11] "The title was absolutely suggested by the Chagall picture," concurs producer Harold Prince. "I think Chagall hovered over the look of the show for a long time."[12] This was literally true, since set designer Boris Aronson was told "to capture the flavor and special essence of Chagall."[13] The Chagall connection goes beyond the coincidence of one picture and the painter's personal history, however. In another, "The Dead Man," which depicts a mourning or funeral scene, the figure of a fiddler is shown actually sitting on the roof of a nearby house while playing. Indeed, many Chagall pictures have fiddlers in them.

> Certainly the fiddler had always been in Chagall's mind. Ever since 1908 he had constantly appeared in a variety of scenes. He was a central figure in the festivities of the Jewish community in the Russian suburb, and his tune accompanied the basic events of life—birth, marriage, and the funeral. By making his appearance at these important moments in life, he became an almost legendary figure—the attendant of human destiny—in the life pattern of the community. He appears as such in Chagall's pictures of births, weddings, and funerals.[14]

Thus, when the collaborators hit upon the image of a fiddler on the roof, they not only discovered a suitable title, but borrowed an authentically ethnic metaphor that would symbolize the most ambitious and dramatic theme of the play.

For what distinguishes *Fiddler on the Roof* from other ethnic musicals is its attempt to place the ethnic identity of the play not in the background but at the center of its dramatic theme. The mute fiddler figure who appears to Tevye at various important junctures is made into a symbol in the opening speech:

> TEVYE: A fiddler on the roof. Sounds crazy, no? But in our little village of Anatevka, you might say every one of us is a fiddler on the roof, trying to scratch out a pleasant, simple tune without breaking his neck. It isn't easy. You may ask, why do we stay up here if it's so dangerous? We stay because Anatevka is our home. And how do we keep our balance? That I can tell you in a word—tradition![15]

Rarely is a dramatic action so explicitly defined. Preserving tradition is the key to the community's existence, and the fiddler who represents it in the play takes on the same symbolic value as he does in Chagall: he is "the attendant of human destiny."

Such a theme puts ethnic identity in the center of the drama because tradition is where ethnic identity resides. The music accompanying this

Ex. 10-7 Bock and Harnick, *Fiddler on the Roof*,
"Prologue—Tradition" (No. 1), mm. 35–47.

exposition then quite rightly establishes the principal commonplaces of
the Jewish musical idiom. The solo violin tune (Ex. 10-5) is heard even
before Tevye begins to speak, reaffirming the symbol and introducing
the modal scales so important to the sound of this play. The first singing
then elevates into music what Tevye has just said. Now the lowered second step first heard in the violin tune is expanded into a full harmonic

Ex. 10-8 Bock and Harnick, *Fiddler on the Roof*,
"Prologue—Tradition" (No. 1), mm. 119–27.

progression, so that the C major chord (mm. 35–37) moves to the exotic D-flat major (m. 38). In measure 44 the D-flat is used in a new motive, which repeats incessantly under the forthcoming explanations of the various community traditions, becoming associated with them. Meanwhile, the traditional roles of "the papas," "the mamas," "the sons," and "the daughters" are told to the audience with four different tunes, which then combine in a rather raucous counterpoint. Perhaps it is not coincidental that "the daughters" tune is that of the opening fiddler tune. Since it is Tevye's daughters, in *Fiddler on the Roof* as in Sholem Aleichem, who cause him to upset the balance of tradition that he has just proclaimed, how appropriate it is that the original fiddler tune is now allied with a lyric emphasizing the tradition of arranged marriages. The tune ends the entire lengthy prologue in grand fashion as Tevye recapitulates the fiddler metaphor one more time.

Ex. 10-9 Bock and Harnick, *Fiddler on the Roof*,
"Prologue—Tradition" (No. 1), mm. 232–240.

The dramatic focus on tradition does not come from Sholem Aleichem's stories. Tevye's Jewishness is essential, but it does not derive
from blind adherence to tradition, nor does tradition bind him to a
community of Jews. In Sholem Aleichem's stories Tevye's is the only
Jewish family in the immediate locale; he does not live in Anatevka but
some miles distant. When the poor tailor Motel Kamzoil informs him
that he and his daughter Tzeitel have pledged themselves to be married,
Tevye does not agonize over a broken tradition. He is hurt at being left
out, but he quickly recovers. "He talked me into it" says Tevye simply.[16]
No, the tradition theme is a transformation wrought by Joseph Stein,
perhaps as a response to director Jerome Robbins's constantly pestering
question: "What is the show about?"[17] For their part, Bock and lyricist
Sheldon Harnick created the "Prologue—Tradition" at Robbins's behest
to make the dramatic theme crystal clear.[18]

Having been so boldly asserted, tradition then becomes the bone of
contention in each of the crises brought about by Tevye's daughters. Each
crisis concerns the marriage traditions. Yente, the comic matchmaker
(completely invented by Stein), has arranged a match for Tevye's oldest

daughter, Tzeitel, with a rich butcher, but she has long ago fallen for Motel. She begs Tevye to give her permission to marry him instead, leaving Yente without her accustomed role, and her fee. Next, his second daughter, Hodel, loves Perchik, a visiting revolutionary student. When he is sent away, they inform Tevye that they would like his blessing, but will marry in any case. Finally, his third daughter, Chava, runs off to marry a Christian boy, and she tearfully begs Tevye to accept them. With each crisis, Tevye goes into a recitative-like soliloquy while the action freezes Ex. 10-10). Tevye's rising fourth is the same interval, in the same metric pattern, that set the chorus singing "Tradition" in the prologue. Later that tune is recalled explicitly, along with the accompanying instrumental motive. And so Tevye weighs, with much struggle, the costs of holding fast against the costs of "pulling out a prop."

But after all, aren't the preservation of tradition and the struggle with changing times, even the loss of homeland, experiences common to

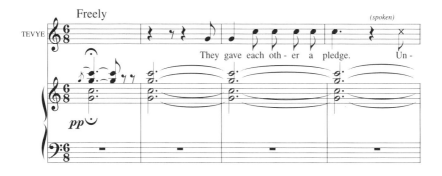

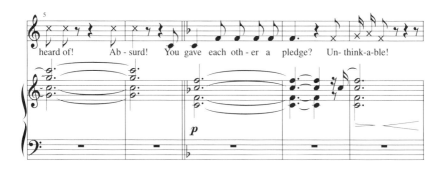

Ex. 10-10 Bock and Harnick, *Fiddler on the Roof*,
"Tevye's Monologue" (No. 9), mm. 1–9.

people everywhere? Why is this an ethnic issue? There can be no doubt of the theme's universal appeal. The history of foreign productions of *Fiddler on the Roof* is full of stories about well-intentioned advice that any play about small town Jews in Russia would not work in Amsterdam, in London, in Paris.[19] All were proven wrong. Joseph Stein, attending the Tokyo production, is reported to have been approached by a young admirer who was astonished that the musical had done well in New York, because "it is so Japanese."[20] But that is precisely the point. As Stein himself has said, it is not the Jewishness of the play that is essential; that is only the particular vehicle chosen for ethnic expression, but what is expressed—the struggle to maintain an ethnic way of life—is a truly ethnic issue that evokes universal response. That is why the dramatic premise of *Fiddler on the Roof* is so special.

Despite a premise of such profundity, despite such a sure-footed opening, the musical fails to play out the tradition theme on the highest level of dramatic action.

Tevye's three monologues, which should be among the most dramatically powerful moments in the play, are colossal disappointments. Here, when he ponders aloud the consequences of sacrificing tradition to his daughters' wishes, the principal drama of the play is brought to the fore, and yet very little happens. The fault is not in the libretto or lyrics; it is a musical failure, a gross awkwardness in the handling of recitative texture (Ex. 10-11). The transformation of the "tradition" motive makes a fair beginning, but Bock can do nothing but repeat the same idea in different keys, winding his way around the circle of fifths, and to the flat side at that, which in classical tradition is associated with declining, not rising musical tension. There is not the slightest change to convey the moment when Tevye begins to see the other side; the music that vainly expresses his outrage must also express his tenderness. Even when he recognizes the depth of his daughters' love, nothing.

When the release of emotion contained in these struggles does come, there is little use of the "Jewish" idiom Bock has labored to create, and so there can be little connection to the dramatic dissolution of tradition. "Matchmaker," sung by the three older daughters in naive anticipation of their arranged marriages, "Miracle Of Miracles," sung by Motel in celebration of his victory, and "Now I Have Everything," Perchik's own song of triumph, were singled out by critics as "catering to Broadway taste."[21] In fact, each of these songs does have some reminis-

Ex. 10-11 Bock and Harnick, *Fiddler on the Roof*,
"Tevye's Monologue" (No. 9), mm. 31–41.

cence of the ethnic setting. "Matchmaker" has a gypsy dance in the
middle of it when Tzeitel parodies the machinations of Yente; the citation of biblical miracles in Motel's song is accompanied by a modulation to the subdominant minor with appropriate suspensions in the
cadences; and "Now I Have Everything" also has a section in the subdominant minor. But the Jewish characteristics are not integrated in

such a way as to signify a victory over an oppressive tradition, and so they do not make musical-dramatic sense.

At the end of *Fiddler on the Roof*, the Jews are thrown out of Anatevka by an edict from "the authorities." They sing a nostalgic song, "Anatevka," and leave. The final scene shows Tevye dragging his wagon with what is left of his family on to America, accompanied by a halting tonic-dominant ostinato and disjointed fragments of the various tradition tunes from the prologue played in various keys. What is one to make of this? Do the fragments mean that the tradition that has held the community together is now but a fleeting memory? Then why was the same fragmentation technique used in "Prologue—Tradition?" Are Tevye and his family taking tradition with them as they take their last leave of friends and loved ones? Then how can the play be about tradition as the essence of a community?

There is little sense to be made of tradition here because tradition has no part in the end of the play. It is true that the edict is not totally unexpected, since such treatment of Jewish communities in Russia is part of history and was introduced by the "unofficial demonstration" that spoils the wedding celebration at the end of the first act. But as regards its relationship with the play's dramatic theme, the edict might as well have been a hurricane or a plague. There is simply no connection between the gradual breakdown of community tradition and the action of the authorities, not in the play at any rate. Such a criticism appeals first of all to the old-fashioned notion that a tragic result should be contained in the premises of the drama, but even if that standard is judged too severe, how can one justify the complete absence of the dramatic premise at the play's final curtain?

The show succeeds much better in Sholem Aleichem's original form, on the level of the short story. Although the four stories on which the play is based were knit together quite convincingly by Joseph Stein, the plan of the numbers clearly reveals that the integrity of each individual story survives (Fig. 10-2). Only the placement of the "Perchik and Hodel Dance" interrupts the continuity of each individual story. Under the arch of the tradition theme, then, *Fiddler on the Roof* presents three well-defined love stories on a lower level of dramatic structure, each with its familiar pattern of conflict and resolution.

The high achievement in all of these little dramas is the railway station scene (Act II, scene 3), when Hodel takes leave of her family and

	"To Life" (No. 6)
	"Tevye's Monologue" (No. 9)
"Modern Children"	"Miracle of Miracles" (No. 10)
	"The Dream" (No. 11)
	Wedding Scene (Nos. 13-19)
	"Perchik and Hodel Dance" (No. 8)
"Hodel"	"Now I Have Everything" (No. 22)
	"Tevye's Rebuttal" (No. 23)
	"Far From the Home I Love" (No. 26)
"Chava"	"Chava Sequence" (No. 30)
	"Anatevka" (No. 31)
"Get Thee Out"	"Final Scene" (No. 32)
	"Curtain—Act II" (No. 33)

Fig. 10-2 Comparison of Sholem Aleichem's stories
with the order of numbers in *Fiddler on the Roof.*

all that she knows to join Perchik at his Siberian camp. This is one of the most poignant scenes in Sholem Aleichem, with Tevye assuring the reader throughout that he is "no woman," only to break down at the end. He cannot comprehend the sort of love that draws his beloved daughter away from him, and that gulf between father and daughter is the subject of Bock's best song of the play.

The harmonic progression and high melody played by the accordian immediately define the melancholy of the moment, and yet by using the emphatic ethnic motive of the lowered second (in the harmony in measure 3, the melody in measures 3 and 4), the melancholy begins to be related to the loss of community. Hodel's melody is heard against the accordian melody, a counterpoint that is rhythmically equivalent until measure 6. Here sorrow is surpassed by her inexplicable steadfast devotion, expressed by the repeated Gs, insistent even when they no longer fit the harmony below them.

The two phrases in minor are balanced by a repetition of the same, now converted to major (Ex. 10-13). The change is consistent, of course, with the idiom of the play, but here it is also expressive of the lyric that

Ex. 10-12 Bock and Harnick, *Fiddler on the Roof*,
"Far From The Home I Love" (No. 26), mm. 1–12.

reflects on Hodel's past life. The change of mood here is effected not
only by the change of mode, but in Don Walker's orchestration. The
accordian is missing. Bock's penchant for expression through form
shows up at the end, just as in "If I Were a Rich Man." Again, two phrases

Ex. 10-13 Bock and Harnick, *Fiddler on the Roof*,
"Far From The Home I Love" (No. 26), mm. 13–20.

in the minor. At measure 37, the major version begins. But just as the
listener expects a second phrase in major, as before, the accordian
enters and its high E-flat, converting the music prematurely to minor,
confirms with great emotion how quickly her former life dies away.
Hodel's last cadence is the most expressive, as she sings for the first time
the D-flat that has colored her accompaniment throughout. In that
instant, the music comes closer to uniting the ethnic idiom with the
action of the drama than at any point in the play.

The failure to follow through with ethnic tradition as the focus of the
drama is disappointing not only on its own terms, but also in that there
is no lack of other potential dramas in Sholem Aleichem. Critics have
pointed to the Tevye stories as a deep "psychological analysis of a father's
unhappy love for his daughters."[22] The song "Chavaleh" deals with this
point in a nostalgic sort of way, but such analysis might have been the

HODEL

Oh, what a mel-an-chol-y choice this is, Want-ing home, want-ing him.

Clos - ing my heart to ev - 'ry hope but his; Leav-ing the home I

love. There where my heart has set - tled long a - go.

Ex. 10-14 Bock and Harnick, *Fiddler on the Roof*,
"Far From The Home I Love" (No. 26), mm. 29–46.

central focus. Another focus appropriate for an ethnic play about Jews would be the messianic. "Messianic thinking, with its peculiar blend of pessimism and hope, is the spiritual base for most of Sholem Aleichem's comic monologues. The most sustained example of hope that survives disaster and even seems to derive from it is the series of stories devoted to *Tevye der Milkhiger*."[23] Finally, there is the relationship between Tevye and God, which in *Fiddler on the Roof* is turned to comic effect, but which is capable of more serious and lengthy treatment:

> Other religions may have their folktales about men who debate with and even rebuke God, but only in Jewish tradition, I believe, are such stories taken with high seriousness, the behavior in question being regarded . . . as the highest form of religious service.[24]

Any of these would have maintained, or even insisted upon, the Jewish ethnic identity and made it even more essential. Of course, in the limited format of a musical play one is foolish to expect the thematic range of literature, but it is still regrettable that, especially in the second act, the collaborators of *Fiddler on the Roof* chose sentiment at the expense of consistent dramatic action. "Do You Love Me?," sung by Tevye and his wife Golde to console one another after Hodel's announcement, rarely fails to make the handkerchiefs appear, but it is music of strong emotion unrelated to the higher purposes on stage. It is not that sentiment itself is always undesirable or false. As Isaac Bashevis Singer points out, Sholem Aleichem himself is a genius who writes with sentiment, "but his sentimentality is redeemed by its utter genuineness, which shows no trace of artifice and is therefore never vulgar."[25] When the action on stage is not dramatic, the traces of artifice show up.

There is yet much of value here, as its apparently immortal popularity all over the world might well attest. The libretto is skillfully crafted and very funny, and the whole pacing of the show, with its mixture of monologue, dialogue, dancing, dreams, and crowd scenes, proclaims the domineering vision of Jerome Robbins. And the songs, if not always dramatically centered, are in themselves meticulous compositions for the most part. Sheldon Harnick's lyrics are simple and natural expressions in the mold of Oscar Hammerstein, and the comic ones derive their humor from situation and character, not from verbal trickery. The little dramas of the short stories look forward to dramatic constructions in musicals of the next decade. The vignettes of the play can indeed be cherished; it is only the shape of the whole that is flawed. That has hardly diminished the world's affection for the play, only the claims of *Fiddler on the Roof* to dramatic art.

Chapter 11

Religious Experience as Musical

... to weave God's spell over the audience ...[1]

John-Michael Tebelak

In the early spring of 1970, a young drama student named John-Michael Tebelak was losing interest in his graduate work. Then, on March 29, Easter Eve, he went out to church.

> I had been working on my masters thesis for Carnegie Tech's School of Drama, but put it aside. Then I went to the Easter Vigil service at the Anglican Cathedral in Pittsburgh. It was snowing, and I was aware of the proper setting for a tremendous religious experience. But the people in the church seemed bored, and the clergymen seemed to be hurrying to get it over with. I left with the feeling that, rather than rolling the rock away from the tomb, they were piling more on. I went home, took out my manuscript and worked it to completion in a non-stop frenzy.[2]

Such a frenzy, born of a disappointment in what should be the most triumphant moment of the Christian liturgical year, produced that most unlikely of events in theater history: a significant debut for both playwright and composer. *Godspell* indeed has been a most unorthodox success story.

It is no coincidence that nearly all the significant works of the Broadway tradition were preceded in their history by vast experience in every department. It should be no surprise that the early works of Kern, Gershwin, Rodgers, Porter and Bernstein form no part of this repertoire, that their highest achievements come much later in their careers, and that those achievements are supported over and over by the same names in production and direction: George Abbott, Rouben Mamoulian, Jerome Robbins, Moss Hart, Harold Prince. History has shown that experience provides the fine tuning of the collaboration that even the most mature dramatic vision requires.[3]

Godspell was dominated by amateurs from the beginning. Tebelak formed a cast of friends and acquaintances from the Carnegie Tech School of Drama, had them set some old Episcopal hymn texts to original music, and mounted some trial performances at the school. The show eventually moved to Cafe La Mama in New York City. The response there convinced producers Edgar Lansbury and Joseph Beruh that the show might be a commercial success if a new score were composed. In March of 1971, they called another schoolmate of Tebelak's, Stephen Schwartz, who at the time was in New York trying to interest producers in his own *Pippin*. "To this day, I don't know why they called me about the score. . . . I can hardly believe, given my inexperience, that I was anyone's first choice."[4] Schwartz finished the score in five weeks, and *Godspell* opened formally at the small Cherry Lane Theater, off-Broadway, on May 17, 1971, less than fourteen months after the snowy Easter of 1970. There were no name producers or directors, certainly no stars, and for all its subsequent success, including a move uptown in 1976, the play seems not to have launched any careers on Broadway with the important exception of its composer-lyricist. Stephen Schwartz was enlisted by Leonard Bernstein to help write lyrics for his *Mass* in July following *Godspell's* opening. In 1974 he won wide acclaim for his *Pippin*, and followed that with the somewhat less well known *Magic Show* and *Working*.

Upon reflection, it seems that this contravention of all Broadway's sacred ways, taking the million-to-one chance in a small off-Broadway theater, may have been *Godspell's* only chance. Clearly, Tebelak tried to create the religious experience he expected but missed at the Easter

Vigil, to "weave God's spell over the audience," as he put it.[5] Would any savvy producer have underwritten such an idea? Would any seasoned director have agreed to do it? The very idea of putting religious experience on a stage and trying to communicate its essence to an audience seems, if anything, antidramatic, but frequent local revivals over the last twenty years and a major one on Broadway in 1988 argue to the contrary. It is not too late to wonder at *Godspell's* most unusual conception, how it is that religious experience can be dramatized.

Dramatizing religious experience can be immediately distinguished from setting a religious story. Sacred histories such as are found in the oratorios of Handel use plot in an entirely conventional way. Even an agnostic can sympathize with the plights of Saul or Jephthe. He regards the divine element in Old Testament stories just as he would the pantheon of Greek mythology; it requires a suspension of disbelief, nothing more. The distinction is subtler with the passions of J. S. Bach. Here, faith and spirituality are premises taken for granted by the composer, and so certain events of the plot take on significance that they would not otherwise have, which is why extraordinarily lyrical recitative is reserved for a simple meal called the Last Supper. Those ignorant of these significances must ignore an entire level of dramatic meaning and fall back to admiring the musical ideas and construction for their own sake. But even the passions do not dramatize pure religious experience in any direct sense because they assume such experience on the part of the faithful listeners. "Everything takes place in the mind of the Christian, or in Bach's mind, or in the mind of the communal singer," writes Joseph Kerman.[6] The drama may draw on that assumption in such a way that deepens and invigorates it sublimely, but it does not communicate the fundamental experience, since it is already there. A true dramatization of religious experience would demand that the audience be taken along in a progressive action that is analogous to the experience itself. How can such an experience be expressed in a way that does not just preach to the choir?

The central problem is that there seems to be no such progression. Nothing can happen; spirituality just is. "Plain spirit in the popular arts can last just about four and a half minutes, and after that it has to start explaining itself. In drama, particularly, we expect the issue to be defined in human terms as soon as possible."[7] But there is one crucial sort of religious experience which is itself an action, which requires no explanation even for the agnostic because it is at base inexplicable, and which has no specific religious content or doctrine: the conversion.

The "Prologue" of *Godspell* makes it clear that this is a play about the experience of conversion, the "turning toward" the divine. When the cast first appears on stage, each member wears a sweatshirt bearing the name of a famous Western thinker: Socrates, Aquinas, Luther, Da Vinci, Gibbon, Nietzsche, Sartre, and Fuller. Each person pronounces his philosophical sentence to the music of the "Prologue," after which all sing them simultaneously in an "ivory tower of Babel." They are silenced by a note from the shofar, the traditional ram's horn of Jewish ritual, and by the appearance of John the Baptist who sings the famous verse from Matthew (3:3, quoting Isaiah 40:3): "Prepare ye the way of the Lord!" The others are amazed. Shortly after they join in his singing, shed their sweatshirts, don clown costumes, and receive his baptism. They are converted.

The contrast in the music of the first two numbers, no less than the action, attempts to express the essence of this conversion. For the construction of the "Prologue" Schwartz chooses one of the most learned of devices, the chaconne, or repeating chord progression.

E: I-V^2/V
  C♮: IV^2-ii^7-V-I-V^2/V
    B♭: IV^2-ii^7-V
      G: VII-I-I^7-IV^7-VII
        E: N^6-V^2/V-iv-V-I

Fig.11-1 Repeating chord pattern of "Prologue" from *Godspell*, showing principal keys used and progressions within each.

Now it is true that certain rock styles live on repeating chord progressions, mostly very brief and simple ones, but this example truly deserves to be called a chaconne because of its length and multilevel harmonic design, and because over it the singing of each philosopher makes a set of continuous variations on the harmonic pattern. The device makes it possible to babble all the pronouncements simultaneously at the end without essential dissonance.

This ancient demonstration of musical learning is replaced by a piece of the most simple design and lyric. There are but two phrases to

"Prepare Ye," an antecedent and a consequent, over a bass that repeats many times with the lyric, but which despite its repetition is as far from the spirit of the chaconne as can be. In the juxtaposition of musical forms is dramatized the conversion of the philosopher, who replaces his vain and ostentatious wisdom with simple assent.

The clown costumes, particularly on the person of Jesus, create a startling stage presence that has elicited a variety of explanations from critics: "a metaphor for Christian grace";[8] a means of "making high theater from the immediate emotions of the child";[9] a rainbow of "ethnic suggestions" that universalizes the themes of the play.[10] Tebelak himself, however, points much more directly to *The Feast of Fools*, a theological essay by Harvey Cox published in 1969, which argues that humanity must recover its lost capacity for festivity and fantasy if civilization is to survive.[11] Cox saw signs of such a recovery in the vigorous political movements, youth culture, and rock music festivals of the late 1960s, but any lasting effect would require a complete renovation of stale church traditions, including a new theological image of Christ himself:

> Christ has come to previous generations in various guises, as teacher, as judge, as healer. In today's world these traditional images of Christ have lost much of their power. Now in a new, or really an old but recaptured guise, Christ has made an unexpected entrance onto the stage of modern secular life. Enter Christ the harlequin: the personification of festivity and fantasy in an age that had almost lost both. Coming now in greasepaint and halo, this Christ is able to touch our jaded modern consciousness as other images of Christ cannot.[12]

Such an image supplies for *Godspell* the stage premise for all the high jinks, the infectious quality of playing that impresses even the skeptic. Playing is nothing less than Cox's prescription for church reform:

> Only by assuming a playful attitude toward our religious tradition can we possibly make any sense of it.
> Only by learning to laugh at the hopelessness around us can we touch the hem of hope. Christ the clown signifies our playful appreciation of the past and our comic refusal to accept the spectre of inevitability in the future. He is the incarnation of festivity and fantasy.[13]

The essay also gives the nod to the often outrageous juxtapositions of what is spoken in parable or sung in lyric and what is portrayed in the acting, such as when one of the female characters sings the traditional hymn text "Turn Back, O Man" to brothel music with stage gestures and humorous ad libs between the lines to fit. Such juxtapositions for Cox make up a necessary ingredient of festivity.

But whatever theological cues from *The Feast of Fools* have turned up in *Godspell*, the most decisive dramatic effect of donning the clown suits is to symbolize a profound inner change in those who wear them. For what can be more opposite to a philosopher than a clown? In such an image, Tebelak has dramatized the Pauline proclamation that God has made "foolish the wisdom of this world" (1 Corinthians 1:20).

But is not conversion an instant's event, a blinding flash in the desert? What is left for the dramatist thereafter? To dramatize its effects in individual lives, especially in a religious tradition that exalts rather than subsumes the individual person. That is why it is important in *Godspell* that the characters other than Jesus are drawn with much more anonymity than is usual in a musical play. They do not have stage names; rather, they carry their own real names, but only first names, so as not to specify their characters too much: they could be anybody. But each gets his own solo music, his own response to conversion. Listeners recalling the play remember the individuals not by who they are but by what they have sung. "The performers are or create the illusion of being ordinary people sublimating their erstwhile secular talents,"[14] or rather turning those talents to the divine call.

The music of the first act, then, expresses the range of religious experience that comes from conversion. Such expressions are prayers, but in so being they do not give up the spirit of festivity and play that is the premise for *Godspell*. Cox maintains that "in several ways prayer and play are strikingly similar. Both are acts of disciplined fantasy. . . . There are four traditional forms of prayer: supplication, intercession, thanksgiving, and penitence. Each can be understood as a form of play."[15] All of these forms are represented in the musical: intercession in "Save the People," thanksgiving in "Bless the Lord" and "All Good Gifts," penitence in "We Beseech Thee," and supplication in "Day by Day."

The music of "Day by Day," in particular, concerns the deeper form of religious experience known as contemplation. The text is medieval, attributed in the Episcopal Hymnal 1940 to St. Richard of Chichester.

The music, like all the music in *Godspell*, in written in one of several popular styles, but its specific construction is unlike that of any other song. What is the key of this song? There is no simple answer to this innocent question, as it turns out. Initially one hears F major as the most likely tonal center, but beginning with the F major seventh chord introduces an ambiguous dissonance immediately, and the ambiguity is heightened by the unusual device of having the singer enter on the seventh factor E and then prolonging the modal D. The initial impression of F seems to be confirmed with the B-flat major seventh (which would be IV⁷) at the beginning of the second phrase, but the confirmation is soon shattered when the B-flat is replaced two bars later (m. 7) with a B-natural. The key now seems to be G major, but again it is compromised with the major seventh chord. The third phrase (mm. 9–12) sounds the first clear triad, so that the progression acts like a strong ii⁷-V in yet another new key, D major. The fourth phrase (mm. 13–16) does not yield the expected D cadence, however, but translates the third

Ex. 11-1 Stephen Schwartz, *Godspell*, "Day By Day" (No. 4), mm. 1–16.

phrase down one step as a modulating sequence, and the ii⁷-V progression now directed toward C does make a cadence, but with a C major seventh. This harmony not only withholds the sense of firm conclusion, but progresses naturally as a substitute dominant back to the F major seventh to begin the next verse.

On the lower level of structure, then, there is a succession of weak tonal centers or keys, and on the higher there is really none. The song is held together by a tight, motivically consistent melody that ends on the same note with which it began, and by an intelligent use of seventh chords which, in addition to giving the song its popular flavor, makes each tonal center just credible without the harmonic commitment of a cadence.

The lack of high-level tension and resolution recalls impressionism. The structure almost seems to have no beginning and no end, and the constrained range of the melody (from C to A only) also contributes to the sense of a devotion that is effortless and yet ecstatic. And how else can the endlessly repeating text be understood, except as the contemplative's centering prayer or mantra?

For a play that in 1971 seemed so innovative in its portrait of Christian religious experience, the extent to which *Godspell* depends on traditional Christian materials and forms is striking. Almost all of the book is taken directly from the Gospel of Matthew, as are some of the lyrics to the songs. As Figure 11-2 (on the following page) indicates, many of the remainder come from traditional hymn texts selected by John-Michael Tebelak.

Even the form of the whole show is traditional, comparable to the Service of the Word of the very same Easter Vigil rite that inspired Tebelak in the first place. In that part of the rite, choice readings from the Old Testament are alternated with responsorial Psalms sung by the congregation. In *Godspell*, the readings are replaced by the book, which is little more than readings from Matthew, and the Psalm responses are replaced by the songs, two of which are Psalm adaptations.

The theatrical conception could not do without these traditional texts, forms, and symbols. Tradition adds a cultural weight to the proceedings that ensures that the antics of these converted clowns cannot be dismissed out of hand. The language of the texts themselves, replete with "Thee" and "Thou" and other anachronisms of the King James usage, affirm the gravity of what they express at the same time they act in juxtaposition to the popular styles of music to which they are set. The wonder is that it all works so smoothly.

At least part of the reason must be the extent to which Schwartz's music captures some essence of these texts and translates it into a popular idiom. "Day by Day" is a fine example. Another, more sophisticated one is his setting of Psalm 103, "Bless the Lord."

Although the text for "Bless the Lord" is taken directly from James Montgomery's adaptation in the Episcopal Hymnal, Schwartz's setting accentuates certain aspects of the text in a way that brings it closer in spirit to the original Psalm. Consider first the following comparison of Psalm 103 (King James version) with its paraphrase as it appears in the song. (Numerals refer to traditional verses of the psalm or to the order of the quatrains in the song. Brackets indicate lyrics by Montgomery that have no direct parallel in the psalm. "R" refers to refrains interpolated by Schwartz.)

Song Title	Source
No. 1 "Prologue"	Various philosophical and historical sources, adapted by Tebelak
No. 2 "Prepare Ye"	Matthew 3:3 (Isaiah 40:3)
No. 3 "Save the People"	Episcopal Hymnal 1940, No. 496; text by Ebenezer Elliott, 1850
No. 4 "Day by Day"	Episcopal Hymnal 1940, No. 429; text by St. Richard of Chichester, 1197–1253
No. 5 "Learn Your Lessons Well"	Original lyric by Stephen Schwartz
No. 6 "Bless the Lord"	Episcopal Hymnal 1940, No. 293; text by James Montgomery, 1819; adaptation of Psalm 103
No. 7 "All for the Best"	Original lyric by Stephen Schwartz
No. 8 "All Good Gifts"	Episcopal Hymnal 1940, No. 138; text by Matthias Claudius, 1782
No. 9 "Light of the World"	Adaptation of Matthew 5:13–16
No. 10 "Turn Back, O Man"	Episcopal Hymnal 1940, No. 536; text by Clifford Bax, 1919
No. 11 "Alas for You"	Adaptation of Matthew 23:13–37
No. 12 "By My Side"	Original lyric by Jay Hamburger
No. 13 "We Beseech Thee"	Episcopal Hymnal 1940, No. 229; text by T. B. Pollock, 1871
No. 14 "Day by Day" (reprise)	
No. 15 "On the Willows"	Adaptation of Psalm 137
No. 16 "Finale"	Original lyric of Stephen Schwartz; reprise of Matthew 3:3

Fig. 11-2 Sources for the lyrics to *Godspell*.

1 Bless the LORD, O my soul!	1 O, bless the Lord, my soul! [His grace to thee proclaim!]
And all that is within me, bless his holy name.	And all that is within me, joins, To bless His holy name.

2 Bless the LORD, O my soul!

And forget not all his benefits:

3 Who forgiveth all thine
iniquities;

Who healeth all thy diseases;
4 Who redeemeth thy life from
destruction;

Who crowneth thee with loving-
kindness and tender mercies;
5 Who satisfieth thine advancing
age with good;
Thy youth is renewed like the
eagle's.
6 The LORD executeth
righteousness and judgment
For all who are oppressed.
7 He made known his ways unto
Moses,
His acts unto the children of
Israel.
8 The LORD is merciful and
gracious,
Slow to anger, and plenteous
in mercy.
9 He will not always chide:
Neither will he keep his anger
for ever.

20 Bless the LORD, ye his angels,
Who excel in strength, who do
his commandments,
Hearkening unto the voice of
his word.

2 O, bless the Lord, my soul!
[His mercies bear in mind!]
Forget not all His benefits,
[The Lord to thee is kind.]
4 He pardons all thy sins,

[Prolongs thy feeble breath;]
He healeth thy infirmities,
And ransoms thee from death,

R O, bless the Lord, my soul!
5 He clothes thee with His love
[Upholds thee with His truth]
And like the eagle, He
renews
The vigor of thy youth.

3 He will not always chide;
[He will with patience wait;]
His wrath is ever slow to rise.
[And ready to abate.]
R O, bless the Lord.
6 Then bless His holy name,
[Whose grace hath made
thee whole;]
Whose love and kindness
crowns thy days.

21 Bless ye the LORD, all ye his hosts;
   Ye ministers of his, who do his pleasure.
22 Bless the LORD, all his works
   In all places of his dominion:
   Bless the LORD, O my soul.   O, bless the Lord, my soul.

Psalm 103 belongs to the class of psalms known as hymns (as distinguished from the laments or penitential psalms, thanksgivings, blessings, curses, and didactic psalms) and shares its form with others in the group. There is the laudatory invocation at the beginning, a recitation of reasons for praising, then a closing that uses the same formula as the beginning. Psalm 103 is extraordinary, however, in that its praise formulas are repeated so often, suggesting that the psalmist can barely contain his joy. "Few psalms are better known or more beloved. All the evangelical theology is here, for here is present the evangelical experience in all its fullness."[16] Indeed, there is a natural progression at the end from the description of

Ex. 11-2 Stephen Schwartz, *Godspell*, "Bless The Lord" (No. 6), mm. 1–14.

human frailty to the hope of the Lord's grace, which is "from everlasting to everlasting." The refrain "Bless the Lord" returns four times, accelerating the pace of the verses until the last recalls the first.

It is just this sense of acceleration that Schwartz restores to Montgomery's adaptation, on several levels. The song begins with a typical repeating rock bass line in a dorian version of A minor. The second verse begins with the same line as the first (mm. 13–14), as per the Montgomery adaptation. That verse, however, is followed by a new section of music, faster and in the parallel major, which begins to use that text as a refrain. The faster tempo and major mode begin here to reflect the joyful tone of the psalm, but no less an important aspect toward this end is

Ex. 11-3 Stephen Schwartz, *Godspell*, "Bless The Lord"
(No. 6), mm. 21–39.

the integration of the refrain with the harmonic construction. Barely two chords, a prolonged tonic (mm. 21–28) and a prolonged dominant (mm. 30–38), make up this faster section. The great tension of the dominant is prepared by a single measure of very fast harmonic rhythm with a metric syncopation (m. 29). The dominant then arrives along with the first use of imitative counterpoint among the voices, with ever decreasing time intervals between entrances to increase the pace, and the refrain "O, bless the Lord" finally bound to this acceleration.

The long dominant resolves quite classically back into A minor to begin the third verse (m. 39), and the whole pattern repeats. When the faster section arrives for the second time, it ends with all voices singing "O, bless the Lord, my soul" in the accelerating counterpoint (mm. 72–80). This leads into the coda. The tempo of the coda is faster still. There is only one text, the refrain. And Schwartz here shows his sense of form by alternating the major and minor modes within the coda as more voices are layered on, emphasizing the change by placing the C-sharp or C-natural in the top melody, thus summarizing an important premise of the composition. The pace is increased again by doubling this alternation and cutting the text down to "Bless the Lord."

Ex.11-4 Stephen Schwartz, *Godspell*, "Bless The Lord" (No. 6), mm. 85–92.

Ex. 11-5 Stephen Schwartz, *Godspell*, "Bless The Lord"
(No. 6), mm. 101–102.

The refrain is restored for the last cadences, and the "tag" sung by the soloist after the last structural cadence has already sounded (m. 115) embodies once more the burst of emotion at the end of Psalm 103, an unceasing urge to praise (Ex. 11-6). Yet, Schwartz has made the small gesture almost necessary for the music too, since the previous phrase included as its melodic high note the C-natural of the A minor mode, while the harmonic destiny of the piece is clearly A major. The last call to praise brings a most classical ending to a great piece of poetry.

The drama of conversion and its various manifestations dominate the first act of *Godspell*. The major dramatic problem with this musical arrives with the second act which, with the exception of the very beginning and the singing of "We Beseech Thee," takes the form of a traditional passion play. This transformation is uncomfortable at best.

> The first act is located in non-linear theatrical time, the time of the revue, or more precisely, the artistic time of the clown, the time of not telling a story but of enacting an identity. But halfway through the second act, we careen into an arbitrary shift of gears, suddenly crammed into narrative sequence to accommodate the Passion and Crucifixion.[17]

The shift is from the personal to the historical, from who Jesus and his believers are to what happened to Him. It seems arbitrary because the virtues of the first act now become vices, severing all connections. The subtle anonymity of stage people about whom nothing is known except their first names makes no sense in a traditional narrative that must

Ex. 11-6 Stephen Schwartz, *Godspell*, "Bless The Lord"
(No. 6), mm. 111–118.

depend on clearly drawn characters who motivate the action. Schwartz's setting of Matthew's castigation of the Pharisees, "Alas for You," is rhythmically and harmonically imaginative and appropriate for its rather harsh text, but can such passion come from a clown?

A musical passion play demands a much tighter relationship between songs and specific actions. Schwartz comments that Psalm 137 was chosen for the Last Supper "because it was about 'believers' isolated and persecuted by a hostile society,"[18] but such subtleties are in the domain of the biblical exegete, not the musical theater audience. Unfortunately, when the crucifixion music in the "Finale" tries to be explicit, it falls far short of expressing anything of the complexity of what should be the central event in the narrative. The use of rapid harmonic rhythm seems no different than in other happier songs, and the jamming of the electric instruments is but a superficial substitute for dramatic expressions drawn from more essential musical elements. The lyrics here too are absurdly simplistic. There is some saving grace in the reprise of "Prepare Ye" which ends the show, for it at least rounds its form, but otherwise the end of *Godspell* is fodder for the cannons of those who claim that rock is essentially undramatic music.

Of course, *Godspell*, no more than *Les Misérables*, is not really a "rock musical" as some have claimed, for its diversity of popular styles is far too broad for that label to do it justice. The vacuity of the passion sequence and the various light touches of the first act have led some to charge that the musical presents an image of Christianity without teeth. "One wonders if a true religion does not call for a certain moral toughness and spiritual fiber as well as a sense of humor?"[19] But the teachings from Matthew heard before and after every song are not soft ones. It is true that in musicals, music speaks louder than words, but the cumulative weight of the Lazarus parable, the unjust servant, the Sermon on the Mount, and the Last Judgment must have their sobering effect.

It is the deliberate inclusion of such crazy ideas about throwing away one's hand or one's eye that shows *Godspell* to be a theater of the festive religious spirit. It is curious that it does not appear so to its composer:

> I never saw *Godspell* as a "Christian" show, or indeed, as a show about "religion". To me, the basic dramatic event of the show has to do with the formation of a community. . . . The idea of community and the need for people to understand and support one another seems to me to transcend any specific religion or creed.[20]

Godspell's peculiar genesis should perhaps be remembered here, the most unusual feature of which is that Schwartz was called in after the show had already attained its form. His role in shaping the music drama is as essential as any theater composer's, but limited to the extent that he was able to reconcile Tebelak's conception of a clown Christianity with the traditional texts given him. In most respects he did that admirably. If he sees *Godspell* only in the most general terms of community formation, he does admit of "the idea of community" and "the need for people to understand." Even that idea and that need demand some sort of conversion, and the dramatization of that spiritual action remains the play's best achievement.

Chapter 12

History as Musical

We tried to put over what we think might have happened.[1]

Andrew Lloyd Webber

A drama with a particular historical setting need be no different than one using any other kind of fictitious plot. The setting may strike a tone, conjure a period atmosphere, or simply provide a certain convenience in designing the background of the plot. Like a historical novel, it may take advantage of what the setting has to offer while refusing any and all associations that frustrate its artistic purpose. But when history itself is dramatized, when events of the past step out from merely coloring the action to be the action itself in a way that involves historical personages, then the dramatist is challenged in peculiar ways. The principal events that articulate the action are now beyond control; contradiction of well-known facts and episodes cannot be admitted, otherwise what is the use of history at all? It would be better, certainly simpler, to make a plot from scratch. The history must be carefully chosen, so that the potential for drama is there in the foggy patches of a character's biography or in the ambiguities of recorded events. Despite such peculiarities, history has attracted dramatists from time to time, for there are compensatory advantages. The plot is ready made, credible, and often fascinating. In the most famous episodes, the plot premises and even small details of action need no explanation. Most important, the stakes of the story, what motivates the characters, are abundantly clear from the beginning.

The Broadway musical tradition has occasionally tried its hand with history. Jule Styne's *Gypsy* (1959) and Jerry Bock's *Fiorello!* (1959) are biographies that create dramatic interest by filling in the flat public images of Gypsy Rose Lee and Mayor Fiorello LaGuardia. Sherman Edwards managed a humorous, visually striking and occasionally moving account of the Continental Congress in his *1776* (1969). But no composer has incited such controversy while making the dramatization of history the foundation of his young career as has Andrew Lloyd Webber, who with his lyricist Tim Rice took the world of popular music by storm in 1969 with his recorded opera *Jesus Christ Superstar* and then followed seven years later with another, *Evita*.

Although far removed from one another in time and place, the two operas share some principal themes. One would expect operas about Jesus and Eva Peron to be about religion and politics, but as director Robert Brustein remarks, these seem to be secondary concerns:

> But the political implications of *Evita* are the least convincing aspect of the work, just as religion was the one thing missing from *Jesus Christ Superstar*. What apparently attracts [the authors] to Eva Peron is her surefire blend of sex, show biz, and ambition; she is, in short, another superstar who experiences a similar rise from poor beginnings to great influence. I suspect that the real subject of Rice and Webber is success, its rewards and human cost, and that has about as much political, religious, or intellectual significance as one finds in *Aida* or *Madame Butterfly*.[2]

It is no coincidence that the crowd or mob plays important roles in both operas, and that they call both Jesus and Eva Peron "saviour."

To refer to *Jesus Christ Superstar* as a historical drama rather than a religious one might appear to miss the obvious, but the authors' own comments prove without doubt that they were interested in Jesus as a historical personage who happened to be a religious leader, not as a God-figure who intervened at a certain point in history. Consider how librettist Tim Rice prepared for his assignment:

I used the King James and Catholic versions—whichever was handier—interchangeably. They're quite similar, actually. My biggest aid was Fulton Sheen's *Life of Christ*, in which Bishop Sheen calibrates and compares the Gospels. Andrew and I examined the books of the Bible—Matthew, Mark, Luke, and John—to write the libretto. Each book differs on their accounts. Matthew, Mark, and Luke seem more dependable, even though John is supposed to have been present most often. He tends, however, to lean more on the supernatural and visions. I only wanted to work from one established perspective, and the Bible and Bishop Sheen are about as established as you can get.[3]

His complete ignorance of the modern Scripture scholar's view of what the Gospels represent and his concern for "dependability" and "one established perspective" can only mean that he read them as biographical documents, not as spiritual tracts. The interpretations of religious traditions were purposefully excluded. "We read the gospels very carefully and that was it. What we did not read was eighty-three other people's interpretations of Christ . . . ."[4] Indeed, the principal complaint of picketers who protested the Broadway opening was that Jesus was not portrayed as a divine figure.

The form of both *Evita* and *Jesus Christ Superstar* is explicitly operatic, with the libretto entirely sung, and borrowing heavily on the traditional devices of aria and recitative. This departure from the norm of the partly spoken, partly sung musical play owes something to Webber's preferences for continuous music[5] but also to the curious history of the two works. Both were introduced to the listening public as record albums, produced entirely in the London recording studios of Decca and MCA. Only after their enormous commercial success as albums were they put into stage production. *Jesus Christ Superstar* opened officially at the Broadway theater on October 12, 1971. *Evita* was presented first at the King Edward Theatre in London on June 21, 1978; an American production, including a number of revisions by the authors, premiered on May 8, 1979, at the Dorothy Chandler Pavilion in Los Angeles.

Thus the conventional procedure of putting a dramatic work on stage and letting its popularity justify a cast recording was completely reversed. Such a change might have been predicted on the basis of a number of shows in the 1960s whose record albums earned more than the Broadway productions that generated them, but in any case, the record album is no less legitimate a source for a staged opera than a novel or previously written spoken play. The album, however, does create an unusual problem for the critic. Is it to be evaluated, more than the subsequent staged version, as the "original" conception?

Generally not, except that the Broadway production of *Jesus Christ Superstar* was by most accounts so outlandish that it might be unsound to relate the music to any of the stage activity. Frank Corsaro of the City Center Opera was the original director-apparent, consulting with Webber and Rice even before he had a contract. "Corsaro envisioned Christ's last seven days as a series of vignettes, strong on dramatic experience with little emphasis on theatrical titillation. He stressed that it should be a very human play."[6] When Corsaro was hospitalized by an auto accident, still without contract, he was summarily replaced by Tom O'Horgan, who had produced *Hair* in 1967. Apparently he turned Corsaro's vision of the opera on its head, and asked little advice of the authors, who were virtually excluded from production decisions. When the opera opened, the audience saw Jesus rise from the floor in a giant silver chalice, and that was only the beginning. "There were too many purely decorative effects, artistic excrescences dreamed up by the director and his designers . . . that seemed to make us gasp and our blood run cold," wrote Clive Barnes.[7] "Let's just say that we don't think this production is the definitive one," remarked Webber politely.

One new song, "Could We Start Again, Please?", sung by Mary Magdalene and Peter just before the trial scene, was added for the stage production and would need to be included in any detailed study, but considering the circumstances, the impression given by the original recording alone may be at least as reliable as that of the staged version. There is also a certain validity in thinking that, if the authors' views are important, the recordings of *Jesus Christ Superstar* and *Evita* represent the best evidence of them, since Webber was involved in every stage of the recording and editing process and was rather fussy about the results. The original recording of *Jesus Christ Superstar* required sixty sessions and 400 hours of studio time at an extraordinary cost of $65,000.

To attribute the operatic form of these works to their origins in recording alone, however, is to underestimate Webber's own preparation for them. His father directed the London College of Music, and

Andrew himself was trained on the piano, violin, and horn. Opera and theater interested him from his childhood. His first successful collaboration with Tim Rice was a children's cantata on another biblical theme called *Joseph and the Amazing Technicolor Dreamcoat* (1966), which was eventually staged in New York. If he and Rice had been given the backing for a staged production of their drama about Jesus in 1969, there is no reason to think it would have been altogether different in form.

In dramatic histories the focus is on character more than action. That is why four of the best-known musical histories of the Broadway tradition are biographical. In a story that involves someone famous, the interest is naturally in the person more than in the framing event which is already familiar. The audience wants to know, not what happened to Ben Franklin, but what he was like. The desire squares well with the constraints of factual history, since character is the part of a history most easily given to the dramatist's extrapolation beyond what is known. In this way Judas, Mary Magdalene, Pilate, and Caiaphas, barely sketched in the Gospels, can be fully drawn. Says Tim Rice, "It's all complete fiction—the way it might have been. I used the information available and took certain liberties."[8]

In one of the few scholarly essays on *Jesus Christ Superstar*, Ulrich Prinz rightly claims that the various characterizations are the best aspect of that opera, and that they derive from an often cited feature: its eclecticism.[9] Although the work is commonly termed a "rock opera," only a fraction of its songs are thoroughly composed in a rock style, though certain characteristic elements of rock may be found throughout. Webber avails himself of a number of popular and serious styles, choosing one or another to express best a particular situation or, most often, the nature of a particular character. So Mary Magdalene sings in the gentler popular folk style ("Everything's Alright" and "I Don't Know How to Love Him") and the ostentatious King Herod is given a music hall rag ("King Herod's Song"). The song of the Apostles, "The Last Supper," a critical scene, "is like a caricature of a Gregorian chant sung by a troop of tired and self-satisfied monks,"[10] with its simple quarter-note rhythms and melodic contour. The crucifixion scene abandons popular idioms altogether and relies for its wordless acerbity on tone clusters reminiscent of Ligeti and Penderecki.[11]

The diversity of styles does wonders for the art of characterization, but since style is the principal means by which an opera is made to sound all of a piece, the aural mediation between the action in one song and another, the introduction of various styles in *Jesus Christ Superstar* makes an issue of the high-level structure. How is any kind of musical-dramatic continuity to be maintained in the opera as a whole? Webber must have been aware of the problem, at least subconsciously, for he arrived at a solution unique to the Broadway theater tradition. Although styles may differ within the opera, he creates musical points of reference by using compositions over and over again, not as reprises, but in the manner of what the musicologists of early music call *contrafactum*.[12] This term refers to a piece of vocal music whose text has been replaced by an entirely new one, usually unrelated to the original. In the Middle Ages and Renaissance it was not uncommon to convert a sacred piece into a secular one simply by according it a new set of words.

"This Jesus Must Die," from *Jesus Christ Superstar*, is first heard when the high priests, including Caiaphas and Annas, are plotting to arrest Jesus. Later, after Judas explains to them why he is betraying Jesus ("Damned for All Time"), they reply to him in the music of "This Jesus Must Die" with completely new words and a different dramatic situation. Later still, when Judas is horrified at what they have done to Jesus ("Judas' Death") the music returns again to set their replies to him, and his line about being dragged through slime and mud. The same music returns one last time at the beginning of "Trial Before Pilate," when Caiaphas asks for the sentence of crucifixion.

The following schematic shows how thoroughgoing is this technique of contrafactum. The first eight songs are new; thereafter the pace of borrowing increases as the opera progresses.

Melodic Material in *Jesus Christ Superstar*

Number in Opera	*Source of Melodic Material*
1. Overture	
2. Heaven on Their Minds	
3. What's the Buzz	
4. Strange Thing Mystifying	
5. Everything's Alright	
6. This Jesus Must Die	
7. Hosanna	
8. Simon Zealotes	

9. Poor Jerusalem	Simon Zealotes (lines 1-7)
10. Pilate's Dream	Poor Jerusalem
11. The Temple	
Moneylenders	
Jesus	I Only Want to Say (fragment)
Crowd of Sick	Moneylenders
12. Everything's Alright	(brief reprise)
13. I Don't Know How to Love Him	
14. Damned for All Time	
15. Blood Money	This Jesus Must Die
16. The Last Supper	
Jesus' speech	Everything's Alright (minor verse)
17. I Only Want to Say	
18. The Arrest	What's the Buzz
	Moneylenders
	Strange Thing Mystifying
	(fragment)
19. Peter's Denial	Strange Thing Mystifying
20. Pilate and Christ	Hosanna (including reprise)
21. King Herod's Song	
22. Judas' Death	Damned for All Time (fragment)
	This Jesus Must Die
	I Don't Know How to Love Him
	(reprise)
23. Trial Before Pilate	This Jesus Must Die (fragment)
39 Lashes ostinato	from Heaven on Their Minds
24. Superstar	
25. Crucifixion	
26. John Nineteen Forty-One	I Only Want to Say

There is no doubt that the method helps to unify the opera. By restricting the amount of melodic material, there is simply less music to unify. But there are dramatic connections to be perceived as well. The example of "This Jesus Must Die" is consistent in that the music is always associated with the high priests. The music which sets the dramatic exchange between Jesus and Judas in "Everything's Alright" early in the opera returns to set a similar confrontation during "The Last Supper." The connections can be ironic, as when the music of the moneylenders and merchants in the temple is used for the pleading of the sick and poor for miraculous cure, suggesting perhaps some shallowness in their common appeal. At other times, the relationship between contrafacta seems far-fetched. Why should "Peter's Denial" have the same music as Judas's reproach of Jesus for befriending Mary Magdalene ("Strange Thing Mystifying")?

Webber's contrafactum method expands and in some ways replaces the time-honored device of reprise. While reprise operates, in the best instances, by revealing the dramatic relevance of an earlier expression to a new dramatic context, the contrafactum, in changing the lyrics, actually changes the expression, and therein is the price paid for its use. The leitmotif idea, from which both reprise and this operatic contrafactum ultimately derive, depends on a consistent association of music with some kind of dramatic expression, be it words or some physical action. When Webber drastically alters the lyric to a certain melody, there is less dramatic association between the melody and action, and he risks a fatal weakening of the melody's dramatic function.

When compared to *Jesus Christ Superstar*, *Evita* seems much more unified in its use of musical style. It depends on just two styles. One is an easy soft rock, often tinged with Spanish effects, such as the tango bass in "Don't Cry for Me Argentina." This style is used by all the major characters, but is reserved for occasions that call for some kind of dissembling or pretense, which are many in this cynical opera. Public speeches, small talk, political slogans, and all the music relating to Eva Peron's love affairs are set to this style (Ex. 12-1). The expression of real feeling is given to the second, rather modernistic style. After Eva and Juan Peron have told one another of their mutual attraction, they face away and sing this curious waltz to themselves, which states that every lover, regardless of gen-

Ex.12-1 Webber and Rice, *Evita*, "There Is No One" (from No. 7, "Charity Concert/I'd Be Surprisingly Good For You").

der, has used his partner for ulterior purposes. The heavy syncopations, accentuated by notes that are dissonant not only with one another but with a strong tonal background, remind one of Stravinsky.

The distinction in styles in *Evita* has nothing to do with characterization, but instead governs two domains of expression for all characters: pretense and cynicism. One might expect, then, that Webber's contrafactum method would no longer be necessary, since the problem of musical unity for the whole opera is taken care of by a singularity of dramatic purpose for each style. It is shocking to discover that not only is the method very much a part of *Evita*, it is more prevalent than in *Jesus Christ Superstar*.

Melodic Material in Evita

Number in Opera	Source of Melodic Material
ACT I	
1. Cinema	
2. Requiem for Evita	
Oh What a Circus	
Sing You Fools!	
3. On This Night of a Thousand Stars	
Eva and Magaldi	
Eva Beware	
4. Buenos Aires	
And If I Ever Go	
5. Goodnight and Thank You	Eva Beware
There Is No One	
6. The Art of the Possible	
Eva on the Air	
7. Charity Concert	On This Night of a Thousand Stars (reprise)
I'd Be Good for You	
There Is No One (reprise)	
8. Another Suitcase in Another Hall	
9. Peron's Latest Flame	And If I Ever Go
Army Theme	
Aristocrat Theme	
10. A New Argentina	I'd Be Good for You
	Eva on the Air
	Eva and Magaldi (fragment)
ACT II	
11. Don't Cry for Me	Oh What a Circus
12. High Flying Adored	

13. Rainbow High	Eva and Magaldi (fragment)
14. Rainbow Tour	
15. The Actress Hasn't Learned	Aristocrat Theme
	Another Suitcase
16. And The Money Kept Rolling In	
17. Santa Evita	Oh What a Circus
18. Waltz for Eva and Che	There Is No One
	And If I Ever Go
19. She Is a Diamond	Army Theme
20. Dice Are Rolling	I'd Be Good for You
	There Is No One
21. Eva's Final Broadcast	Oh What a Circus
22. Montage	Oh What a Circus
	Eva Beware
	A New Argentina
	High Flying Adored
	Sing You Fools!
23. Lament	Requiem for Evita

Not only are contrafacta more prevalent, they are more baffling. Why should Eva, when dismissing her lovers one by one like so many hired hands in "Goodnight and Thank You," sing the same music that Magaldi used when he warned her not to go to Buenos Aires ("Eva Beware of the City")? Why is the lovely song of Peron's mistress, "Another Suitcase in Another Hall," converted to become Eva's subversion of the aristocracy's society charity ("The Actress Hasn't Learned")? And what is the audience to understand when it hears the tune known by the world as "Don't Cry for Me, Argentina" sung at the opera's beginning by the leftist Che to the cynical lines "Oh, What A Circus, Oh, What A Show!"? The contrafactum method in *Evita* has become a rather careless infatuation with Webber's not inconsiderable powers of melody.

It is possible that the contrafactum technique in the two operas resulted quite naturally from the authors' working methods. Tim Rice remembers that with *Jesus Christ Superstar*

the music came before the lyrics. We would discuss the scene, and I'd say, "Right, this number will be Judas saying so-and-so," and Andrew would say, "Right, therefore, we want this kind of music, we want an agitated kind of song, or a ballad, or a love song, or vaudeville, or whatever." So Andrew would write his tunes, and I would be given a tune that was obviously sympathetic to what I wanted to say.[13]

If the authors truly operated with the naive belief that a kind of music by itself reflects dramatic action, it is all too easy to see how they could decide that one dramatic situation might be similar in character to another, so why not use the same music again, with different words? In *Evita*, which depends on just two styles, the repetition has no justification save the sort of dramatic connections and ironies that music can make. Whatever sensible connections are in the opera, however, have their impact diffused by other absurd contrafacta which have none.

Jesus Christ Superstar works better because its principal action depends almost totally on its characterization, which the stylistic diversity creates and the musical repetitions in the contrafacta help to reinforce. The juxtaposition of conflicting characters singing contrasting music has its own dramatic interest that is especially effective when subsumed within a single, often symmetrical musical form. "Everything's Alright," which Mary Magdalene sings as she annoints Jesus with the precious ointment, has such a form: A B A B A. The beginning section of the song brings a clear and simple action: she is trying to calm his indignation after Judas questioned the political wisdom of his associating with "women of her kind."

Ex. 12-2 Webber and Rice, *Jesus Christ Superstar*,
"Everything's Alright," mm. 5–7.

The lyric, to the effect that Jesus should try not to become anxious about the day's troubles, makes the intention explicit, but the music makes it credible in the constrained melodic range, easy sequential patterns (mm. 5–8), and above all in its 5/4 meter, which by obliterating the sense of regular strong beats within easy rhythmic subgroupings gives the melody an almost chantlike flow.

In the B section Judas charges that Mary's attention has been wasteful.

Ex. 12-3 Webber and Rice, *Jesus Christ Superstar,*
"Everything's Alright," mm. 19–22.

The musical contrast is made in the change of mode, from E major to E minor, the more active bass line and faster harmonic rhythm. Rhythmic accents are stronger. Nevertheless, the meter remains in 5/4, and Judas's melody, though different enough to articulate his character, is based on the same rhythmic motive as Mary Magdalene's melody, thus justifying the continuity of form underlying the contrast. The second B section, with Jesus' reply to Judas, has the same contentious music. Between them is Mary's more gentle insistence to calm down. The rondo-like return to her verses is well prepared by Webber's harmonic scheme for the B sections. Both Judas and Jesus rise to climaxes of passion, expressed by the strongest syncopations of the song and a sustained dominant harmony (Ex. 12-4). The resolution of the dominant prolongation into Mary's music at one stroke makes the form more continuous and makes more palpable her insistence that calm is needed in the time of greatest tension, for that is what this moment portrays in its musical progression. The only disappointing feature of the form is its ending.

Ex. 12-4 Webber and Rice, *Jesus Christ Superstar*,
"Everything's Alright," mm. 41–49.

Here Webber resorts to the recording industry's all-purpose answer for
composers who cannot end their songs properly: the fade-out. Unfortunately, several of the principal numbers in *Jesus Christ Superstar* drift off
in this fashion, including "Heaven on Their Minds" and "Superstar,"

and in this regard the compositional technique of *Evita* shows a certain maturity, for the fade-out is not used once in that opera.

A similar rondo arrangement is made out of "The Last Supper" with the Apostles' song serving as the returning section. Between the repetitions are more loosely ordered, but more dramatic sections containing Jesus' predictions of denial and betrayal and the last face-to-face confrontation with Judas, set once again to the minor mode music from "Everything's Alright." Again, the rondo usage of the Apostles' song functions not just as a structural device but as a means of symbolizing their utter obliviousness to the significance of the action within the scene.

This juxtaposition of characters within single musical forms is complemented in the opera by a longer-range development of two characters, Jesus and Judas. All other personages in the opera are static; these two undergo dramatic changes. The changes are brought about in a flash, although neither is unprepared. Jesus has an indignant tone of sure righteousness until he sings "I Only Want to Say," Webber's dramatization of the Gethsemane scene. The portrayal of indecision, near failure of nerve, and almost childish pout is so stark that this piece singlehandedly created the image of an abased Jesus that the listening public took away, forgetting his earlier remonstrance of Judas ("Strange Thing Mystifying"), bracing of his disciples ("What's the Buzz"), and castigation of the temple merchants ("The Temple"). But there is a hint of this weakness earlier, when he cannot endure the crowd of sick who press him. The transformation of Judas is easier to take, since it follows the expected course, but it traverses a greater distance. His opening words, the first words of the opera, "My mind is clearer now," are ironically recalled in his last words while still alive, sung to the same music: "My mind is darkness now." This number, "Judas' Death," is a patchwork quilt of contrafacta, but it also includes the most important reprise of the opera. When Judas sings one verse of "I Don't Know How to Love Him," the audience recognizes that even though Jesus has brought him, in his mind, down a torturous path to the brink of insanity, Judas cannot help feeling something mysterious for this man he has betrayed.

Evita fails to create any similar character action. In an opera in which the most beautiful music is given to pretended emotion and a modernist style can express only the cynical, all becomes passionless. There is no character action because there is no room given for development. Eva and Juan Peron are cold opportunists from beginning to end. Che is a cynical leftist commentator from beginning to end. The opera fairly starves for emotional expression, which is perhaps why Webber lavishes one of the best songs, "Another Suitcase in Another Hall," on Peron's teenage mistress, a nameless character who is on stage for five minutes. The authors make no use of historical evidence suggesting that Peron and Eva had more than a marriage of convenience, which at least might have lent some contrast between the public and private characters.[14]

Another opportunity for character action was provided by the authors' insertion of Che as a commentator, or one-man chorus. He might have been someone who was initially enthusiastic about Peronism, only to be disillusioned, or someone whose liberal inclinations were revolted by the political methods of the First Lady but who at the same time could not deny her effectiveness in raising living standards of certain segments of the working classes, in ridding Argentina's railroad and principal industries of foreign ownership, and in enfranchising women for the first time in Argentine history. But the opportunity is missed. Instead he is Che Guevara, the Argentine-born aide to Fidel Castro, who in the final version comes off as a negative image of Eva, nothing more. The attempt to conflict these images at the opera's end in "Waltz for Eva and Che" fails utterly. They snipe at one another with clever and cynical words, but they sing the same pretty music, so nothing substantial comes of the contrast. This woodenness of character, which reduces the opera to little more than a political editorial, may have been exacerbated by certain changes made when it was brought to Broadway. The London premiere was greeted by a number of notices and letters complaining that the opera glorified fascism, and American producers hesitated to carry the project further. "I had qualms when I saw the show in London," said one, "but when I learned how Hal Prince was going to reshape it, I was pleased and thrilled. Hal persuaded the authors to change four minutes of dialogue and develop the character of Che Guevara as a counterpoint to Evita, so that now Evita's critic and opponent is just as important as she is."[15] The London Che cannot be as clearly identified with Guevara, for he is actually an inventor with capitalist designs through much of the opera and makes only intermittent political comments. The new Che is clearly in the image of Guevara and plays in virtually every scene. Webber, stung by the London criticism, went so far as to say of the new version, "The basic point of *Evita* is that it's very anti-Eva."[16] The politically sensitive held their peace on Broadway, but not so the critics. "The purpose of the rewrites, obviously, was to take the appeal out of *Evita*. In this they have absolutely succeeded. The evening is now emotionally icy, psychologically chromatic, a cut-and-dried sermon . . ."[17] The revisions do not materially change the opera's statement—Eva and Peron, for example, are virtually the same in both versions—but they do remove even what little remained of the ambiguity on which the dramatist of history thrives.

To be sure, the history of the Perons is more problematic than the Christ story. The nature of Eva Peron's demise, which of course is quite out of the authors' hands, is undramatic. The crucifixion in *Jesus Christ Superstar* develops naturally from the action of the characters, but the cancer that kills Eva Peron comes from nowhere and has no explanation. One almost wishes that the authors had defied the historical fact and fabricated their own ending that would somehow clarify what preceded it. As it stands, the plug is suddenly pulled on Eva's career, and on the opera, too.

But the crucial difference is simply that the Peronist history is so much less well known. In *Jesus Christ Superstar*, the authors had the luxury of simply sketching a rather obscure episode such as Mary's annointing of Jesus in the song "Everything's Alright" without having to explain it. The assumption of a certain historical literacy in the audience is clearly on their side in that opera, but it could not be with *Evita*. When she was First Lady of Argentina from 1946 to 1953, Eva Peron was world famous, but the younger generations of the 1970s had never heard of her, and the details of her story were the preserve of Latin American historians. So it would not do to try to interpret what had happened; first it had to be explained, and in some detail. This required that a substantial portion of the music be given over to an expository function, and historical events that took place in distant places or over a considerable period of time, such as Eva's "Rainbow Tour" to Europe, had to be narrated without actually being shown. Critics complained about the violation of the off-stage action rule and labeled *Evita* a secular oratorio.[18] That it might be an oratorio has little to do with its success or failure, for many of Handel's finest choral numbers describe off-stage action too, but they never fail to reflect on that action even as they describe it, or else they are immediately followed by such reflection. This is really the root problem: in an opera which trivializes all emotion as mere means to an end, there is no possibility of dramatic reflection.

The failure to move beyond exposition is what distinguishes *Evita* from Rice and Webber's earlier, though partial, success in *Jesus Christ Superstar*. "No one expects a musical to be a political handbook. . . . But when Rice and Webber chose this subject, they assumed some obligation to make the Perons' rise to power credible in the theater, rather than relying on the extrinsic fact that they *did* rise to power, just as they had some obligation to shape the materials into a cumulative and discerning drama rather than relying on the fact that the actual lives were dramatic."[19] Even as a study of power, *Evita* does not work well because Eva is only shown singing about, never moving among, her *descamisados*, her people, the source of her power, something that she did in fact do very well. Jesus, on the other hand, is effectively shown as the object of the crowd's adoration in the elegant "Hosanna," and later as the object of their derision, made ironic through the use of the same music, in the Pilate scenes.

The portrayal, in both lyric and music, of Eva, Peron, and Che as political symbols rather than as human characters eliminates the ambiguous aspects, the hidden dimensions which can make drama out of history. The contrast with *Jesus Christ Superstar* is quite instructive. In that opera, it is the authors' unorthodox images of Judas and Jesus that move that drama forward, that reinterpret the famous events that follow in a fairly consistent way. What the Gospels have only sketched is clarified for a dramatic moment. History is not left on its own.

Chapter 13

Frame Story as Musical

I wanted to do a show with dancers.[1]

Michael Bennett

The dramatic conceptions that underlie musical plays or operas may be adapted from most any source that has some potential for dramatic action. Legitimate plays are perhaps the most common source in the Broadway tradition, simply because their adaptation is so much more straightforward than other sources, but even this limited survey has encountered inspirations in many other forms: novels, legends, short story collections, the New Testament, historical biography, and sound recordings. The translation of these latter forms onto the stage has always come with some difficulty, even as the resulting musicals realize some, even extraordinary success. The luxurious length and detail which are the very fiber of novels and legends proved too overwhelming for *Show Boat* and *Camelot*. The thematic consistency of Sholem Aleichem eluded *Fiddler on the Roof*. The dichotomy of religious experience and religious narrative melded so well in St. Matthew's Gospel was the undoing of *Godspell*. Is it any wonder that the majority of the most critically acclaimed American musicals—which might include, but not be limited to *Porgy and Bess*, *Carousel*, *My Fair Lady*,

The Most Happy Fella, and *West Side Story*—sprang from conceptions already staged?

Imagine, then, the prospects of staging a musical play whose only source is an extended conversation:

> It all began at midnight in a dance studio on January 18, 1974, when I met with 22 dancers, including me, and we danced for an hour and then just talked, one at a time, about why we had start-ed dancing. The subtext of that evening became the play. We did it twice, and I had thirty hours of tape.[2]

That is how Michael Bennett recalled the birth of *A Chorus Line*.

In retrospect it seems that the spark for such an experiment could only have come from Bennett, or someone very much like him. His career epitomized the meteoric rise to fame in the theater world. He broke in on Broadway at age seventeen as a chorus dancer and was designing dances for shows in his mid-twenties. These included *Promises, Promises* (1968), *Coco* (1969), and two important Sondheim musicals, *Company* (1970) and *Follies* (1971). He wished to present a show that captured the experience of dancers on Broadway, not in star-ring roles, but as everyday chorus dancers, as "gypsies." His own expe-rience both as chorus dancer and director made him sympathetic to the very idea and to see its dramatic possibilities. It is no surprise that his own personality is stamped on *A Chorus Line*'s Zach, the unseen direc-tor whose voice booms from the back of the theater, and Bennett admit-ted that Zach was modeled on himself. "He's cut off, dehumanized in a sense. That's a period I went through."[3]

Bennett organized the tape sessions out of conviction that the typical routines of composing a Broadway show would not permit him to real-ize his conception. In his view of the norm, "The director sits in a room with the composer and lyricist for a year. The costumes and sets are designed. Orchestrations are done." After auditions and hurried rehearsals, "You cross your fingers and hope it comes together."[4] Ben-nett brought in James Kirkwood, an actor and playwright with one off-Broadway show to his credit (*P.S. Your Cat Is Dead*), and Nicholas Dante, one of his midnight dancers, to convert the raw tape into a script. Joseph Papp, director of the New York Shakespeare Festival, generously granted Bennett a place to run a workshop to refine the idea, including funds to pay participating dancers $100 per week. Only then were the composer Marvin Hamlisch and lyricist Ed Kleban hired on. Bennett had turned the normal procedure on its head, taking a cue from experiments in modern legitimate theater:

> The book, the songs and the dances were worked out as they went along, from materials that came out of rehearsals, including the lives of all the participants. This is clearly the appropriation by Broadway musical people of a method that has been developed, not by Off Broadway but by Off Off Broadway—in "matrix" groups, such as Joseph Chaikin's now disbanded Open Theater, which evolved their productions out of the contributions in rehearsal of all the participants, with writers and composers (if used at all) as collaborators in the evolution. In fact one moment near the beginning of *A Chorus Line*—when a dance ends with the line of dancers holding up their photographs in front of their faces—is strongly reminiscent of a similar device in the Open Theater's *Mutation Show* (1973).[5]

How could such a source material as the taped conversations—extremely honest in expression, without artifice, very loose, totally unrelated except by the theme of dancing—be converted into a script without spoiling its nature?

Bennett's solution was to stage an audition, a competition for eight places in the chorus line of an unnamed Broadway musical. Because the chorus dancers would be required to act small parts in this show, the director Zach asks each of the seventeen finalists to step out of line and talk about himself, so that Zach may make judgments about the characters he is hiring. They resist at first, but soon begin to open up through a series of musical numbers. The "autobiographies" are drawn from the original tapes. "It is their lives, although they are not necessarily telling their own stories," said Bennett about the actors in *A Chorus Line*.[6] "It is a psychological striptease," wrote Clive Barnes in review of the opening on May 21, 1975, "and slowly the kids undress in a series of sad if funny vignettes."[7]

Bennett's conception is the frame story, a literary form with a long history, whose most conspicuous example in English is Geoffrey Chaucer's *Canterbury Tales*, "a single narrative within whose framework are placed other and distinct narratives."[8] As the pilgrimage to the shrine of St. Thomas à Becket of Canterbury is the occasion, or excuse really, for the telling of stories of exceptional variety in both genre and content, so are the audition and Zach's extraordinary request the excuse for the autobiographical revelations of the dancers. It is a curious coincidence that, although there is no evidence that Michael Bennett thought of the *Canterbury Tales* while creating *A Chorus Line*, the pilgrims' tales are encouraged and orchestrated by the Host, "the director of the proceedings, firm, commanding, and gracious,"[9] who makes the storytelling into a competition.

The conception of *A Chorus Line* as a frame story enabled Bennett and his writers to preserve the individuality and honesty of the original autobiographies without having to weave them into some plausible plot line, an impossible task. *A Chorus Line* is a frame story because its stories are neither episodes of a high-level plot nor subplots, which abound in more traditional musicals as a means of articulating the main action. Such episodes and subplots relate directly to the main plot and affect it in important ways. Without the bantering relationship of Bernardo and Anita in *West Side Story*, the action of the final scenes cannot be understood. If Mary Magdalene does not sing "I Don't Know How to Love Him," then the listener has much less sense of Jesus' mysterious and powerful attraction in *Jesus Christ Superstar*. But the various autobiographies in *A Chorus Line* could be altered significantly, have their order of presentation changed, or be replaced by new ones without the slightest effect on the show as a whole. That is because the high-level plot, the competitive audition, the excuse, is divorced from the low-level events which fill up the stage time.

Indeed, the dramatic structure of a frame story emphasizes the low-level events, that is, the individual stories, at the expense of overall plot. The frame story sacrifices high-level tension and resolution, and puts in its place a series of small dramas, little waves of tension and resolution. Now, Helen Cooper, in her overview of frame story practice,[10] points out that in some examples the frame functions as the focus of attention, and this is perhaps the case in *Company* (1970), the show that begins the mature period of Stephen Sondheim, which at least one critic cited as *A Chorus Line*'s natural model.[11]

Company dramatizes the situation of Bobby, a thirty-five year old handsome bachelor, and five couples, his friends, who are in various states of matrimony. Each scene involves Bobby with one or more of these couples and amounts to some comment on marriage. There is very little directed plot; Sondheim called it "non-linear." Some of the individual scenes could probably be reordered without much effect, as in *A Chorus Line*. But the overall theme of how Bobby will deal with his unmarried state is still dominant in the play. In fact, the last song, "Being Alive," forms a real dramatic climax as Bobby admits that being alone in life isn't enough. Sondheim, who was persuaded to replace a more satirical piece, "Happily Ever After," with this song, never thought that it worked dramatically—"When Bobby suddenly realizes that he shouldn't be alone at the end of the scene, it's too small a moment and you don't believe it"[12]—but nevertheless it ensures that the frame is the primary dramatic focus.

That is surely not the case in *A Chorus Line*. If the audition were the real plot, then who wins would matter very much at the end of the play. But anyone who has seen it will not be able to name the winners, except for one or two personal favorites, perhaps. The fact is that the audience never learns the reasons for Zach's particular selections at the end, and it doesn't matter who wins the audition. Where is the development of the theme of competition, the plotting of strategy, the dreams of victory? There is none because that is not the true subject of the play. And the weightiest evidence of all is that there is no musical expression for the drama as competition after the opening number, "I Hope I Get It," which functions mostly as a curtain raiser that establishes the frame. Harold Clurman's characterization of the play is therefore most apt: "There is hardly any 'story' except for the stories of the young people on the line."[13]

Paradoxically, the retreat of the frame into the background of the drama does not mean that the choice of frame was unimportant. If one could imagine *A Chorus Line* as a bunch of interviews taken by some feature magazine writer in a crowded dressing room, for example, it becomes immediately clear how much the frame influences the character and effect of the stories without affecting their contents. "When you see the sixteen [sic] boys and girls competing for eight jobs, there's something so naked about it," recalls James Kirkwood, who collaborated on the book. "You want everyone to get the job, but you know only half can. And that's the pull."[14] Certainly, knowing what is at stake in the personal confessions colors the confessions themselves. Nevertheless, the competition can affect only the tension in the little dramas that are the autobiographies; it is not a vehicle for high-level dramatic action.

The frame story changes the nature and purpose of the songs in the play. Rather than contribute to a developing action by defining character or dramatic movement through music, Marvin Hamlisch and Ed Kleban had to create complete dramas in miniature. It is not that the songs had to be complete narratives in themselves, but they had to have a dramatic role in the storytelling. This role might be as simple as a character definition, as in the comical "Sing." Very much in the mold of *Oklahoma!*'s "I Can't Say No," "Sing" supplies an answer to Zach's question—Val dances because she can't sing—and closes her story. Generally the pieces have more ambitious dramatic functions and therefore have more complex structures. It was a demanding assignment, and although there are a number of clever moments in the score, even the best attempts of Hamlisch and Kleban are flawed.

In "At the Ballet" three of the women—Sheila, Bebe, and Maggie— explain that they began dancing to escape from troubled home lives, as a way to be beautiful. The verse and refrain form of each section contrasts music that stands for the reality against music that expresses the fantasy life offered by the ballet school. The opening melody is an admirable image of the loveless home Sheila is trying to recall. An insistent, monotonic A, very fast, clashes with a prevailing G minor harmony, creating a subdued but ever present tension (m. 1).[15] Metrical asymmetry in the phrasing increases the bitterness (m. 2). After another verse on the same music, there is a transition to the refrain, which expresses how beautiful everything is "at the ballet." Here Hamlisch resorts to an imitation of a classical waltz, which, especially in the accompaniment, suits well the fantasy world of the ballet (mm. 20–36). Yet, the anachronistic texture can still be expressive, as when the vocal melody becomes chromatic (mm. 29–32), seeming to modulate out of A major, only to return forcefully on the word "Hey" (m. 33), with its sudden yet appropriate emphasis on the tonic just before the cadence. The second part of the refrain is composed in the parallel minor, which prepares the next verse.

The form of the entire song is more ambitious than a simple verse-refrain alternation for each character.

"At the Ballet"

| Verse 1 | (Sheila) | G minor |
| Verse 2 | (Sheila) | G minor |

Refrain — part 1	(Sheila)	A major
— part 2	(Sheila and Bebe)	A minor
Verse 3	(Bebe)	A minor
Verse 4	(Bebe)	A minor
Refrain — part 1	(Bebe and Maggie)	D major
— part 2	(all)	D minor
— interlude	(spoken dialogue)	G major
Development	(all)	C♮ minor
Refrain — part 1	(Maggie)	D major
— extension	(all)	D major

The development is a rendition of the refrain tune in C-sharp minor, over which fragments of the verses are sung intermittently by the three women. The section is important, for it makes clear how much the three women love their ballet for the same reason, and since its texture is less continuous it creates a higher- level tension. This tension sets up the most expressive moment: when the key and melodic continuity are stable again Maggie extends a chromatic passage, singing three times the key words of the title (mm. 134–143).

This peak moment of the song is made possible by the varied pattern within the form, the development and interlude sections which make the return to the familiar refrain more dramatic than it would have been otherwise. Yet, for all its ambition and imagination, the structure of "At the Ballet" is a puzzling one. Why does Hamlisch forgo the powerful tensions and unity that a central key can provide? The use of various keys for both expressive variety and structural articulation is of course a necessary component of tonal form, but their deployment in "At the Ballet" seems just haphazard.[16] The form lacks the tonal unity, and therefore the expressive power, it might have had.

Defects in the details, too, detract and distract from the song's dramatic function. The change from duple to triple meter and from minor to major mode at the end of the first verse (mm. 8–10) might serve as some preparation for the waltz to come, which is in triple and in major. But the tonal preparation is lost when, at the same point in the second verse (mm. 20–21), the music remains in the original G minor. That makes the modulation to A major incomparably more distant and, since there seems to be no call in the material for such a modulation, grating. Indeed, most of the changes of key in the piece strike the listener as ill-conceived and clumsy. The lyrics for these important measures do not match up well with the musical content, an intermittent problem characteristic of the entire play. Why should the music change to major when Sheila recalls her mother's marriage (mm. 8–10)?. After an entire verse in minor, the change of mode romanticizes the marriage, when just the opposite is intended.

The tonal unity missing from "At the Ballet" finds its place in "Montage," the most ambitious structure in *A Chorus Line*. It is a rondo-like form using the refrain "Hello twelve, hello thirteen, hello love" as its recurring theme. "Montage" involves the entire cast of seventeen, many having solo bits which describe their own teenage years. The piece is therefore a frame within a frame, for within the entire confessional scheme of *A Chorus Line*, "Montage" constructs yet another artifice in which a considerable number of the dancers can reveal themselves.

Plan of "Montage"

Part I	Refrain ("Hello Twelve")	(all)	E major
	"Gonorrhea"	(Mark)	F#-A major
	"Four foot, ten"	(Connie)	C major
	Refrain ("Goodbye Twelve")	(all)	E major
	"Four foot, ten"	(Connie)	C major
Part II	"Nothing" (verse 1, 2)	(Diana)	E-flat major
	"Nothing" (verse 3, coda)		E major
Part III	"The summer I turned"	(Don)	E major
	Refrain ("Goodbye Twelve")	(all)	E major
	"Please take this"	(Maggie)	B major
Part IV	"First time I'd ever"	(Judy)	—
	Refrain ("Goodbye Twelve")	(all)	E major
	"Gimme the ball"	(Ritchie)	E minor
	Refrain ("Goodbye Twelve")	(all)	E major

The plan given here shows only the lengthy solos. There are innumerable short interjections, both sung and spoken, throughout the sections between the refrains, and the refrains themselves are often overlaid with other words and melodies. But it makes clear how the key of E major acts as the principal tonal center and, in conjunction with the refrain, organizes this sequence of twenty minutes.

The security of the overall form cannot ensure success in the composition of details, however, and defects in handling the musical continuity from section to section and once again in the match of music and lyrics undermine the potential of such an ambitious piece.

The lyric begins with a promise that is never fulfilled. The refrain line "Hello twelve, hello thirteen, hello love" introduces the theme of adolescence, it is true, but there is nothing in the song about love. All of the lyrics, save perhaps Maggie's message to her mother, are directed back at those who sing them. They are too busy talking about themselves to consider love. It makes a clever refrain, nothing more. At other places in "Montage" the lyrics simply do not fit the music, which is not a failure of imagination, but of craft.

A striking example of this failure is Diana's song about her acting class in high school, "Nothing," Part II of "Montage." The tune, one of the best in the play, has as its most identifiable feature the leap of the chromatic major seventh, from B-flat to A on the words "to feel" (mm. 22–23), introducing a sequential motive in the following bars. The word *feel* in measures 23 and 25 receives a great musical emphasis because of the leap and the length of the note and the prominence of the melody given by the meter. All to the good, because in this context, *feel* is the active word of the line, and the chromatic leap seems to express the kind of intense, longing effort required of the budding actors. But this rather positive association is soon subverted. The same music in the second verse emphasizes *be,* a much less active and emotional word. But the worst comes in the next phrase, when the melodic peaks bring out ex*cept* and *try* as Diana recounts how her teacher singled her out of the class with a plea to try harder, while actually ridiculing her. The first case is simply poor, but the second actually distorts the whole dramatic premise of the song. By emphasizing *try* in the same way it emphasized *feel,* the music paints the teacher, Mr. Karp, in rather sympathetic, not villianous, tones as Diana intends. The third verse crowns the effort with an egregious dangling modifier that Oscar Hammerstein could never have condoned. The phrase pattern of the earlier verses only makes it stand out.

The problems in musical discontinuity perhaps derive from the ambitiousness of "Montage." It covers a great deal of verbal and emotional ground, perhaps more than it should. The sections between the refrains are filled with extended solos, short vocal interjections, and spoken dialogue. There is no attempt to treat the melodic lines or accompaniment with any motivic consistency, so the entire burden of organization is put on the refrain, and the continuity between refrains is therefore carried entirely by the text. Hamlisch and Kleban might have succeeded had they used recitative exclusively, but when that texture is used intermittently with spoken dialogue, there must be some dramatic justification for the inherently greater emphasis and expressive weight that music gives to a text. In the following lines from "Montage—Part III"

> Well, she really took to me. I mean, we did share the only dressing room and she did a lot of dressing . . .
>
> Anyway, she used to come and pick me up and drive me to work nights.

why should the text up to "a lot of dressing . . ." be spoken and the rest sung? Recitative in the right hands can be an expressive resource of great profundity, but in "Montage" its use, once again, seems haphazard.

A Chorus Line is performed without intermission, probably because the fragile continuity of the frame story could not tolerate a lengthy break, but there is a kind of visual intermission when Zach lets the dancers have a break out in the hall. The stage is now empty except for one dancer, Cassie. As Zach speaks with her, it becomes clear that they were once lovers, and that although she was once a star dancer, she now needs "a job." When she joins with the others in a unison dance number ("One"), Zach criticizes her dancing as too special, and the argument soon turns into an old-fashioned lovers' quarrel.

It is difficult to understand why Bennett wanted this scene, except perhaps as some autobiographical expiation of his own, because it has no dramatic premise and does grave injury to the device of the frame. Zach, who instigates all the storytelling from the beginning, is really the personification of the frame. When he enters into this little "plot," the distinction between the frame and the stories is critically blurred. It is an attempt to create a high-level dramatic tension where none should exist. To confound the inconsistency, Cassie's song, "The Music and the Mirror," has nothing to do with the past love affair; it reverts to the self-portrait, like the others. It is no wonder that a number of critics objected to this scene and to the knee injury scene which follows.[17]

Perhaps the greatest difficulty of the frame story is closing it in a way that brings the stories together in some sort of artistic whole, a difficulty Chaucer neatly avoided by leaving his *Canterbury Tales* unfinished. The composer of the variation set faces the same structural issue: after having linked a number of small, essentially closed forms, how does one compose the last in a way that seems not to simply break off in stride, but conclude in a summary way?

As the dancers are rehearsing the big ensemble number, "One," which in dramatic terms is a prop-song because it belongs to the show for which they are auditioning, one of them, Paul, falls on a turn and hurts his knee.[18] After he has been taken to the hospital, Zach faces the rest and asks the summary question: "What do you do when you can't dance anymore?" The question is intended to evoke responses from the dancers about dancing, and isn't this a musical play about dancing? Their reaction is the show's most popular song, "What I Did for Love," sung at first as a solo by Diana but then by the whole chorus. The undeniable impression is that the song, and the whole episode, is forced, an impression which producer Joseph Papp had from the beginning.

> In Mr. Papp's judgment, Marvin Hamlisch's song "What I Did for Love" did not belong in the musical. Mr. Papp recalled having "a little go-round" with the composer and to this day he can hear Mr. Hamlisch's insistent plea: "Joe, listen, I've got to get something on the charts!"[19]

Hamlisch concurs: "Joe Papp didn't want it. . . . It was written to be a hit. . . . It doesn't fit in as well as the other ones."[20] But why doesn't it? Because, once again, it is inconsistent with the dramatic premise and form of the play, the frame story. Contrary to the opinion of many, *A Chorus Line* is not a show about dancing, but a show about individual characters who happen to dance. If Zach's last question had been asked at the beginning, then the frame would have been constrained in such a way as to dramatize the role of dancing, but there is no such constraint. The stories, and the songs, touch on a great variety of themes and personal experiences, many of which have nothing to do with dance.

The effort to end the frame story drama suitably goes beyond "What I Did for Love" and the final selection into the curtain call. After the stage empties to the applause of the audience, the entire cast reappears after a quick change into opulent gold top hats and coats, dancing the ensemble number to "One." This elaborate curtain call has occasioned a variety of critical comment, a token of the effectiveness of the trick.[21] Is it a stunning revelation to the audience of the great dream of the chorus line dancer, symbolized by the utter contrast of audition rags and show costume? Then why is the whole cast included, even the losers, whose dreams have been shattered once again? Does it show the audience, in Bennett's words, that "the transformation of people it has come to know as individuals into a mechanical unit is the sad truth of the matter"?[22] Or is it something much simpler, much more traditional, the reprise of a prop song to bring the curtain down, to send the audience home with, to quote Bennett again, "the kind of happy show-biz number they've been waiting for all evening?"[23]

The controversy provokes an important question. Perhaps criticism of the shortcomings of the music in *A Chorus Line*, or more precisely the music drama, is misdirected. Perhaps this musical, coming at the end of three decades in which the role of dancing in the Broadway tradition has grown steadily more significant, from the dream ballets of Rodgers and Hammerstein to Jerome Robbins's dance episodes in *West Side Story*, is the one in which dance succeeds music as the conduit of dramatic meaning. Bennett himself seems to have sought this power in his dancers: "The really good dancers are dramatic dancers. They're not just watching their bodies. Something is going on in their heads."[24] He believed, too, that dance had not only the potential, but the duty to be expressive in a dramatic way:

> Choreography is not about steps, just steps, in terms of shows. I like to think I make the best dances I can, but I'm also interested in dancing being right for a character. Most importantly, dancing has to continue the story line. And it's got to have a point of view. It's got to be about something.[25]

But it is one thing to maintain that dance can be expressive of a particular moment or of a particular part of the dramatic action—few who have seen *West Side Story* would argue with that—and quite another to say that dance can carry dramatic action over the course of a two- or three-hour play. Can physical gesture take on character identification or dramatic meaning as easily, and develop them as flexibly, as a musical theme or harmonic progression?

In building *A Chorus Line* as a frame story, Bennett greatly simplified the theoretical problem for himself, since in that form there is little need to carry the action for a long time, only as long as an individual story. Cassie's universally acclaimed solo dance, certainly, is a fine demonstration of how dance might fulfill the drama of an individual story within the frame, as are some of the pantomimic routines in "Montage." And yet, there seem to be few other moments when dance acquires that importance. "For a show built around dancers, 'A Chorus Line' is loath to release any of its meaning through dance,"[26] reflects Arlene Croce, the *New Yorker*'s articulate dance critic. It is possible that the premise of the play actually compromises the meaning of individual dances, because it is characters as dancers who perform them. The line between the expressive dance and the "prop dance" runs thin; is what they are doing a dramatic expression of themselves, or are they showing off for Zach?

The dances of *A Chorus Line* provide a spectacular visual element, no doubt, but as recent megamusicals have inadvertently proved, spectacle by itself is not drama, and in the absence of a consistently dramatic dance, the play must fall back on its songs and lyrics, its music. For its composer and lyricist, the brilliant originality of *A Chorus Line*'s conception proves too great a challenge. Their music, however inventive and memorable at times, fails to make convincing drama out of the frame story.

Chapter 14

Thriller as Musical

I've never been conscious of trying to further the theatrical language. It comes from a feeling of not wanting to cover the same material twice or to bore yourself.[1]

Stephen Sondheim

W hen Stephen Sondheim was awarded the Tony for Best Musical of the season in 1988 for *Into the Woods*, Broadway more or less officially recognized a domination of the American musical theater over the last two decades reminiscent of an earlier reign during the 1940s and 1950s by Rodgers and Hammerstein. In retrospect, Sondheim seems to have been bred, like an heir apparent, for such a crown. Beginning at age fifteen, he composed a number of "studies" in musical drama under the tutelage of his friend and neighbor in Pennsylvania, Oscar Hammerstein II. His debut on Broadway was the most auspicious imaginable, as the somewhat reluctant lyricist (he wished to be a composer-lyricist from the beginning) for Leonard Bernstein's *West Side Story* (1957) and Jule Styne's *Gypsy* (1959). His first offering as the complete songwriter was a commercial if not artistic success, an adaptation of Plautus called *A Funny Thing Happened on the Way to the Forum* (1962). Yet his domination of the Broadway musical from 1970 onward is difficult to characterize, best described, perhaps, as a triumph of integrity over commercial interest, marked by an unflagging seriousness of purpose and an astounding dramatic range:

> In his 13 shows . . . Sondheim has staked out a turf as big as the emotional landscape of post–World War II America. Even when the shows have been set abroad or in the past, their themes have addressed contemporary topics—or universal ones, Sondheim might aver—by way of metaphor. This is particularly true of the Sondheim shows since 1970. He has treated the travails of modern marriage in "Company," the corrosion of American optimism in "Follies," injustice and revenge in "Sweeney Todd," idealism and compromise in "Merrily We Roll Along," and Western imperialism in "Pacific Overtures."[2]

It is the range that makes choosing a representative work of Sondheim's quite impossible, much more difficult than choosing one of Rodgers and Hammerstein's. No one would say that the older men wrote the same show many times, of course, but there are common elements that unite all their great ones, principally the dramatic organization around a resolution of conflict in a romantic couple along with a contrasting subplot. There is nothing so consistent in Sondheim's plays. "He doesn't duplicate himself, does he?" mused Michael Bennett. "He'll tackle things no one else would think of. You can't think of any Sondheim show that's like any other."[3] The choice of *Sweeney Todd*, however, is not entirely capricious. Because it is virtually through-composed, it is the most ambitious of Sondheim's scores, and it is one whose composition and production he initiated.[4] And, while all Sondheim's mature musicals offer severe challenges in dramaturgy, those inherent in the adaptation of a thriller are particularly formidable, as are the composer's attempts to meet them.

Sondheim's domination of the musical theater differs further from his predecessors' in that it has not been accomplished by overwhelming public success or critical acclamation. His commercial successes are few, and the critical reception for each show is invariably divided and controversial. The reaction of Walter Kerr to *Company* (1970) seems typical of the critical frustration. After describing a multitude of virtues, he writes:

> Now ask me if I liked the show. I didn't like the show. I admired it, or admired vast portions of it, but that is another matter. Admira-

tion stirs in the head; liking sends out its signals somewhere lower in the anatomy, the pit of the stomach maybe, and gradually lets you know that you are happy to have been born, or to have been lucky enough to have come tonight.[5]

There has never been any dispute over Sondheim's powers as a lyricist. He is routinely compared with Lorenz Hart and Cole Porter for sheer virtuosity of rhyme and construction. The statement of playwright Arthur Laurents, with whom Sondheim worked closely in *West Side Story*, *Gypsy*, and the early failure *Anyone Can Whistle* (1964), contends that he surpassed even those masters in his deeper understanding of the lyric's dramatic responsibilities:

> Without question, Steve is the best Broadway lyricist, past and present. Any lyric he has written can be quoted to illustrate this contention. Steve is the only lyricist who writes a lyric that could only be sung by the character for which it was designed, who never pads with unnecessary fillers, who never sacrifices meaning or intention for a clever rhyme, and who knows that a lyric is the shortest of one-act plays, with a beginning, a middle and an end. Moreover, he knows how the words must sit on a musical phrase. His approach to writing for the musical theater is nothing less than remarkable.[6]

Yet the same voice pronounces a devastating sentence upon the first Sondheim works directed by Hal Prince, which include *Company*, *Follies* (1971), and *A Little Night Music* (1973), award winners all:

> I can only point to the shows that Steve and Hal have done together and say that they are all cold . . . which may be their aim. But I've never liked the theory of alienation. I think it's an intellectual conceit. The gloss and technical excellence of those shows should have made you care.[7]

Most of the criticism has been directed at Sondheim the composer. The charge: a general lack of feeling, a "salon music that revels in an Old World sophistication, with hardly a trace of jazz that excited Gershwin, Weill, and Bernstein."[8] One occasionally hears that Sondheim's melodies are "unhummable," a characterization which incenses the composer.

I don't understand it entirely. Quite often the stuff I write is not simple. I think I'm getting more and more accepted, but sometimes my work is too unexpected to sustain itself very firmly in the commercial theater. The only shows of mine since *West Side Story* and *Gypsy* that paid back their investments and went into profits on Broadway were *A Funny Thing Happened on the Way to the Forum*, *Company*, and *A Little Night Music*. It would be nice to have a smash.[9]

Sondheim's vocal melodies are neither "unhummable" nor unmemorable in the pejorative sense, but they can be difficult to remember on just a few hearings. The cause is not extreme chromaticism in the melodic line, nor his much vaunted dissonance, but rather an assymetrical phrasing, and most of all a harmonic language that is essentially nonfunctional.

Until quite recently, the harmonic idioms of all American popular styles have been firmly based on functional harmony, the harmonic language that has dominated Western music since the seventeenth century. Chords are chosen not only to harmonize with the prevalent melodic note, but also to construct relationships with the chords preceding and following them. Progressions have a syntax, an expected order. Such an idiom is known as "functional" because the various chords within a key have assigned syntactic roles or "functions" in the construction of harmonic "sentences" or progressions. Functional progressions have an integrity all their own, quite distinct from the melody which they set or the rhythm with which they are imbued. For that reason functional harmony has great power to create the articulations so necessary to music, and when joined to a melody, these articulations offer powerful memory cues like signposts for the listener. The chords themselves seem to direct the melody to its predestined goal.

It is no accident that Sondheim counts Ravel, Prokofiev, Copland, and Britten among his most important models,[10] for his harmonic language derives from the nonfunctional progressions of early twentieth-century impressionism and its derivatives. In *Sweeney Todd*, except in the parody numbers, there is an almost complete absence of harmonic function, conventionally ordered progression, on the low level of structure. Here in the opening number of the opera,[11] the tonal center of F-sharp minor is clearly established, but not by any harmonic progression, rather by a sustained pedal in the bass. The first change of chord (m. 4) makes little sense in a functional idiom. The E-natural, stressed in the upper voice, is dissonant against the D in the bass and does not act as a leading tone to F-sharp because it is the lowered seventh step. The vocal melody is completely diatonic yet receives no accompanying harmonic articulations, not even in measure 6 where some form of authentic cadence might be expected. In a structural sense, the notes of the melody are simply ignored by the harmony.

Ex. 14-1 Stephen Sondheim, *Sweeney Todd*, The Demon Barber Of Fleet Street, "The Ballad Of Sweeney Todd" (No. 1), mm. 1–25.

On the higher levels of structure, the chords may form a functional progression. In the "Ballad," for example (Ex. 14-1), the long F-sharp in the bass moves to D (m. 15), then to C-sharp, then to F-sharp, sketching the conventional progression of i-VI-V-i. But the triadic rhythm is so slow that the syntactic relationships are strained, and the progression still does not coordinate with the vocal melody; the return to tonic harmony occurs at the beginning of the last phrase (m. 24), even though the sung notes do not imply that F-sharp triad that arrives there. Elsewhere in the opera, even the high-level progressions in *Sweeney Todd* are nonfunctional, and harmonic organization and coherence are accomplished with sustained pedal tones and inconspicuous ostinato figures. These alternative methods of musical organization were perhaps the focus of Sondheim's compositional studies with Milton Babbitt, undertaken after he graduated from Williams College. "I learned from Milton the means of holding an ear over a period of time, how you keep someone listening for 45 minutes so that at the end they feel they've heard a piece."[12]

The great advantage of such an idiom is the enlarged harmonic vocabulary and wealth of fresh harmonic progressions so familiar from Debussy and Ravel. Nonfunctional harmony is the true source of Sondheim's free dissonances so often noticed by listeners and critics, for it makes unnecessary the rigid coordination of melodic and harmonic articulations. Traditional rules of harmony control dissonance to maintain the clarity of functional progressions. When those progressions are absent, dissonant intervals can become the norm, the stable terms of a composition. Notice that the first verse melody of "The Ballad of Sweeney Todd" (Ex. 14-1, m. 25) ends on the second scale step, G-sharp dissonant against the F-sharp tonic in the bass. This can only make aural sense when it is heard as the same ninth that opened the opera (see m. 1), established then and there as a relatively stable sound.

The nonfunctional idiom encourages Sondheim's penchant for modal melodies, founded on scales other than the traditional major and minor. The traditional scales have "tendency tones" built in to reinforce the syntax of the supporting functional harmony. But if there is little harmonic syntax to sustain, the tendency tones can be altered or dispensed with entirely. The opening phrase of the "Ballad of Sweeney Todd" (Ex. 14-1) has a tune clearly centered on F-sharp, yet the lowered seventh, E-natural, is used in place of the more functional E-sharp. Modal tunes are particularly appropriate for *Sweeney Todd*, set in nineteenth-century London, since they can be reminiscent of old-fashioned English folk music, and lend a musical substance to the fiction that the tale is some hoary legend.

Of course, in abandoning traditional functional harmony Sondheim gives up a great deal, particularly its power to create and sustain the harmonic tensions and resolutions which have been so important to musical expression in Western art. On the highest levels of structure, it means that the motion away from a tonal center and back may be a colorful event but does not generally produce, by itself, a significant tension. The lovely "Green Finch and Linnet Bird" of Act I, for example, contains several modulations away from its main tonal center of F. Each return is marked by the main motive, but this motive is used in the other keys as well, and none of the returns has any trace of the high-level resolution or arrival heard in, say, "Tonight" of *West Side Story*. The absence of high-level harmonic functions may explain why Sondheim, after taking care to organize the opening scenes of *Sweeney Todd* around the tonal center of F-sharp, does not mind ending the opera in G, even though the same "Ballad" is the final piece. The penultimate piece is also in G. Apparently the lower-level connections are more important to him than any overall tonal organization.[13]

Without functional harmony, the onus of musical tension falls on other elements. The middle section of the opening "Ballad" begins as follows.

Ex. 14-2 Stephen Sondheim, *Sweeney Todd*, The Demon Barber of Fleet Street, "The Ballad Of *Sweeney Todd*" (No. 1), mm. 102–9.

Although this music changes the tonal center from F-sharp to E, the bass register is entirely forgotten, so that the change can hardly assume structural significance. The important element is the phrase rhythm. The first measures establish a four-bar period, which is carried on in the second phrase (mm. 106–109). But the rhythm of "Back of his smile, under his word" already suggests a potential foreshortening of the phrase, an acceleration of the rhythm. This suggestion shortly erupts into the climactic entrance of the title character. The F-sharp harmony returns well in advance of the true arrival of the climax (m. 136), and has little to do

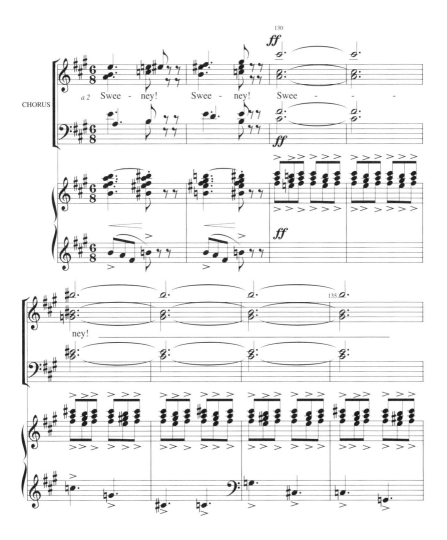

Ex. 14-3 Stephen Sondheim, *Sweeney Todd*, The Demon Barber of Fleet Street, "The Ballad Of Sweeney Todd" (No. 1), mm. 128–43.

with it. It eases the transition, nothing more. But Sondheim has drawn almost every other element into play: texture, in the slow adding of the choral voices, and in the withholding of the bass register; harmonic dissonance, not in the functional sense, but in the acoustic sense of dissonant intervals in the choral writing, particularly in the sustained final chord (mm. 132–135); rhythm, in the use of the short periods predicted earlier (mm. 128–129); and dynamics and orchestration. In a traditional harmonic idiom, such marshalling of forces might sound grossly out of proportion, even histrionic. Without the idiom, they are just sufficient, and make a very satisfying musical climax.

When Sondheim restricts himself to only a few of these musical forces, the effects are much more understated. Sweeney Todd's first aria, "There Was a Barber," one of the dramatic linchpins of the opera, depends entirely on phrase rhythm and melodic contour for its effects (Ex. 14-4). The song is in two sections. The first describes an unknown barber married to a beautiful, virtuous woman. Todd is, of course, describing his own past. It is fairly even in tension and ends inconclusively. The second begins as the first, then expands its melody. There is no question about the sense of climax at the end of this passage, but what produces it? Certainly not the chord beneath. The high D on the last "beautiful" is the highest note Todd sings, but that alone would not be sufficient. It is rather the preparation for that upward contour by the phrase rhythm.

How are phrases even articulated without a syntactic harmony to indicate beginnings and endings? Sondheim relies on characteristic rhythms consistently placed. The three eighth notes that begin the vocal melody are made into a clear anacrusis (upbeats), for example, by the onset of the accompaniment in measure 230. That must be the downbeat, the beginning of a phrase event. Then the harmony changes on the 6/8 measure, "beautiful." A return to the G harmony (m. 233) along with the same motive in the melody indicates the second phrase. So the listener has one rhythmic figure associated with phrase beginnings, another, the dotted figure, with endings. In effect, Sondheim has defined his "phrasing grammar" for this particular song.[14] Yet no sooner is it defined than it becomes purposefully ambiguous. What should be the ending of the second phrase is in precisely the same rhythmic position as the 6/8 measure, and has the same pitches and harmonic change underneath, but the note rhythm of the melody has been altered to accommodate more syllables, and now sounds suspiciously like a phrase beginning. This is the justification for a most subtle acceleration in the phrase rhythm, the shortening lengths of the phrases that move ever higher in pitch. The third phrase has no "ending" at all. Instead, the fourth anticipates itself by augmenting the three pick-up eighth notes into quarters ("Then there was") which lead into the downbeat of four eighths.[15]

First	"There was another man"	(mm. 229–232)	26
Second	"A pious vulture"	(mm. 232–235)	23
Third	"Removed the barber"	(mm. 235–236)	12
Fourth	"Then there was nothing"	(mm. 237–242)	31

Fig. 14-1 Phrase diagram of "There Was a Barber," second verse. Numerals in the right column count the number of eighth note beats in each phrase.

Ex. 14-4 Stephen Sondheim, *Sweeney Todd*, "There Was A Barber" (No. 2), mm. 229–244.

The fourth phrase goes on for what seems an excruciatingly long time, because it denies the ending rhythm as Sondheim has defined it, denies it against the insistent pattern of ever shortening phrases, until the peak of the melody, "beautiful" once again, makes it resound with feeling.[16] The acceleration of the phrase rhythm, free and gentle because of the lack of strong meter and Sondheim's ingenious preparation, has created Todd's slow but dangerous fire.

The use of harmony in "There Was a Barber" shows that changes of chord in a nonfunctional idiom are neither unimportant nor haphazard. Indeed, the clarity of the most musically dramatic moment in the whole opera depends on a chord change (see Ex. 14-15). In "There Was a Barber" the harmonic changes help to define the phrase grammar. But in a syntactic harmonic accompaniment, there would have been no need to define one, for its functions are already known by the culture. Paradoxically, when nonfunctional harmony must articulate structure, the harmonic changes often must be more carefully deployed than if they were functional.

Such a harmonic idiom lends itself to certain types of expression and not others. "Mood" and "atmosphere" are likely strengths that come to mind first, and it is no surprise that such powers would attract Sondheim, for his ability to fashion a musical ethos of a stage work is perhaps unsurpassed in the Broadway tradition. "Once you have a musical atmosphere—which could be anything from a running figure to a chord change—you have a way to start some melodic ideas. They're not related to a conscious lyrical phrase, but it gives you a basic melodic rhythm and that can spring into other things."[17] The highly extroverted dissonances which the idiom allows contribute mightily to the acerbic cynicism that pervades *Company*, the sense of contrivance in *A Little Night Music*, and foreboding, mysterious evil in *Sweeney Todd*.

"Atmosphere" is, in this sense, opposite to dramatic action, and perhaps it is this preference for atmosphere, with a coherent musical style to support it, that makes Sondheim's mature shows seem like tableaux, an impression that becomes explicit with *Sunday in the Park with George*, in which tableau merges with drama. But there is a corresponding lack of overall tension that makes one scene demand the next. The music is intent upon atmosphere, feeling, idea, but not action. When Joseph Kerman writes, "Each of the short scenes gets something done, but their effect is of a 'slice of life' with a drabness and incoherence characteristic enough of ordinary living,"[18] could he not be describing *Company* instead of Debussy's *Pelleas et Melisande*?

The exception is *Sweeney Todd*. This tale of an honest barber who returns to take revenge on a corrupt judge and, failing that, madly turns his razor on anyone who happens along, this horrific thriller would not seem to be a likely choice for a composer whose style seems ill-tuned to complicated action. Yet, Sondheim chose this story on his own.

He was in London in 1973 when *Gypsy* was revived with Angela Lansbury. On a free evening he went to see a melodrama called *Sweeney Todd*. "I'd always been interested in Grand Guignol and had heard about this play . . . I went to see it, thought it was terrific and bought all the published versions—which were all terrible."[19] They all derive from a play by a popular Victorian dramatist, one George Dibdin Pitt, written in the 1840s but never published. The source of the story is unknown. Montague Slater, editor of a 1928 printed version, suspects that it was a popular legend, since "Pitt usually borrowed the plots of his plays, and this one seems too good for him to have invented."[20] Others cite a novel by Thomas Preskett Prest,[21] and playwright Christopher Bond claims that Pitt "based it on a 'penny dreadful', a newssheet containing sensational descriptions of depravity, violence and grotesque murder with a few lines of pious editorial humbug at the end . . ."[22]

The play has enjoyed a curious popularity over the years. Brian J. Burton added music and lyrics to it in 1962, and a film version was directed by Herb Roland and produced by the Canadian Broadcasting Corporation in 1972. The version that Sondheim enjoyed so much, however, was written by Bond. It is a play that not only transmits the core plot from Pitt but borrows heavily from other melodramatic sources to make a better play.

> I have "borrowed" from, amongst others, *The Count of Monte Cristo*, *The Revenger's Tragedy*, *The Spanish Tragedy*, the family green-grocer, and Shakespeare, as well as Dibdin-Pitt's original melodrama. My object has been to add to the chair and the pies an exciting story, characters that are large but real, and situations that, given a mad world not unlike our own, are believable.[23]

He succeeds fairly well. In the mostly Pitt versions,[24] Sweeney Todd is simply a madman who kills his customers to enrich himself—a pure villian. Even as such he is incredibly overdrawn by standards of modern taste; here the too-often used critical phrase "cartoon character" really fits, for as he points his pistol at his accomplice, Mrs. Lovett, he actually gloats, "Now say your prayers,"[25] so anticipating Yosemite Sam and Bugs Bunny by a century.

In Bond, there is something of a dramatic motivation. Todd first appears just having been returned to London by the sailor Anthony. After an encounter with a crazed beggar woman who seems to know him, he meets Mrs. Lovett in her pie shop under his old establishment. She recounts how the former tenant, a handsome barber, was transported for life by a judge who desired his wife. Then, feigning repentence, the judge lured the wife, Lucy, to his house where he raped her as part of the fun at a masked ball. She took poison, leaving her daughter Johanna to become the judge's ward. Todd now reveals himself to Mrs. Lovett as the barber and together they plan his revenge on the judge and his beadle who aided him. Meantime, the sailor Anthony tells Todd that he has fallen in love with a beautiful ward of a certain Judge

Turpin, who of course is Johanna, Todd's daughter, but the judge intends to marry Johanna himself. An early opportunity for revenge presents itself to Todd when the judge himself arrives for a shave, but as he is about to slash his throat, Anthony barges in to announce that Johanna has agreed to elope with him. The judge leaves indignantly, swearing to lock his ward away. Todd, his chance lost, now swears revenge on all comers until a second opportunity arrives. Mrs. Lovett, privy to this confession, sees a new sort of filling for her failing pie business and the curtain falls on the mad laughter of them both.

The second act opens upon a prosperous pie business. Mrs. Lovett has even taken on a hired boy, Tobias Ragg. When Anthony finds Johanna imprisoned in an asylum, Todd sends him off disguised as a wig-maker in search of hair to free her. At the same time he lures the judge back to his tonsorial parlor with a letter telling about Anthony's rescue. Then the beadle comes around to inspect the bakeshop because of complaints about the curious stench. Todd tricks him into sitting in his special chair, and down the chute he goes. But as Todd waits for the judge to arrive, the mad beggar woman enters. Fearing to be caught with questionable company once again, he slashes her throat just before the judge arrives. After he kills the judge, Mrs. Lovett's screams summon him to the bakeshop, where he discovers that the old beggar woman was his wife Lucy. Enraged, he throws Mrs. Lovett into the oven. As he mourns his error, the boy Tobias, now half-mad with discovery of what has been going on in the shop, appears from the shadows, picks up Todd's razor, and slashes Todd's throat as Anthony, Johanna, and the rest of the company run on.

When Sondheim inquired into the rights, he found that Richard Barr and Charles Woodward were already negotiating to put on the play in New York. After Sondheim proposed a musical version, they agreed to wait until he had finished up his commitment to *Pacific Overtures*, which opened in 1976. Hugh Wheeler adapted the Bond version quite faithfully into a book from which Sondheim could work. The premiere of *Sweeney Todd* was March 1, 1979, at the Uris Theater.

The decision to set such a thriller brought with it at least two pervading problems. First, how to manage a story of such pacing and complexity without having it bog down in hours of music? Music dramas with plots of comparable complexity do exist, of course, but they are mostly comedies, where the quick pacing is essential to comic effect.

The comic elements in *Sweeney Todd* are very important, but it is clear that Sondheim wanted to preserve the dark tone and atmosphere of the original, and he recognized the pacing difficulty: "It is highly plotted. You can't spend a lot of time saying, 'It's a lovely day today.'"[26] Second, how does one prevent the story from overwhelming the musical commentary that accompanies it? There is no question that the increased pace toward the end of the second act and the surprise conclusion are stunning when first encountered, but what happens the second time around, when the listener knows the end?

The plot complexity demands a musical construction that can accommodate the large number of significant events without sacrificing either clarity or pacing. In short, it demands a unified musical continuity. This excerpt from the first number of the opera after the "Prologue" is brief, and yet it contains three characterizations and two important events. At the beginning, Anthony sings happily of his return to his most wondrous city, his melody and its accompaniment of altered chords echoing the bells of London. When Sweeney Todd interrupts him, his bitter mockery of Anthony's sentiment is immediately felt in his substitution of the G-flat for Anthony's G-natural, changing the mode of the tune from major to minor, and in the mysterious chromatic accompaniment that will come to stand for his obsession. Then, in the underscoring, the opening motive of "There Was a Barber" is heard (m. 22), although its significance is yet undefined. This music is suddenly interrupted by the appearance of the Beggar Woman (m. 26), her depravity and her insanity both imaged by her descending, chromatic motive beginning at a tritone over the bass. All this in 25 measures, with no stop in the musical flow.

This dexterity in handling extended musical forms, which Sondheim traces back to his work with Bernstein on *West Side Story*,[27] allows the

Ex. 14-5 Stephen Sondheim, *Sweeney Todd*, "No Place Like London" (No. 2), mm. 6–30.

composer to include many events in each number, rather than one or two. Thus there are not too many little pieces to be organized for the listener, and fewer higher-level structures than there might have been.[28] The intermittent snips from "The Ballad of Sweeney Todd" not only offer choruslike comments on the action but set the musical boundaries of each scene, as well as for the opera as a whole.

Essential to this continuity are leitmotifs for each character and important dramatic theme. "The notion of using motifs is to pique the audience's memory, to remind them that this theme represents that idea or emotion. They're guideposts along the way. In a sustained piece you have to do that . . ."[29] In other words, Sondheim's use of leitmotifs is purely Wagnerian: they contribute to the musical-dramatic expression at the same time they build a thematic unity into the musical texture.

The heavy reliance on a texture of leitmotifs means that the accompaniment of the singer may well be as important at times as the music that he or she sings. Counterpoint is therefore an essential aspect of this musical thriller. The ostinato figure that underlies "There Was a Barber," for example, is responsible for the particular tone and subliminal unease of that statement.

Ex. 14-6 Stephen Sondheim, *Sweeney Todd*, "There Was A Barber"
(No. 2), mm. 215–217.

That is because it derives from the source of mystery, the ostinato in
"The Ballad of Sweeney Todd."[30] It is equally important that this figure,
and the end of Todd's song, merge with the "obsession" leitmotif which
accompanied his very first words after the prologue (Ex. 14-7). This,
too, is formed from "The Ballad," from the brassy interpolation that
occurs between each of Todd's phrases as he sings after rising from the
grave, the musical climax of the prologue (see Ex. 14-3, mm. 142–43).

Counterpoint, then, is the chief means of developing the musical-
dramatic action in a manner sufficiently economical for the pace of the
plot. Because leitmotifs may be used as accompaniment, they have great
power to color what is sung in words around them. When Mrs. Lovett
begins to recount the tale of Todd's misfortune, she reprises, logically
enough, "There Was a Barber" (Ex. 14-8).

How quickly essential information is conveyed in these three measures. Sondheim's clever alteration of "And he was beautiful" immediately hints at Mrs. Lovett's longstanding attraction to Todd, later made
more explicit. At the same time, even though she sings Todd's earlier
melody, it is missing its haunting effect, because the crucial ostinato
figure is gone, replaced by sustained chords.

Counterpoint also quickens the pace of certain ensembles for comic
effect. The comedy of the opera is of many kinds and has many sources,
and greatly helps to justify the unflagging pace of action. There is the
grisly sort, of course, which brings the curtain down on the first act in
"A Little Priest," but Sondheim's humor appeals more often to the intel-

Ostinato from "Prologue"

Ostinato from "There Was A Barber"

Fig.14-2 Comparison of accompanimental figures from "The Ballad Of *Sweeney Todd*" and "There Was A Barber."

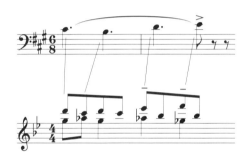

Fig. 14-3 Transformation of "obsession" motive from "The Ballad Of *Sweeney Todd*" to the conclusion of "There Was A Barber."

TODD

So lost and oh, so   beau-ti-ful.

Ex. 14-7 Stephen Sondheim, *Sweeney Todd*, "There Was A Barber" (No. 2), mm. 241–244.

Ex. 14-8 Stephen Sondheim, *Sweeney Todd*, "There Was A Barber"
(No. 4), mm. 5–7.

lect. He sets the title line from "The Worst Pies in London," Mrs.
Lovett's first song, to a romantic waltz melody. He parodies the venera-
ble British ballad when the beadle, about to inspect the bakeshop, sits
at a harmonium and sings "I am a lass who alas loves a lad who alas has
a lass in Canterbury." At other times, however, the comic effect derives
from clever use of contrapuntal texture. The comments of the
bystanders and customers in "Pirelli's Miracle Elixir" and "Mrs. Lovett's
Meat Pies" (the second a contrafactum of the first) are set in counterpoint against the sales pitch of Tobias Ragg, making the construction
itself funny.

There is one other ensemble which actually compresses the action in
a way that finds virtue in the inherent pace difficulties of the thriller.
The one significant change introduced by Sondheim and Wheeler into
Bond's play is to bring on stage the early encounters between Anthony
and Johanna. The first of these elicits the purest love song Sondheim
has written for the theater, Anthony's "Johanna."[31] The second shows
them secretly meeting in her room, planning what to do next. Here it is
the counterpoint between the vocal parts that increases the pace of the
action. The opening music, especially Johanna's, is comic in effect, like
a pattersong, but the expression changes abruptly at measure 8, a
change which comes naturally out of Anthony's exasperation at getting
her to listen to him. At the same time the suddenness of it, and the
chromatic C-natural in the vocal parts for the first time, shows some

Ex. 14 9 Stephen Sondheim, *Sweeney Todd*, "Kiss Me" (No. 13), mm. 1–9.

real feeling in what appears to be comic relief. Then Johanna resumes her fretting and the music recapitulates until this point:

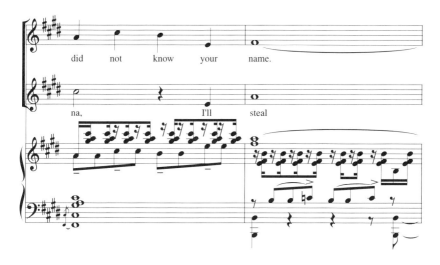

Ex. 14-10 Stephen Sondheim, *Sweeney Todd*, "Kiss Me"
(No. 13), mm. 18–27.

Now the pace of musical events picks up. Johanna, comprehending at last, responds to Anthony's melody, filling up beats that were vacant or sustained before. By measure 20 there is motion on every eighth note before "Kiss me" resumes. The rhythmic acceleration is played out again, intensifying its effect. Much more important, however—and here Sondheim teaches another advantage of his harmonic idiom—is how the chords begin to move after sustaining a single harmony, E major, since the beginning. All this reaches a musical climax at measure 23, just when Anthony begins a reprise of his love theme. This is a moment of true contrapuntal art, a coordination of rhythmic preparation, of the two singing together for the first time, and of the ineffable rightness of Anthony's sustained theme which cancels all memory of pattersong, all concentrated on a single point of time. It all builds, of course, the dramatic image of the besieged couple who are so much in love that they cannot take their own danger seriously enough. Curiously, it is the duet's compression of several dramatic necessities, information, and feeling in a brief number that creates its effect, one of the most enduring of the opera.

There seems little to complain about and much to admire in *Sweeney Todd*'s first act. There is no piece without its dramatic function, and the thrilling plot loses none of its power to absorb. The second act is disturbed by some puzzling problems of pacing just opposite to what one might expect from the plot: the music appears to run out of episodes; at least, the "Johanna" ensemble and Mrs. Lovett's music hall number "By the Sea" add little to the story. On the whole, however, the musical construction of *Sweeney Todd* is a triumph of counterpoint and imagination.

But the craft and continuity of Sondheim's music ensures only that it is able to carry the plot of the thriller. Does it make of the story something it could not be on its own? Does the music allow, even reward, a second and third hearing of the opera?

Sondheim needs to go beyond his intellectual cues such as the old "Dies Irae" sequence in "The Ballad of Sweeney Todd" and other places, and the theme linking the Beggar Woman to her true identity. Music needs to be made the substance of a dramatic issue. For Sondheim, that issue is obsession.

> I was using the story as a metaphor for any kind of obsession. Todd is a tragic hero in the classic sense that Oedipus is. He dies in the end because of a certain kind of fatal knowledge: he realizes what he has been doing.[32]

Obsession takes on the musical identity of a leitmotif, drawn from the opening ballad and first given clear identity in the confession song "There Was a Barber." But Todd's horrific progress from an obsession with revenge on the judge and his beadle to an obsession with revenge on all humanity, at any cost, must be made palpable in musical terms. That is the reason for "Epiphany."

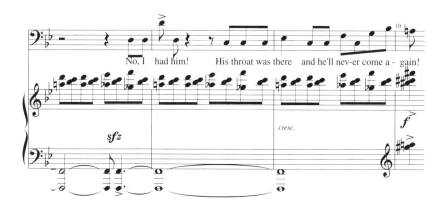

Ex.14-11 Stephen Sondheim, *Sweeney Todd*, "Epiphany"
(No.17), mm. 4–10.

"Epiphany" is perhaps Sondheim's best improvement on Bond's melodrama. In Bond, this progress of Todd is without motivation. When Judge Turpin escapes Todd's razor in Act I, the barber simply says: "A second chance may come. It must, it shall! Until it does, I'll pass the time on less honored throats."[33] Compare how the sudden entrances of the bass under the "obsession motive" convey Todd's inexpressible rage in the Sondheim version. Then his resolution follows, and his mad explanation of why all deserve to die has yet a musical rationale. For the first time, Todd sings his obsession. The A, B-flat, and C setting "all of the whole human race" are the notes and intervals of the obsession leitmotif, amplified by the accompaniment (Ex. 14-12). The progress is shown in musical terms. It is also given depth by a new theme growing out of the lyricism which sets his oath. It is odd that the theme invoking Johanna sets a variety of lyrics, invoking Lucy,

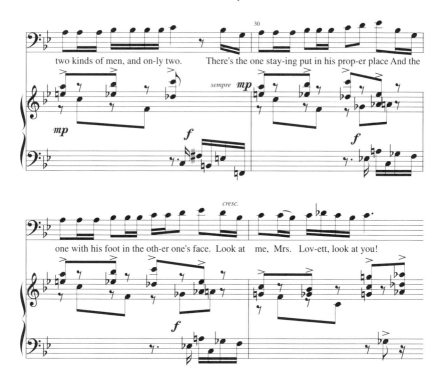

Ex.14-12 Stephen Sondheim, *Sweeney Todd*, "Epiphany"
(No. 17), mm. 27–31.

invoking vengeance in general (Ex. 14-13). At the end it crowns Todd's insane proclamation of himself. The last chords show once again the peculiarly expressive powers of Sondheim's dissonant harmonic idiom. The fortissimo B-flat chord in measure 82 has no dissonance in it. For that reason, it stands out against the whole composition, interpreting Todd's last high F,

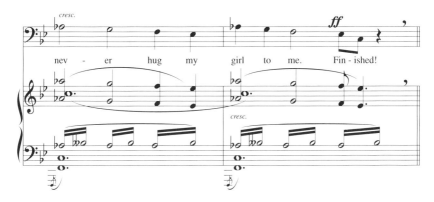

Ex. 14-13 Stephen Sondheim, *Sweeney Todd*, "Epiphany"
(No. 17), mm. 38–44.

"joy," with a terrifying clarity, only to give way once again to the diminished octave (m. 83) characteristic of the obsession motive (Ex. 14-14).

"Epiphany" is the central moment of the music drama. After this, all is really denouement. The corresponding event in the second act is the revelation to Todd of what Sondheim calls the "fatal knowledge." The Beggar Woman's leitmotif and the lyrical theme from "Epiphany" have always been related, both derived from long descending half-steps, but only here is the relationship made explicit. The inner voice counterpoint is maintained as Sondheim succeeds one motive with the other, but, ironically, this dramatic moment is revealed most clearly by the harmony. The beggar woman's motive has always begun with a tritone over the bass, while the lyrical theme began as a consonant third factor. When the chord changes from a harmony based on C in measure 1 to one on D-sharp in measure 3, the melodic F-sharp is brilliantly reinter-

Ex. 14-14 Stephen Sondheim, *Sweeney Todd*, "Epiphany" (No. 17), mm. 75–83.

preted and identified, matching the horrible realization in Todd's mind. The only thing missing: he is not singing.

Sondheim's idea of having Todd sing at last by choking on the lyrical theme in halting fashion is a beautiful one, but it is defeated by the counterpoint, of all things (Ex. 14-16). First, the complex inner part writing, and then Mrs. Lovett's babbling at much faster speed steal the listener's attention and obscure what should be the paramount expression. Even in the purely instrumental rendition (mm. 1–4, Ex. 14-15),

Ex. 14-15 Stephen Sondheim, *Sweeney Todd*, "Final Scene"
(No. 29), mm. B, 1–4.

the effect of the essential chord change is almost too subtle. The impact is also diffused because the dramatic associations with the lyrical theme are not clear. What exactly does it mean? Is it the price of revenge, or the sorrow at the loss of another loved one?

The opera ends with Todd's reprise of the first section of "There Was a Barber," followed by his death at the hands of Tobias and a recapitu-

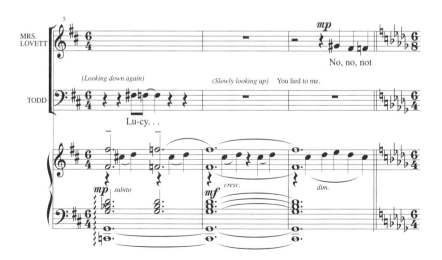

Ex. 14-16 Stephen Sondheim, *Sweeney Todd*, "Final Scene"
(No. 29), mm. 5–8e.

lation of the opening ballad by the cast. Todd's death seems necessary in some vague sense of tragic justice, but to use Tobias as the instrument is unconvincing. It is clear that the boy has a maternal affection for Mrs. Lovett, best expressed in the lovely "Not While I'm Around" in the second act, but by that time it seems too late, contrived. If he had given some sign of his deep gratitude when she fed his ravenous hunger with pies in the first act, that thread might have held.

The reprise of "There Was a Barber" also falls short of its intention. Since it is immediately followed by "The Ballad of Sweeney Todd," the reprise creates a structural symmetry with the beginning of the opera, but what does it offer besides elegance of form? What does it do for the moment? It recalls what the opera was about, of course, but such a reminder seems hardly necessary just after the disaster, and there is no transformation or alteration in the music suggesting that Todd has been changed, or that he has learned anything since then. One wonders whether Todd cared more for his wife or his justice. If the former, then the reprise is lacking in grief; if the latter, the scene of horrible recognition loses its power. The instructive comparison with this moment is the reprise of "Somewhere" in *West Side Story*. That song communicates what Tony and Maria have lost—their love, their hope for a life together—in musical terms that show how that loss grows from the tragic story. The transformation in setting and the extension at the end differentiate the new context of the song without losing its accumulated meaning. When Sondheim's finale fades, the question of what Todd has lost still lingers.

A number of writers criticized *Sweeney Todd* for a lack of dramatic focus. "The horrors are not entirely Grand Guignol jokes. They are not entirely tragic statements about the human condition, or protests of social rottenness, or studies of abnormal psychology. They attach themselves at one point or another to all of those things, but without a real hold on them."[34] Director Harold Prince fairly admitted as much: "I suppose people who are collaborating should be after the same thing, but Steven and I were obviously not with respect to Sweeney. I think it's also about impotence . . . . The reason that the ensemble is used the way it is, the unifying emotion for the entire company, is shared impotence. Obviously, Sweeney's is the most dramatic, to justify all those murders."[35] The disjunction may have had its effect on the New York production as a whole, but when the music and libretto are considered alone, the opera is admirably consistent in its musical dramatic point. Sondheim's idea of Sweeney obsessed is there in the notes for all to hear, but presented so subtly that it is too easily missed or overpowered by other aspects of stage production. A more sympathetic production would surely make this theme more powerful.

Within the purview of Sondheim's career it is surprising that *Sweeney Todd*, surely one of his most brilliant musical creations, is a show that violated principles of musical theater that he once proclaimed. Take the notion of converting a legitimate play:

Now lots of things can be a challenge—such as making a musical out of "Pygmalion." But personally, as much as I enjoyed "My Fair Lady," I don't think the challenge was really worth it. If I'd been asked to do it, I'd have said no. It was a fine play, so why mess around with it?[36]

Sweeney Todd, of course, comes from a play which the composer thought was "terrific." Next, the uses of rhyming in lyric:

One function of rhyme is that it shows intelligence and a controlled state of mind. . . . For the songs for the character of Fredrik, the lawyer in *A Little Night Music* . . . I used heavy rhyming because he is a man who rationalizes everything and does a lot of thinking.[37]

By this standard, Tobias Ragg merits a doctorate in literature for his masterful "Pirelli's Miracle Elixir," and yet even the stage directions describe him as a "simple-minded assistant." On the musical reprise:

I find the notion that the same lyric can apply in the first and the second act *very* suspect. Most of the time the character has moved beyond, particularly if you're telling a story of any weight or density.[38]

Yet, *Sweeney Todd*, with leitmotifs as the basis for its musical continuity, is a study in reprises. Finally, in a discussion of *West Side Story*, Sondheim's view on the theater's dependence on character:

. . . the show isn't very good . . . because the characters are necessarily one-dimensional. They're not people. What lasts in the theater is character, and there are no characters in *West Side*, nor can there be.[39]

How many "types" are there in *The Demon Barber of Fleet Street*?

Now it is not really fair to put Sondheim on trial as drama theorist, for his calling is a much higher one, and if these comments dating mostly from the early 1970s sound extraordinarily doctrinaire, perhaps

it is because they come on the heels of three award-winning shows—
Company, *Follies*, and *A Little Night Music*—that reflect very well that
atmospheric, static sort of drama that Sondheim's impressionistic style
serves so well. But how remarkable it is that the composer could adapt
such a style and predilection to the packed action of a thriller!

It seems more remarkable that he would go after such a project himself, without prodding from writers or producers who could not have
realized the immensity of the musical task. But then, Sondheim has
been accused of being intentionally and outlandishly innovative, of
tackling "things no one else would think of," and all of his mature
works contain a dramatic problem that appeared insoluble from the
start: the end of *Company*, the central theme of personal histories in
Follies, the reverse chronology in *Merrily We Roll Along*, the great chasm
of time and mood between the acts of *Sunday in the Park with George*,
coloring the subtlest shades of passion in *Passions*.

To every innovation, Sondheim can bring to bear the formidable
power of his lyrics, which at their best go beyond the cleverness and
jocularity of a Hart or Porter. Alan Rich described the experience of listening to an evening of Sondheim's music: "you constantly found yourself thinking—about words, about music, about great singers singing
great songs. It's not such a bad thing, now, is it—being treated in the
theater as if you just might be a grownup with a grownup's intelligence?"[40] But can the musical theater consist of thinking alone, without
feeling? The matter of Sondheim's music is brought round once again,
for in the end, the vitality of the work depends on its music, the language of feeling, even more than its lyrics.

Specifically, the fate of Sondheim's works rests on their vocal melodies,
what the singers have to sing, and of all musical aspects simple melody
is the deepest mystery. No one understands it. There is no theory that
accounts for melodic invention, that distinguishes the profoundly great
from the mundane. "Sondheim, side by side or upside down or right-
side up, is simply defective in invention. He can supply the necessary
changes for numbers like the opening chorus or the patter songs, which
are really only matters of mild rhythmic acuteness, music which need
not be—and isn't—memorable in itself. But when melody is absolutely
required, as in the love songs, Sondheim just spins series of notes,
which could just as easily be other notes."[41] A great deal of Stanley
Kauffmann's impression derives from the harmonic idiom, whose lack

of syntax makes the tunes at times seem equally undirected. But he touches on a severe critical question, whether Sondheim's music is capable of the deep emotions certain dramatic situations require. The paucity of popular hits, compared to, say, Rodgers and Hammerstein, could be a symptom, and the excuse that the songs are too closely wed to the situation for them to stand on their own will not do, not for the whole corpus. The music and lyrics of "I Got Plenty O' Nuttin'," "To Life," even "Non più andrai" for that matter, relate specifically to their situations, yet as separate songs and tunes they have done all right. Does so singular a harmonic idiom require a period of acculturation, perhaps, or is it fundamentally inappropriate?

If any show could make apology for Sondheim's emotional power, it would be *Sweeney Todd*. The love music for Anthony seems undeniably right, and even if the audience is never sure whether Todd feels more for his vengeful obsession than for his wife, the melodic climax in the first-act version of "There Was a Barber" shows what Sondheim's harmonic idiom can achieve.

All operas are flawed, of course, and Sondheim's shows, because they reach higher than any other current Broadway composer's, seem to ask for more severe critical standards. Thus their faults sometimes eclipse their virtues, but their virtues are nevertheless formidable. All have a dramatic integrity unsurpassed in the American musical theater, untainted by gimmicks or star vehicles.[42] They never insult the listener's intelligence and give back much for the effort the listener contributes, rewards, perhaps, other than emotional ones. Sondheim may well be Broadway's answer to Eric Bentley, who criticized the tradition in particular and opera in general as an unthinking medium. His place in American musical culture is indeed special, if not unique. One test of the vitality of contemporary music is to wonder who are the composers to whom the listening public eagerly looks for a new musical play. That public has of late become broadly commercialized and far-flung, and among those unwashed listeners Sondheim has little chance, but among theater *cognoscenti* there really is no one else.

Chapter 15

Epic as Musical

Vous me demandez ce qui me force à parler? une drôle de chose, ma conscience. . . . Ce n'est pas assez d'être heureux, il faut être content. *[You ask me what forces me to speak? a strange thing, my conscience. . . . It is not enough to be happy, one must be at peace.]*[1]

Jean Valjean

"I had always considered the idea of a French musical as a contradiction in terms," remarked Cameron Macintosh, recounting the production history of *Les Misérables*.[2] It is true that the French showed little patience with light opera in the twentieth century, and that even the most significant achievements of the Broadway tradition have bombed in Paris, but the real mismatch that should have given Macintosh no little pause is not between the musical and French tradition, but between the musical and the epic.

It is the epic and the drama that contradict one another, for all the defining features of an epic are precisely what the theater cannot have. The epic must have limitless horizons of time and space, not merely as backdrop for a story, but as a visceral component of the experience. We must feel the weight of the *Odyssey*'s twenty years and measure every foot of the universe from the pit to the empyrean in Dante. How can a three-hour production on 300 square meters accomplish the same? While the epic most often unifies around the fortunes of one man, an

Aeneas or a Ulysses, it encompasses dozens of other characters of all dimensions, a cast that particularizes the vast scope of the story through time and space. What drama can afford to establish so many roles? Indeed, the old classical unities of the theater—time (twenty-four hours), place, and action—amounted to wise counsel on the economy of means for a young dramatist, and they categorically exclude the epic.

If music is then added as a dramatic agent, music that almost always protracts every dramatic action while intensifying its emotional effect, it becomes clear why the epic opera is such a rarity. On those occasions when composers tried it, the stories are almost always transformed so that they are no longer epics. Thus the great Claudio Monteverdi, setting the Odyssey in *Il Ritorno d'Ulisse in Patria*, restricts himself to the psychological drama of Penelope caught between her desire for her husband's return and the pressure of the suitors to settle affairs. The opera is misnamed—it should be called *Penelope*—since Ulysses, deprived of the great wanderings and adventures, is ancillary to this central action. Monteverdi's work is constrained to one place and a single day, and as a measure of theater's economy the original 108 suitors are reduced to one countertenor, one tenor, and one bass. A great music drama it is, but it is not epic. Yes, Wagner's *Ring*, on the other hand, is indeed a true epic music drama, but remember that he requires four linked operas sung over four evenings to accomplish the feat.

Now consider that Victor Hugo's *Les Misérables* is an epic of epics. He wrote it in five "parts" of normal novel length, each of which is divided into many "books," which are further divided into chapters ranging from 1 to 20 pages. It is something over 560,000 words, about twice the length of *David Copperfield* and seven times that of *The Divine Comedy*. While the scope of the immediate plot runs only from 1817 to 1833 and takes place mostly in Paris, its components allow Hugo great digressions through French history and culture on topics ranging from Napoleon's defeat at Waterloo (60-odd pages) to the social significance of slang, from a comparison of monasticism in France and Spain to the medieval origins and structure of the sewers of Paris. The novel is nothing less than an encyclopedic tour of French civilization and in the reading one cannot avoid the impression that Hugo knows just about everything worth knowing in 1862.

He recognized the dimensions of his achievement. "At the end of his career, surveying his own works, he was more than ever convinced that the novel—his kind of novel—was a drama too big to be performed on any stage," writes Victor Brombert in *Victor Hugo and the Visionary Novel*.[3] It is true that many film directors have attempted *Les Misérables*, but no film version has made the cinematic canon, and in any case, the magic of montage has advantages over the stage that can begin to meet the demands of epic. As far as opera goes, Giaccomo Puccini agreed with Hugo when, after serious consideration and the success of *La Bohème*, he declined to take up the challenge of *Les Misérables* in 1901. Why, then, did two French collaborators, Alain Boublil and Claude-Michel Schönberg, take it on in the late 1970s?

Encouragement came from several sources. One was that of a successful, established collaboration. Boublil and Schönberg had already composed a rock opera, *La Révolution Française*, in anticipation of the bicentennial.[4] Another was the musical adaptation of a similar kind of novel of Charles Dickens, Lionel Bart's *Oliver*, which Boublil saw in London in 1979, the character of the Artful Dodger inspiring a musical Gavroche. Yet another must be the stature of *Les Misérables* in French culture. It is like *Huckleberry Finn*; every student preparing for the national BAC exam must read it, although few read all of it. Such a monument has a ready-made audience, while at the same time "I was well aware at the outset that such an enterprise would be regarded by the guardians of our heritage as an act of desecration."[5]

At first blush the potential for dramatization in *Les Misérables* must appear to be an embarrassment of riches. One could do a heroic biography of Jean Valjean as the moral progress of an individual, as Dickens has in *Nicholas Nickelby* or *David Copperfield*. Or, more generally, there is the well-tried triumph of good over evil:

> Le livre que le lecteur a sous les yeux en ce moment, c'est, d'un bout à l'autre, dans son ensemble et dans ses détails, . . . la marche du mal au bien . . . [The book which the reader has in front of his eyes at this moment is from one end to the other, in the whole and in its details, . . . the march from evil to good . . .] (*Les Misérables*, Part V, Book I, Chapter 20)

There is the love story between Cosette and Marius, complete with obstacles occasioned by political unrest and her father's illegal status. And there is the potential to make drama out of the novel's social criticism, although the history of such tracts on the musical stage is spotty.

All of these dramatic themes, and more besides, work beautifully in the novel, in part for the simple but essential reason that Hugo allows himself so vast a canvas that he can accommodate them all without the sacrifice of detail that drama must make. Traces of these themes are easily found, too, in Boublil and Schönberg's popular opera, but here such tradeoffs must be made and take their toll.

As a heroic biography the opera traces Jean Valjean's rise from the misery of a prison chain gang to the post of mayor of a small town near Paris, his rescue of the orphan Cosette from the hands of the evil couple *les Thénardiers*, how he saves her lover Marius on the street barricades of the revolutionaries by carrying him through the sewers, and finally how he dies a fulfilled and forgiven man, apparently of old age. Much of this has musical expression, which is all to the good because it provides a dramatic weight to make up for the lack of detailed narrative, but if the central action of the opera is Jean Valjean's life, why has he no part in the most stirring number, "Do You Hear the People Sing?" This inconsistency in the middle of the opera might be forgiven as an irresistible musical indulgence, but when the entire opera ends with this song utterly unconnected with Jean Valjean, the integrity of the heroic biography is negated at its climax.

There are characters galore who can personify the forces of good and evil: the bishop Myriel, the falsely accused Champmathieu, the outcast Fantine, and, blackest of all, *les Thénardiers*. In Jean Valjean himself and in Javert, the police commissioner who doggedly pursues him, there is even the potential to explore the nature of the good and its place in the social order, since Valjean, the good man, is technically a renegade parolee and Javert, the legal hound, merely carries out the letter of the law. Inconsistencies and nonsequiturs, however, defeat this interpretation. The great villains Thénardier get away clean. Even in Hugo this is a moral difficulty, but at least the rationale is clear: Marius must pay his dead father's debt of honor to this rascal who accidentally saved his life attempting to rob his corpse on the field at Waterloo. In the opera they show up unexplained at the wedding of Marius and Cosette and merrily take their leave with the silver, never to be seen again. The factory scene near the beginning of the opera appears as an icon of *les misérables*, that is, the underclass, but works at cross-purposes. If it is a sweatshop, as "At the End of the Day" would proclaim, then how can the owner, Monsieur le Maire Madeleine, alias Jean Valjean, be a good man? Later on, the libretto itself gives away this contradiction, when Jean Valjean, trying to decide in what should be a titanic struggle of conscience whether to reveal his identity to save the innocent Champmathieu, ruefully wonders what will become of his many workers who depend on his factory for their livelihood. The confusion arises from too dense a compression of Hugo, who makes it perfectly clear that Madeleine's factory, far from being an English workhouse, is the economic and civic salvation of Montreuil-sur-Mer, going so far as to detail the town's precipitous decline after Jean Valjean's arrest. It is difficult to play out an essay on good and evil if the symbols are so compromised. And then, what role has the love story in all this?

If the love story is the central action, then the same problem is inverted: what of the rest, the factories, the pursuit, the revolution? The love story in *Les Misérables* produces a lot of music ("Red and Black," "In My Life," "A Heart Full of Love," "One Day More," "On My Own," and even "A Little Fall of Rain") which attempts with some success to match the romantic intensity in Hugo, but he has the luxury of prolonging a simple if profound attraction over hundreds of pages with little hints and vignettes scattered among the principal events, so that when Marius finally approaches Cosette for the first time, her immediate, unblushing response with the intimate form of address strikes the perfect note of innocent passion. The opera must rush things, and the one obstacle, Jean Valjean, hardly surfaces before it is resolved. Inflating the role of Eponine from the waif in Hugo who barely recognizes her own infatuation with Marius to a formidable torchbearer in the opera— she has more love music than Cosette—is how the collaborators try to inject some substance into this love plot, but without more time for development it rings false.

The publicity for the show trumpeted Hugo's theme of political and social consciousness, particularly in the poster child Cosette, and more disingenuously in the slogan evoking "the spirit of 1789," the French revolution that is completely outside the story. As a marketing strategy social consciousness would naturally appeal to Americans, but it does not make dramatic sense in the opera. The virtue of the downtrodden class is compromised from the start when Fantine is cast out by her own comrades at the glass factory ("At the End of the Day"). The contention of critic Laurence M. Porter that Hugo's "major theme is that poverty dehumanizes"[6] cannot explain *les Thénardiers*, who seem not abjectly poor and yet never reform, nor Jean Valjean, who reforms himself with only the help of God.

Then there are the idealistic students, the revolutionaries, and the barricades which made the staging of Les Misérables so famous. Here is the heroic fight for the rights of men, but what rights? Where exactly is the tyranny? "Do You Hear the People Sing?" aims at rousing the blood, and its martial rhythms, brassy orchestration, and above all its climactic harmonic structure succeed admirably on the level of emotion, but on the political level the most specific thing it can tell the audience is that it is the song of "a people that will not be slaves again." It is exciting to watch, but this revolution has no dramatic substance, and that may well be Hugo's intention. Why, if he wished to inspire his readers with fervor for republicanism or socialism or some other politics, would he choose the insurgency of June 5–6, 1832, an uprising so minor in the turmoil of the early 1830s that general histories of France do not even mention it?[7] The politics of the barricades is not at issue here; rather, it is how the futility of the uprising affects the lives of the major characters. In the novel, the military conclusion is forgone before the first shot is fired. Everyone there knows he is about to die. For Marius, and to a lesser extent Jean Valjean, participation, at least initially, is merely an exalted form of suicide.

The insurgency of 1832 is not the story but part of the scenery. Like the small-town life of Montreuil-sur-Mer, like the culture of the convent, the battle of Waterloo, the layout of the sewers, the barricades are one weave of the great tapestry into which Hugo's characters are set. The novel is epic, but also historical, not mythological. Details are real, and the plot is a nexus of story, moral, culture, and history that does not easily admit simplification. This is why the creators of the opera could not settle on any one of the tempting offerings of the novel, for making one a credible dramatic action requires an intolerable disfiguring of the whole that threatens credibility. Shall they cut all the action before Paris in order to focus on the love story? Then Jean Valjean's hatred of Marius is inexplicable. Shall they cut the love story? Then Jean Valjean's final crisis has no motivation and no meaning. It is all intertwined.

And yet the great danger of trying to dramatize everything while falling short is sentimentality, the common criticism of both London and New York reviewers of Les Misérables. Sentimentality here is nothing more than cueing the audience for an emotional response to scenes inadequately prepared. Jean Valjean dies over the pleading of Marius and Cosette and is welcomed into eternal peace by Fantine and Eponine. He sings the same ballad that Fantine sang at her own death; the melody soars upward, the orchestra swells. To paraphrase Joseph Kerman's criticism of *Tosca*, the audience can have a good cry at Jean Valjean's expense. For his melody has been used by Eponine as a torch song ("On My Own"), so its meaning is compromised, and what is she doing here, anyway? What is the meaning of Jean Valjean's death, other than to make the opera stop? The music has no answer.

This conflict of dramatic integrity and musical economy that is the burden of all music dramatists is evident in the great changes that took place between the original French version and the version prepared at the instigation of Cameron Macintosh and his colleagues of the Royal Shakespeare Company. *Les Misérables* followed the trail blazed by Andrew Lloyd Webber with *Jesus Christ Superstar*. Its first incarnation was not a stage production at all, but a "concept album" with French lyrics by Alain Boublil and sung by a French cast. After successful sales, a stage version ran for 105 performances at the Paris Palais des Sports in 1980. Then Macintosh took an interest, asked lyricist James Fenton and then Herbert Kretzmer to make an English adaptation for London audiences, opened it in 1985, and brought it to Broadway on March 12, 1987. The English version is no simple translation, but a thorough revision of the whole opera. (Figure 15-1 compares the two versions.)

The hand of the composer is strongest in the French version with its admirable classical symmetries. Here the opera opens with the sparkling ostinato that comes to be Jean Valjean's leitmotif (see Fig. 15-2, top staff) in the key of A-flat major ("Prologue" in Fig. 15-1). This leads directly to the factory song in the relative key, F minor ("La Journée Est Finie) and the tonality remains focused on F throughout this scene and then into Fantine's first big song, "L'Air de la Misère." This becomes "Come to Me" in the English version, but rather than sentimentalize the daughter who has not yet been on stage, "La Misère" speaks directly to the ravages of poverty. At the end of the opera the A-flat/F polarity is reversed: Jean Valjean sings the melody of "La Misère" with new words in F ("Epilogue"), followed by the F minor introduction to that song which then eases elegantly into the relative A-flat major. Now the "Jean Valjean ostinato" is heard for the last time, in a high register, the ascent to heaven. Schönberg composes the opera's midpoint, the finale to Act I ("Demain"), also

	Work Song
	Valjean Arrested
	Valjean Forgiven
	What Have I Done
Prologue	Prologue
La Journée Est Finie	At the End of the Day
L'Air de la Misère	
Les Beaux Cheveux	
J'Avais Revé	I Dreamed
(La Nuit)	Lovely Ladies
	(Lovely Hair)
	Who Am I?
Dites-moi	
Fantine Et M. Madelaine	Come to Me
	Confrontation
Mon Prince Est En Chemin	Castle on a Cloud
Mam'zelle Crapaud	
La Devise	Master of the House
Valjean Chez Thénardier	
La Valse Fourberie	Waltz of Treachery
Donnez, Donnez	Look Down
	Stars
Rouge Et Noir	Red and Black
Les Amis ABC	
Volonté du Peuple	Do You Hear the People Sing?
Dans La Vie: Cosette	In My Life: Cosette
Dans La Vie: Marius	In My Life: Marius
Voilà Le Soir	
Le Coeur Au Bonheur	A Heart Full of Love
	Plumet Attack
L'Un Vers L'Autre	
La Faute a Voltaire	
La Nuit de l'Angoisse	
Demain	One Day More
Ce N'Est Rien	
L'Aube Du 6 Juin	Upon These Stones
	On My Own
	Upon These Stones

	Javert/Little People
	First Attack
	Little Fall of Rain
	Drink with Me
	Bring Him Home
	Dog Eats Dog
Noir Ou Blanc	Javert's Suicide
La Mort de Gavroche	
Marius Et M. Gillnormand	
	Turning
	Empty Chairs
Le Mariage	Wedding
	Beggars at the Feast
L'Aveu de JV	
Marchange / Révélation	
Épilogue	Finale

Fig. 15-1 Sequence of songs in the French recording and
the English stage production of *Les Misérables*. Directly facing titles
are different versions of the same music (contrafacta).

around the ostinato, but removed to the distant key of A major, and so the
opera's design has a Mozartean harmonic balance, beginning and ending
in one key, with the middle at an extreme harmonic tension.

The French version can also boast of some remarkably efficient
sequences that help relieve the conflicts of epic and drama. The linked
ensembles of "Dites-moi" and "Fantine et M. Madeleine" introduce
Javert's rectitude with a vengeance, and outline the episode of Fantine's
arrest, the mayor's intervention, and vows to help Cosette in less than
three and one-half minutes, no small feat in opera. On the other hand
"Marius et M. Gillenormand" completely fails to compress the complex
relationship of Marius with his guardian uncle, a character whom the
audience has never met before, and this piece was wisely dropped from
the English adaptation.

The English version dispenses with the neat symmetries of musical
structure. It ends with the same F/A-flat sequence even though "Do
You Hear the People Sing?" replaces the Jean Valjean leitmotif, but the

fanfares that open the opera are set, inexplicably, in E-flat minor, which is then abruptly shifted upward to F minor for "Work Song." There is no compositional reason why the English version could not have begun in A-flat as did the French, but perhaps Macintosh and his colleagues preferred to establish the dark atmosphere immediately.[8]

In general, the English version pushes the social and political messages harder, although with a more popular, less feminist, and less moralizing slant; that explains the much expanded music for the barricades. Nevertheless, the four completely new songs "Valjean Forgiven" for Bishop Myriel, "Stars" for Javert, "Bring Him Home" for Jean Valjean, and "Dog Eats Dog" for Thénardier are all important character statements.

The one moment in the opera when the creators manage to harness the complexity of Hugo's plot to the advantage, rather than the defeat, of music drama is the finale to the first act ("One Day More"). At this point the story has most of the main characters in crisis. Jean Valjean begins by wondering about his next move, now that his identity has been discovered by Thénardier and his cronies. Marius and Cosette, cut off from one another, despair of their future life together while the insurgent Enjolras asks Marius where he stands. Javert looks forward to crushing the revolt and *les Thénardiers* lick their chops over the bodies soon to fall from the barricades. The number works very much like the great quintet from *West Side Story*.[9] Jean Valjean sings a rapidly paced solo and then yields the floor as Schönberg layers on the characters one by one. Thus the finale builds, in classic style, from modest beginnings to a full-throated chorus, maintaining all the while the dramatic intensity of separate characters in conflict.

Even the reprise idea from Bernstein's quintet appears here, but much expanded so that it dominates the piece (see Fig. 15-2). The first music is the shimmering ostinato, Jean Valjean's leitmotif, and to that backdrop he sings a new text to the melody of "Who Am I?", which formerly set his agony of conscience over whether to save the innocent Champmathieu. Then Marius enters, soon followed by Cosette in parallel thirds, with a contrafactum for Fantine's "I Dreamed." Javert makes his threats with the same music with which he arrested Fantine. Finally *les Thénardiers* recapitulate, with new lyrics, "Master of the House." Every melody has been heard before, and they all fit contrapuntally, thanks mostly to Schönberg's penchant for a clearly functional, slow harmonic underpinning to his songs. This complex of reprises

Fig. 15-2 The various themes of "One Day More"
superimposed on the repeating bass line.

brings with it a wealth of semantic referents, that is, all the accumulated meanings acquired over the course of the first act, and the experience is rich indeed. Like Bernstein's ensemble, this finale dramatizes by
using music to contrast simultaneous yet dissimilar actions.

And there is one new melody, after all, a repeating, slow, descending
A major scale in the bass, a real *passacaille* that harks back in French
opera tradition all the way to Lully and the *tragédie lyrique*. As a melody
the scale seems like the simplest bass ostinato one could imagine, but it
is a device of great harmonic power, because the moving bass notes give
the impression of changing chords while all the while, on the more
abstract level of experience, they project a rock-solid harmonic center
against which all this motion pushes and pulls.[10]

The principal successes of the music in *Les Misérables* apart from this
finale are mostly in establishing characters and tableaux.

Alain Boublil described his libretto as "three acts, seven tableaux" and
indeed the French recording suggests at times not so much a complete

adaptation of Hugo's story but rather a series of reminiscences, not unlike a musical revue, as a solution to the problem of dramatic epic.[11] *Jesus Christ Superstar*, which figured significantly in Boublil's background, works pretty much in this way. Such a strategy depends upon a knowledgeable audience to fill in with imagination the missing continuity of plot (there are aides-memoire in the recording notes), and in France that could be taken for granted with *Les Misérables*. Thus the song "Mon Prince Est En Chemin" (later, "Castle on a Cloud") explains nothing of little Cosette's plight, yet dramatizes her situation with music of short phrases and simple rhythms, much like a nursery rhyme song, a poignant clash of innocence in her singing and menace in her surroundings. On the other hand, other pieces, notably the rebuke of Fantine in "La Journée Est Finie" and the music of the barricades, are clearly plot-music, with more explanation than reflection written into the lyrics, and so the tableaux reading is weakened. In the English version it is eclipsed altogether.

That does not hamper Schönberg's powers of characterization. Like most modern musical composers, he commands a number of idioms whose semantics can efficiently sketch a character's personality or situation. A good example is the revolutionary summons "Do You Hear the People Sing?", for its rhythms and phrase structure instantly call to mind all the marching songs heard in parade (for instance, the first three phrases have the same rhythm as the American Civil War song "Tramp, tramp, tramp"). Similarly, "The Innkeepers Song (Master of the House)" is a music hall sendup that instantly establishes *les Thénardiers* as a comic duo rather than Hugo's scoundrels, although this impression cannot last. A more sophisticated case is the "Waltz of Treachery," sung by *les Thénardiers* when they negotiate with an obviously well-to-do stranger for the custody of Cosette. The combination of the waltz tempo and phrasing with a modernist, slippery chromaticism that retains the tonality while mixing its mode, alternating major and minor, all strike just the right tone of sycophancy, hypocritical grief, and pretended gentility. When for the last verse the couple sings the odd chromatic waltz in parallel fifths, there is a note of menace, too. In very short order the audience learns just what kind of folk these innkeepers are.

Although such extreme chromaticism is exceptional in the score, in general Schönberg's music has a rich harmonic vocabulary combined with a lucid, almost classical sense of form. "Come to Me," in some ways the signature ballad of the opera and one of the best, is a fine example.

Here is the slow harmonic rhythm carried by the bass line so evident in the finale to Act I, and the excellent use of subsidiary key relations, first to articulate the harmonic goal of the dominant and the end of the second phrase (m. 18) and then as a sudden source of color that sets up a long subdominant (m. 19, V of ii). The phrasing seems periodic to the ear, but the time signature changes evince a subtle metric shifting of the last phrase, so that the half cadence in measure 22 actually comes one beat late (the extra beat is in the 3/4 bar). That is why the cascade of

Ex. 15-1 No. 5 "Fantine's Death," mm. 14–22.

quick syllables so reminiscent of much French popular music projects
a sincere outpouring of emotion here, because it breaks Schönberg's
phrase pattern without seeming to, without violating the structural
integrity of the song.

Ex. 15-2 No. 5 "Fantine's Death," mm. 23–32.

For higher-level expressions and structures Schönberg resorts to real modulations, particularly those of the relative major and minor keys, but sometimes more distant ones. For the release of "Come to Me" (Ex. 15-2) Jean Valjean shifts to the parallel mode, F minor, appropriately enough. Once there, Schönberg can use this simple change to open the door, in a fashion most traditional, to all the other related flat keys. Thus the second phrase already cadences in D-flat (m. 25). Fantine's phrase moves to B-flat minor, another traditional relation, but Schönberg's choice of a G minor harmony for the downbeat of measure 29 is more radical, more expressive than expected, and prefigures the luminous D-natural on Fantine's highest note. This is not only a peak of expressive intensity but also a mode shift which takes the music into the vicinity of the home key of F major to begin the last refrain ("My Cosette . . .").

So Schönberg's harmonic vocabulary can be richly expressive; alas, modulations can also be used wastefully, as when Fantine's last refrain in "I Dreamed" hikes up from E-flat major to F, or when the accumulated harmonic power of A major in the first act finale ("One More Day") is short-circuited by a midway modulation in the English version and terminal modulations in both versions. Compared to the expressions of "Fantine's Death," these are cheap thrills. But not really so cheap, because like any profligate technique, the expressive capacity of a modulation can be weakened much as an overused currency is devalued.

Schönberg's harmonic shifts and clarity of form are generally ill-served by the libretto, particularly the English one. Much of the mismatch derives, once again, from the need to advance this operatically impossible plot as quickly as possible, which works precisely against Schönberg's need to lay out a clear melodic-harmonic form even as simple as A A B A. The composer needs time, and the librettist hasn't got it. Why should Jean Valjean, when he finally pries Cosette loose from *les Thénardiers*, sing the same cynical waltz of theirs? As does Marius as he rejoices to Cosette after having discovered that her father saved him? Dramatically, it is senseless, but the creators cannot afford the stage time to develop a new musical event more appropriate to the expression. So here the interests of musical form win out over fidelity to character and lyric. Sometimes the opposite occurs. When the third verse of "At the End of the Day" suddenly shifts from F minor to F major and launches a chromatic sequence before falling back to its harmonic origin, the changes in rhythm and orchestration do tingle the spine, but there is nothing in the lyric that justifies such a thrill.

At other moments the lyrics can be simply awkward or fall into cliché: "Will we ever meet again?", "What a life I might have known", and "And I swear I will be true." Can these lines, all sung within ten seconds' time in the first act finale, not have already been heard in fifty Tin Pan Alley songs? The first important sung motive of the English version, the insistent fourth always rising from degrees 5 to 1 (i.e., sol–do), will seem odd to any experienced listener when the words are "Look down." Thénardier singing to the moon while deep in the sewers must also puzzle the audience ("Dog Eats Dog"). But the most irritating feature of Kretzmer's lyrics is the unpredictable lapses into blank verse, as if he had suddenly lost the rhyming dictionary. The periodic phrasing and clear forms of Schönberg's songs demand the analogous structure of a rhymed verse. These blank verses fall on the ear like bricks.

One matter of music and lyrics which is surely of joint responsibility is another latent influence of *Superstar*, the abundant reliance on contrafactum in the opera (see Fig. 15-3).

The Broadway tradition has shown time and again how powerful the reprise of a song in a new dramatic context can be, and how, especially in the work of Andrew Lloyd Webber, the general notion of musical referent can be expanded to encompass the contrafactum, the recurrence of a melody with entirely new lyrics that perform a new dramatic function. Moreover, the thorough use of contrafactum can unify an opera that otherwise might be fragmented by the variety of idioms employed for expressive effect, and there is no doubt that *Les Misérables* is so unified. The original music of the piece probably amounts to about forty-five minutes, but this source material is altered and stretched and recombined so that the three-hour opera plays out with abundant self-references. It sounds all of a piece.

The risk of this strategy is a fatal vacuity of meaning for what otherwise might be a powerful song, owing to the fragility of the relations between words and music. The listener learns the meaning of a tune or leitmotif in music drama first by associating the words sung with the music he hears, and with the dramatic situation at hand.[12] But that association is tenuous because in general the semantic potential of a musical passage is broad, that is, capable of many meanings. Should the

NO.TITLE	ENGLISH SOURCES	FRENCH SOURCES
ACT I		
Prologue		
The Chain Gang		Donnez; Bonjour Paris
On Parole		Beaux cheveux
The Bishop		Dites-moi
Valjean's Solil.		Noir ou blanc
1. At the End		La Journée est Finie
2. I Dreamed		J'avais revé
3. The Docks:		
Lovely ladies	On Parole	La nuit; Beaux cheveux
Fantine's arrest	The Bishop;	Dites-moi
4. The Cart Crash	On Parole; Bishop	Beaux cheveux; Dites
Trial (Who Am I?)		Demain
5. Fantine's Death		Epilogue; La Misère
Confrontation	Chain Gang; Dreamed	Bonjour; J'avais revé
6. Little Cosette		Mon prince
7. Innkeeper's Song		Le devise carabetier
8. The Bargain	Dreamed	J'avais revé
Waltz of Treachery		La valse fourberie
10. Stars		
11. The Beggars	Chain; Confront.	Donnez; Bonjour;
12. The Robbery	Parole; Chain;	Beaux; Bonjour;
	Waltz;	La valse
Javert Intervenes	Valjean's Sol.;	Noir ou blanc
	Bishop	Dites-moi
13. ABC Café (Red		Les amis ABC; Rouge
and Black)		et noir;
14. The People's Song		A la volonté du peuple
15. Rue Plumet (In		Dans ma vie
My Life)		
16. Heart Full of Love		Le coeur au bonheur
17. Plumet Attack	Parole	La nuit qui tombe;
		Beaux cheveux;
18. One Day More	Who Am I; Dreamed;	Demain
	Bishop; Innkeeper	

ACT II

19. Building Barricade	ABC; Beggars; Trial;	Les amis; Donnez;
On My Own	Fantine's Death	La misère
Back at Barr.	Red and Black	Rouge et noir
20. Javert at Barricade		La faute de Voltaire
	Bishop;	Dites-moi
Little Fall of Rain		Ce n'est rien
21. First Attack	Parole;	Beaux cheveux
23. The Night:		
Drink with Me		Souviens-toi
Bring Him Home		
24. The Second Attack	Javert at Barricade	La faute de Voltaire
25. Final Battle	People's Song	La volonté
26. The Sewers (Dog Eats Dog)		
27. Javert's Suicide	Valjean's Sol.	Noir ou blanc
The Victims	Lovely Ladies	La nuit
28. The Café Song	The Bishop	
29. Marius and Cosette	Heart Full of Love	Le coeur au bonheur
Valjean's Confess.	Who Am I?	
30. Wedding	Waltz of Treachery	Le mariage; La valse
	Innkeeper's Song	Le devise;
Epilogue	Bring Him Home	
	Fantine's Death	La misère
	People's Song	A la volonté

Fig. 15-3 Diagram of contrafactum use in the English version of *Les Misérables*. Numeration is that of the vocal score derived from the Palace Theatre production in London, published Cameron Mackintosh (Overseas) Ltd., 1986. Nos. 10 and 22 were cut.

same melody be then set to a lyric with a completely different purpose, that melody's power of expression is lost. Imagine a college campus where a new slang word refers to something different with each utterance. Before long it means nothing at all.

The contrafactum can work wonders if the lyric sets are chosen from roughly the same semantic range. It is perfectly right for the "Work

Song" of the convicts and "Look Down" of the beggars to have the same music, and it might even make the political point that poverty and crime are two faces of the same social ill. But what does it mean when Javert, rationalizing his oncoming suicide, sings to the same music that set Jean Valjean's conversion by the bishop? A good stretch of the imagination might conclude that these men are alter egos so that their spiritual wrestling matches deserve the same treatment, but such an interpretation works at cross-purposes with the other dramatic themes of the opera. And this is what happens with overuse of the contrafactum: the semantic edge of the music is dulled to near uselessness.[13] The descending diminished fourths and tritone leaps first heard when the farmer and innkeeper spurn Jean Valjean for his yellow parole passport are heard again when Fantine sells her hair, when the cart crashes, and eventually mean nothing more than "something bad is going on." While it may be reasonable for Jean Valjean to recall Fantine's death song ("Come to me") at his own demise, there is no reason for Eponine to convert it to a torch song ("On My Own"). Similarly, to sing again the evocative, half-mournful, half-hopeful melody by which Bishop Myriel charges Jean Valjean to change his life as a sentimental reminiscence of the dead students in "Empty Chairs" is a waste of a precious resource, musical semantics.

The misuse of the bishop's charge is, upon reflection, particularly regrettable because this music could have played a major role in constructing the opera around Hugo's most obviously dramatic theme: the drama of the conscience.

In the course of this epic novel, Jean Valjean endures four crises of conscience. The first is a conversion: Bishop Myriel's intervention and generosity prompt a classic self-examination of conscience, finding of fault, and resolution to reform. The second is a test of that resolution, an unforgettable portrayal of a dark night of the soul, when Jean Valjean decides to save the demented, unknown, insignificant Champmathieu who is mistaken by the authorities for himself. The third comes when he discovers that Cosette, who taught the hardened convict Jean Valjean how to love another person in her, now loves another. This crisis is the most obliquely drawn by Hugo, but it is no less real, and reminiscent of another operatic Hugo character who loves his daughter too possessively—Rigoletto. Even while carrying Marius through the sewers his spirit contradicts his actions: "Jean Valjean déchira sa chemise, banda les plaies le mieux qu'il put et arrêta le sang qui coulait; puis, se penchant dans ce demi-jour sur Marius toujours sans connaissance et presque sans souffle, il le regarda avec une inexprimable haine." (*Les Misérables* Part V, Book 3, chap.4) [Jean Valjean tore his shirt, bound the wounds as best he could and stopped the flow of blood; then, bending over Marius still unconscious and almost without breath in the half-light, he looked at him with an inexpressible hatred.] The final crisis, compared to which the Champmathieu affair was "nothing," is brought on by the happy marriage. Jean Valjean concludes that his police record threatens Cosette's good name and happiness if he lives in their home. He cuts himself off from her, and the unutterable pain of the separation kills him.

The drama of the conscience ties together all the principal scenes that Boublil wanted to include in his opera. Even the barricades can remain, since Hugo's Jean Valjean, in despair brought on by his discovery of the love-match, joins the revolutionaries at first to get himself killed, and then, in a paradox of spirit, remains to take the wounded Marius away from the carnage. And in fact the two versions of *Les Misérables*, in different ways, realize in music three of these crises, groping, perhaps unconsciously, for the thread of dramatic action that will run throughout the opera.

The great gap in the French version is the missing prologue set in the bishop's town of Digne. This is the clearest sign that Boublil might have originally conceived the opera as selected tableaux that assumed an audience familiar with the plot, since nothing that Jean Valjean does has any motivation without the conversion scene. This essential action the English version provides. The music for that scene begins to dramatize the spiritual progress of Jean Valjean, first in the brief but evocative charge by Bishop Myriel, and then, at greater length, in Jean Valjean's soliloquy. Here the rapid modal shifts between F major and F minor—a principal key of the French version—mirror his struggle, Hugo's darkness and light. Then follows immediately the shimmering ostinato that is Jean Valjean's leitmotif (Fig. 15-2, top staff). It merely covers the scene change, so its meaning is yet unclear. Had Schönberg composed it into the conversion scene, it would have been a succinct and flexible musical symbol of Jean Valjean's conscience.

It nearly takes on that meaning as it glitters above the main melody of "Who Am I?" at the crux of the Champmathieu episode, another interpolation of the English version that clarifies both plot and action. What is needed now is semantic reinforcement and the opportunity comes in the first act finale, into which the ostinato has already been composed. But Jean Valjean's worry here is how he will react to Thénardier's threats. A little massaging of Hugo's plot might have turned this soliloquy within the ensemble into a crisis of conscience over Cosette and Marius, whether Jean Valjean should remove his daughter from a threat to his possession of her, far more important to him than being discovered by the police. Then the original French lyric "Comment faire?" [What to do?] would make more sense here and, most important, the ostinato could become a window for the audience, a window into Jean Valjean's spirit. Then the first act finale would not only summarize the conflicting intentions of all the protagonists but would clarify the dramatic action.

With the last and greatest struggle both versions falter. The French at least recognizes it as a struggle of conscience, as Jean Valjean sings over nonfunctional harmony "Se je me tais, je me damne; si je parle, c'est moi qui me condamne" [If I keep silent, I damn myself; if I speak, I condemn myself]. The English version transfers these lines to the "Who am I?" crisis of Act I, but inexplicably changes the lyrics here to superfluous mumblings about Cosette's welfare. If any moment in the opera demanded a true reprise, this would be it. In both versions, the musical setting of this scene is cursory; Jean Valjean's last crisis has no musical depth.

This reduces the novel's tremendous last scene into a mere ending brought on by the death of the main character rather than the climax of dramatic action it might have been. Porter calls the reuniting of Cosette and Jean Valjean "one of the most pathetic scenes in literature," but remember that it can have such pathos only because the reader has seen with what indignity Jean Valjean slunk out of Marius's household, has seen how every evening thereafter he left his own shabby room simply to approach the street where he knew Cosette lived, has seen how these nocturnal walks became ever shorter until he barely left his room, and then did not leave at all. The reader experiences all the sacrifices of separation and loneliness and, most important of all, knows why they are made. He sees Jean Valjean killed by his own conscience.

Without witnessing all this, the opera finale is not pathetic, merely sentimental. The English version exploits the sentiment by bringing on stage the spirits of Fantine and Eponine to escort Jean Valjean to God. Hugo has a spirit there too, but his dramatic vision is far more consistent: when Jean Valjean is asked if he would like a priest, he replies "I have one."

> Et, du doigt, il sembla désigner un point au-dessus de sa tête où l'on eût dit qu'il voyait quelqu'un. Il est probable que l'évêque assistait à cette agonie. (*Les Misérables* Part V, Book 9, Chapter 5)

> [And he seemed to indicate with his finger a point over his head where one would have said that he saw someone. It is probable that the bishop was present at this agony.]

In the drama of conscience, what better spirit could there be?[14]

The contrafactum of "Come to Me" for Jean Valjean's dying words is semantically appropriate, but in its musical form this song is the least apt for a finale because Schönberg has composed his beautiful melody to lead to a structural half-cadence. The melody has no ending and must lead to something else. In the French version, the composer wisely recapitulates the modal, recitative-like introduction to the main song and then simply allows it to cadence in the relative key of A-flat major with which the opera began. The last thing heard is the shimmering ostinato, which must represent the ascent of Jean Valjean's spirit, but without the English conversion scene that is all it can mean. It could have meant so much more.

The solution in the English version fails its test of conscience and falls into the old Broadway temptation of bringing back a great tune for the last curtain, regardless of its dramatic propriety. There is a pregnant pause on the last tense high C of Jean Valjean's song, sustaining the word "God." After the dominant harmony has disappeared, the C is harmonically reinterpreted also in A-flat major, but with the opening phrase of "Do You Hear the People Sing?" The whole company eventually joins in this intimate scene. This is a complete betrayal of the drama of conscience, or any conceivable dramatic action for that matter, but the anthem does make the audience stand up.

No one can be sure that the drama of conscience would have worked, if only because all the problems of dramatizing an epic with music remain, well, epic. If the ancillary characters have no musical substance, then the sacrifices of conscience are rendered irrelevant. The audience must believe, through music somehow, that Fantine is worth saving, that the factory will go bankrupt, that Cosette means absolutely everything to Jean Valjean, that Marius loves her irrevocably. Subplots which populate the epic may be simplified to an extent but never slighted or made insignificant. They must have the songs that make them real dramatic agents. All of this takes time and space. For the epic these are superabundant; for the music drama, never enough.

Chapter 16

Epilogue

A statistician might well be uncomfortable with conclusions drawn from a sample of seventeen about a population of more than a thousand. Musical plays, however, like other artworks, do not behave like voters, and the power and character of an artistic tradition can hardly be judged by methods of random sampling. Most plays will have barely closed before they are forgotten, but some out of the thousand will make a more lasting impression and bear upon subsequent productions. A very few will become pillars of the tradition, to be heard and studied by everyone who thereafter participates in it; some of them have been the concern of this book. Since their influence on the tradition is out of all proportion to their number, it is fair to make a few observations about this select group of musical plays. What does it say about the tradition of American musical theater?

Any tradition of art is first of all a collection of artists with a common purpose. That purpose, to make music drama, is found in the Broadway tradition again and again, but beyond that there is in this group of two dozen composers, lyricists, and librettists a homogeneity so remarkable that it nearly suggests a predestination for their appointed achievements. To begin with, all are Caucasian males, and all grew up in rather advantageous surroundings. In some cases this simply meant money—Kern, Gershwin, Rodgers, and Bernstein were the sons of successful businessmen—and in others it meant an early appreciation of serious learning and music in particular. Frank Loesser's father and brother were classical pianists of note; Frederic Loewe's father was a world-class opera singer in Vienna; Andrew Lloyd Webber's was the director of the Royal College of Music in London; Stephen Sondheim spent his teenage years living next door to Oscar Hammerstein.

Almost all were American immigrants or sons of immigrants, and the group is completely dominated by Jewish-Americans. Now it is well to remember that the Broadway musical tradition has a geographical center in New York City, which has been home for many Jewish-Americans and Jewish immigrants throughout the twentieth century, but the singular influence of this particular ethnic group is nonetheless astonishing. Of the twenty composers and lyricists studied here, Jewish-Americans are in the vast majority; only Cole Porter, Andrew Lloyd Webber and his partner Tim Rice (both British), and Alain Boublil and Claude-Michel Schönberg (both French) may be counted out with certainty.

Perhaps it is this similarity of family background and experience that allowed the many significant partnerships to work so well. Musical composition is not by nature a collaborative enterprise, but in the theater it must be, and the best Broadway composers seem to have thrived on such collaboration. Indeed, it would be fair to say that several of Broadway's most notable names—Richard Rodgers, Leonard Bernstein, and Stephen Sondheim among them—might not have survived as popular songwriters without the theater. The requirements of drama were a most necessary stimulus.

Collaboration in the musical theater meant not only that a composer might work with a lyricist and a librettist, but also a director, an orchestrator, a choreographer, a set designer, and all the other technicians of the stage, to say nothing of actors and actresses. It is remarkable that this survey, which has sought a wide variety of composers, has repeatedly turned up the same names in all the other posts: Rouben Mamoulian, Moss Hart, Jerome Robbins, Agnes de Mille, Michael Bennett, Harold Prince, Boris Aronson, and Robert Russell Bennett. How necessary their contributions are to the enduring qualities of the best plays is difficult to say, since dance routines, sets, and subtleties of direction are much more fragile and less easily transmitted than music and lyrics, but the list suggests an intricate network of acquaintances that underlay the great variety of musical productions.

One focal point of the network might be Oscar Hammerstein II, who with Jerome Kern wrote *Show Boat*. His most famous and fruitful association was with Richard Rodgers, of course, but he also worked with Moss Hart, who much later directed Lerner and Loewe's *My Fair Lady*. The choreographer for that show, Hanya Holm, also did Cole Porter's *Kiss Me, Kate*. Rodgers and Hammerstein wanted Rouben Mamoulian to direct both *Oklahoma!* and *Carousel* after having seen what he had accomplished with Gershwin's *Porgy and Bess*. Another focal point would be Stephen Sondheim, who began his career working with Leonard Bernstein and Jerome Robbins. Robbins later directed Bock and Harnick's *Fiddler on the Roof*. Sondheim's landmark *Company* involved the talents of director-producer Harold Prince, later the director of Webber and Rice's *Evita*, and choreographer Michael Bennett, the creator with Marvin Hamlisch of *A Chorus Line*. The most improbable line of all, in retrospect, is that which connects the two centers, Sondheim and Hammerstein, since they would appear to represent opposite poles within the limited aesthetic of the Broadway theater. Sondheim once asked Hammerstein to sit in on a run-through of *West Side Story*. Hammerstein, who could never have written such a piece himself, nevertheless admired it, but suggested that the fire escape scene needed a song that "soared."[1] His pupil and Leonard Bernstein turned that suggestion into "Tonight," the central melody of that scene and the great quintet. The connection, however improbable, was real.

The artists of Broadway built a network of collaboration, tutelage, and friendship that is the musical theater. To refer to such a community as a "tradition" is certainly justified; one might even call it an artistic "school."

The history of the tradition has some curious parallels with the history of European opera. Broadway has had its founding father in Jerome Kern, its boy genius who died young in George Gershwin, its long-lived and expert practitioner of inherited forms in Richard Rodgers, and its reformer in Stephen Sondheim. But the dependence of the musical tradition on the techniques and prevailing style of nineteenth-century opera goes far beyond coincidence, to the heart of the tradition.

Simplified though they may be, operatic techniques show up throughout the best musical plays. The ancient recitative-aria scheme survives in the verse-refrain song form in which the verse presents a musical passage lacking in marked periodic phrasing, clear harmonic direction, and occasionally in clear meter. All these produce the introductory texture that mimics the function, if not always the sound, of recitative, the function of preparing the musical and emotional ground for the stability of the refrain to follow, and also the transition from spoken dialogue to song. The refrain, often composed in the modified, miniature da capo of A A B A, expresses unmistakable feelings in well-articulated phrases and directed harmonic progressions. Operatic ensembles more involved than a duet are rare early in the period, but the later shows of the survey include them regularly. The best of them operate in purely classical, almost Mozartean, fashion by allowing each character a solo to explain himself before giving way to contrapuntal invention. Finales, of course, hold sway throughout the tradition, and if they often fail to measure up to their forebears in musical sophistication and dramatic content, their essential character and function of bringing down the curtain remains unchanged.

The cantankerous distinctions, therefore, made between musicals and musical plays on one hand and operettas and operas on the other hand, in the words of Professor Higgins, "by now should be antique." How many times in the annals of criticism has the dirty word *opera,* been used to snub a Broadway production? *Porgy and Bess, The Most Happy Fella,* and *Sweeney Todd* are but a few that have suffered such nonsense. The fact is that one critic or another in one place or another has used the term *opera* or *operetta* to describe nearly every work in this survey. The challenge remains to write a definition of opera that includes *The Magic Flute* but not *West Side Story.* That the New York City Opera and other less famous opera companies mount fully staged productions of these musical plays, that world-class opera singers are rushing to record them, shows how silly the whole terminological business is. The matter at hand is music drama.

The seriousness of the matter among the composers selected here can be heard, not only in their adaptation of operatic vocal forms but in their distinct preference for orchestral "prologues" over medley overtures, despite the overwhelming predominance of medleys in the tradition taken as a whole. Of the seventeen musical plays discussed here, only *Oklahoma!, Kiss Me, Kate, My Fair Lady, Camelot,* and *Jesus Christ Super-*

star follow common practice.[2] The prologue allows the serious musical dramatist to replace a loose collection of tunes, which at that point have no significance other than that they will be heard later in the play, with a succinct summary of the most important terms of the musical drama. The summary may simply contain principal motives, as does the prologue to *The Most Happy Fella*, but it may be more ambitious, establishing an unusual harmonic progression, as in "The Carousel Waltz," or even establishing a harmonic structure for the whole play, as does the prologue to *West Side Story*. The things that are important in prologues are often tiny things—motives, single phrases, harmonic progressions—but they become the structural underpinnings for whole songs and other forms later on. Almost all the prologues are played with the curtain up and some kind of activity on stage: pantomime, dance, or later, singing. The only exceptions are *Show Boat* and *The Most Happy Fella*, whose prologues are very short and come closest in construction to the medley overtures. It is as if composers were unwilling to let the musical statement be as abstract as cultural associations would allow; they preferred some setting, some immediate and specific interpretation. Thus, the community background of *Porgy and Bess* and the violent dancing of *West Side Story*, while retaining a certain abstraction, yet become essential components of the drama. The insecurity seems greater in the newer plays, for the prologues of *Fiddler on the Roof*, *Godspell*, *Sweeney Todd*, and *Evita* narrow the interpretative possibilities further by having their casts explicitly define the dramatic themes in song.

The most signal link of the Broadway tradition with European romantic opera is its dependence on the reprise for incisive dramatic effect. The reprise, of course, is Broadway's answer to the leitmotif, and just as many of Wagner's and Verdi's greatest dramatic statements depend upon a carefully developed leitmotif scheme, so do Broadway's more limited achievements. And how successful the sensitive and timely reprise has been! Stephen Sondheim's argument (quoted in Chapter 14) that to recapitulate a particular song and lyric at a later point in the play is to betray its original dramatic intent assumes that the transfer of meaning between music and drama goes one way only. Music can inform the drama, but drama cannot inform the music. But that is to argue that the dramatic context of a song is irrelevant to it, that the definition of what is going on comes entirely from the music. If the many examples from the Broadway repertoire quoted in this survey have shown anything, it is that the transfer of dramatic meaning is circular: the dramatic context of the play and cultural background of the audience condition and narrow the possible meanings of a piece of music, which in turn specifies the dramatic context and action.

The most effective reprises, therefore, make their point not through changes in the music or lyrics, although such changes may contribute, but because the dramatic situation which calls for their reprise is different from the original. The reprise juxtaposes for the audience both the original context and the new, and thereby gives rise to a host of possible ironies and dramatic meanings. When Billy Bigelow sings "If I Loved You" in the second act of *Carousel*, when Maria helps Tony through "Somewhere" at the end of *West Side Story*, the musical and lyrical alterations are minor. The power of these moments derives from the accumulated meanings of these pieces, which at the point of reprise must be reassessed against the new situations Billy, Tony, and Maria face and against all the action that has happened since they were first sung. These particular examples are two of the best reprises of the Broadway stage because they express in their accumulated meaning the very essence of the actions of their respective plays, and the expression is marvelously appropriate for those moments. That is perhaps why the reprise of "There Was a Barber" in *Sweeney Todd* falls short, because its musical focus on Todd's obsession seems at cross-purposes with what he must be feeling.

Such summations may be accomplished without reprises. "O, Lawd, I'm on My Way" at the end of *Porgy and Bess* and "I Am Ashamed That Women Are So Simple," the finale of *Kiss Me, Kate*, are examples of songs that affect the audience's sense of dramatic action superbly, and yet they are completely new. They are the exceptions to the general rule, in works which have important reprises elsewhere. In this book only *Godspell* and *A Chorus Line* have no dramatic use of reprise (they occur as "bow music") and that is because they have what Sondheim called "nonlinear" plots.

Such plots partly characterize the sea change in the historical tradition beginning in the mid-1960s, a reading which would agree with the opinion of many critics. But the landmark shows of the last four decades part company with their forebears in several respects beyond nonlinear plots: less emphasis on the romantic interest, for instance, and more on modernist concerns about alienation and identity found in legitimate theater. The director's star has been in the ascendant, the composer's has been setting. During this period the economics of the musical theater has seen steady decline. "In 1929, there were about eighty new musicals on Broadway; in 1978 there were fewer than fifteen."[3] In the 1990s the average dropped below ten. Some cite inflated production costs that dampen enthusiasm for new shows. In 1994, *Variety* listed the ten musicals with highest capitalization costs, which ranged from $6.6 million to $11.9 million, six of which failed. But even in artistic terms, revivals of old shows bring more excitement nowadays than almost any new one. Economics does not explain the malaise about the state of popular music drama. Instead there is a more fundamental cause in the medium itself.

As everyone knows, the 1960s saw the rise of rock music as the dominant popular style of American culture. For the first time, the musical language of the culture at large began to grow apart from the musical language of the theater. A chasm opened.

Rock was not the first big change in popular music to confront the theater by any means. The music of Broadway has at several points in its history withstood the assault of various popular currents by absorbing the most useful of their characteristics within its central style of simplified nineteenth-century romanticism. Thus the blues and bop influences permeate the scores of *Porgy and Bess* and *West Side Story* without changing their essential romantic musical languages. Such a strategy succeeded dramatically because composers did not have to yield the powerful resources of the romantic style, and it succeeded commercially because the popular culture at large never abandoned that style for anything else.

But rock finally broke the stranglehold of Tin Pan Alley on American popular music and introduced an irresistible alternative that operated on different principles of music-making. Gone were the rich and often chromatic harmonies of the European Romantics, and gone too were the periodically phrased and yet supple, flexible melodies which those harmonies supported. In their places were much simpler harmonic plans deriving from the blues, energized by insistent downbeats in fast tempo. Melodies are more strictly diatonic, although highly colored by bending pitches, with phrase structures cut from the blues cloth. Even the aesthetics of singing changed. What everyone regarded as a great voice in 1950 would be unacceptable in 1970.

If there can be any credence at all in the notion that an artistic tradition, especially a popular one, reflects in some essentials its parent culture, then any fundamental change in the culture must be accompanied by either the reform or death of the tradition. The domination of rock meant quite simply the reform of the Broadway musical. This impetus ushered in a period of trial and error, experimentation, and rapid change.

One immediate loss was romance. The romantically involved couple, which had been the principal source of dramatic conflict till then, no longer mattered so much. Neither *Godspell*, *Jesus Christ Superstar*, *A Chorus Line*, *Sweeney Todd*, nor *Evita* have people in love at the center of their dramas. The significance caught the attention of Lehman Engel in 1972:

> It should be clear that—to date—no musical without principal romantic involvement has worked. Romance is the fuel that ignites the music and lyrics. But romance has not been a prerequisite for the most significant non-musical plays of almost a century. I think the simplest explanation is to be found in the difference between words (drama) and music (feeling). Shakespeare alone combined both with a grandeur and magnificence that is still unique. And his methods of employing romance are echoed in today's best musicals.[4]

The loss of romance has required plays to dramatize other values, and so they have done: power, revenge, religious experience, political struggle, and, most prosaic of all, getting "a job" in *A Chorus Line*.

The attempts to dramatize such themes, particularly those oriented toward a political or social issue, led naturally to the "concept" musical, for which *Company* is often cited as the landmark but whose roots go back further, at least to *Fiddler on the Roof* with its themes of ethnicity and tradition. A traditional romance requires a directed plot, complete with exposition, conflict, and resolution. "Issues," on the other hand, find better expression in repeated and varied expositions, as the first-act vignettes of *Godspell*, the tableaux of *Jesus Christ Superstar*, and the hopscotch among epic themes in *Les Misérables* show. In this survey, *Sweeney Todd* and, to a lesser extent, *Evita* are exceptions, but the trend is clear. In most of Sondheim's work the directed plot is but lightly sketched and in some, such as *Assassins*, it disappears entirely.

The preference for such dramatic structures may explain the ascendancy of the director over the team of composer and lyricist. Of course, the director was always an essential person in a successful show, but formerly he was not the dramatic visionary for the music drama. That role was played by the composer and, to a lesser extent, by the lyricist. When Rodgers and Hammerstein composed *Oklahoma!*, they did it virtually by themselves. When they finished, they set about raising money, contracting a director, choreographer, stars, and so on, and it was their show. *West Side Story* was billed as "a conception of Jerome Robbins," who became its choreographer-director and a significant influence. That influence increased substantially when he directed *Fiddler on the Roof*, to the point where Robbins defined the dramatic themes for Bock and Harnick and even fiddled with orchestrations. "I think the director should have the final say" in such matters, said he, and he gave a good reason: "a single piece of art is wrought by a single vision."[5] In the case of *A Chorus Line*, it is safe to say that the director, Michael Bennett, is the essential creator. Indeed, composer Hamlisch was called in only toward the end of the process.

There is nothing intrinsically wrong with a director doing these things, but it does change the nature of the art. If the composer is not in control of the essential dramatic materials from the beginning—music, certainly, but also lyrics, plot, how much dancing and when—then it is hard to see how he can be the essential dramatist. The musical theater loses its link to opera and becomes something else.

Four decades of experimentation have failed to validate rock music, in and of itself, as a dramatic vehicle. This is no wholesale indictment of the language; every musical language has its expressive strengths and limits. It is as hard to imagine a Richard Rodgers song effectively protesting the Vietnam War as it is the Rolling Stones writing anything for the character of Ado Annie. The driving beat and sound of the rock band best express powerful but static emotions, semantic ranges that change little over the course of a song. This is death to the music drama, which can accommodate some such moments, of course, but which must have a language that can move the action. The principal means for composers to do this has been through modulation, expressive chromatic shifts, delay of the melodic cadence, and only occasionally changes in tempo or meter. All these except that last are mostly foreign to rock, and its ancestor, the blues. That is why there are no lasting all-rock or all-jazz music dramas.

Well, what about *Jesus Christ Superstar, Evita, Godspell*, and all those other "rock" musicals? (Even *Les Misérables*, incredibly, has been so called by some critics.) The description is quite false, because only a fraction of their music would be suitable for a real rock band. These shows freely supplement their few rock songs with eager borrowings from many other languages: the traditional romantic language that Rodgers used, the folk revival, vaudeville and music hall, ragtime, and even the "serious" languages of Debussy and Stravinsky. These musicals are pastiches.

Pastiche is common in the late twentieth-century musical because it can compensate for the limited dramatic range of rock. If rock is not up to creating a jaunty, jeering King Herod, compose a rag instead; if it is totally inappropriate for the death of Fantine, reach back for a romantic song; if its tonality is too straight for Eva Peron's cynicism, add a little acid from Stravinsky.

Again, there is nothing intrinsically wrong with a bit of pastiche now and then. Frederick Loewe, after all, composed a tango for *My Fair Lady*, quite out of place in turn-of-the-century London. *Kiss Me, Kate* has a madrigal, a minature sonata form, and a "Bowery waltz." But no one would mistake "The Rain in Spain" for an authentic tango, nor "Tom, Dick, or Harry" for a real madrigal. Loewe and Porter mimic these compositional types only in their superficial aspects; they never abandon the Tin Pan Alley chromatic style as the central compositional language that can unify their plays despite the great diversity of effects. "Master of the House," however, could have been written in an early 1900s music hall (except perhaps for the salty lyrics), and its musical language has little in common with "Javert's Suicide," which borrows heavily from modernism.

That is why depending on pastiche for the necessary variety of dramatic elements threatens the musical unity of the show, for how can so many different musical languages sound all of a piece? The answer is Andrew Lloyd Webber's through-composed opera technique, the contrafactum, the use and reuse of a few melodies in various dramatic guises. As *Superstar*, *Les Misérables*, and others have shown, the strategy does have a unifying effect, but at the high cost, at times, of credible music drama.

In the end a music drama that depends on pastiche cannot bridge the chasm between popular theater and popular musical language. Rather it makes the chasm more apparent than ever, for pastiche advertises its own anachronism. That is, after all, how it works: by announcing that it is from the past, composed in a language that is to some extent not the modern listener's own, it brings with it a different semantic baggage that expresses the character of Herod and Eva and the dying sentiments of Fantine. But being foreign, pastiche always operates at a distance from the listener, like poetry in translation. When the classic Broadway composers resort to it, they compose the music in their own idiom and leave just a hint of the anachronism.

In using languages of the past while at the same time aiming to compose utterly new kinds of musical plays, theater composers are treading the same path blazed by Debussy, Stravinksy, and the other revolutionaries of the cultivated European tradition. For they faced the same problem: the growth of a classical repertory, born of a consciousness of history. Music history shows that whenever a tradition of compositional practice is consciously noticed, defined, analyzed, and admired, it is usually already dead. This had certainly happened by 1960. The composers who came after that saw themselves as inheritors of a tradition. But the celebrated legacy of Gershwin, Rodgers, Loesser, and the rest could be, in that most individualistic of all centuries, not only a source of inspiration but of despair. The consciousness of a tradition, that vital, flexible system of conventions and artistic goals, renders it forfeit to those who contemplate it, for how can one compose within it without slavish imitation? The only solution is an equally slavish innovation. As Stravinsky knew, one could borrow from popular music, but to be original in the twentieth century one had to hold it at arm's length. The chasm widened.

Whether the chasm has directly caused or merely contributed to the decline of the musical theater on Broadway is impossible to say, for cultural phenomena like Broadway are obviously complex. But the role of the composer was surely different in 2001 than in 1941, and it is surely less of a dramatic visionary, more of a craftsman hired to create specific effects, akin to a set designer.

Contemporary production strategies virtually assure this state of affairs. The economics of producing a new show is quite a curious affair. Most new musical plays are doomed to failure by astronomical production costs and many other causes; yet a select few will not only succeed but run for years and years. These are the "megamusicals."

Megamusicals—*Cats*, *The Phantom of the Opera*, and *Miss Saigon* are examples—have enormous capital investments behind them in order to aim at an international audience. What is astonishing about them is the level of standardization achieved to appeal to the global market. Sets and sound designs are reproduced in meticulous detail. The satellite companies in cities around the world are cast with actors who have the same kinds of voices and use the same inflections that are on the original cast recording, which becomes the arbiter of what makes a good cast member. And managers from the parent production company visit these satellites to ensure uniformity: if, in New York, Jean Valjean gives little Cosette a doll on the tenth bar of Rehearal J^2 in "The Bargain," he must do exactly the same in Toronto and Tokyo. The explicit intent is to make every licensed production of these pieces the same as every other. To see *Les Misérables* in New York is to see it in London, Tel Aviv, or Sydney.

Here, at long last, the musical theater has capitulated to cinema, for such cloning mimics the film industry. Like a film, the megamusical is produced once and for all. Now even directors are reduced to executors of a chart. The creative vision, once supplied by the composers, then by directors, has now shifted to the producer. Cameron Macintosh is the real creator of the English version of *Les Misérables*.

And how similar is the experience of watching one of these megamusical productions to that of watching a movie, owing to the advanced techniques of sound design! These took off when radio microphones attached to the body became practical on stage, when their combined output could be manipulated by a single engineer. Now Ethel Merman is no longer needed, or even particularly wanted. A ten-year-old Cosette can sing in her little-girl voice and have every word be heard by 3,000 listeners all over the house. The orchestra is never too loud, and all the music is acoustically scrubbed and then sent through loudspeakers until it arrives, pristine in its radio quality, at the ears of the audience. There are some curious side effects. If Cosette turns her back on the audience, once an actor's cardinal sin, the sound does not diminish. It makes no difference which direction she faces. And if the various revolutionaries on the barricades quickly exchange lines, often one cannot tell who is singing, since the normal aural cues are defeated by the loudspeaker and there is no close-up camera to zoom in on one singer before quickly cutting to the next.

The cumulative side effect is more than curious. Can a Cosette who sounds the same regardless of location be an actual girl? An invisible curtain falls between actors and audience when the megamusical imitates cinema. The audience no longers feels engaged with real persons, who once reacted to them, but rather, like the moviegoer, the theater audience now views only an image of real persons, a record of a drama long past. Such an image can be dramatically vital, but it is not music drama. How else to account for *New York Times* critic John Gross's assessment of both music and lyrics from *Les Misérables* as "doggerel" and yet his advice to see it nonetheless?[6] How else to account for the tremendous popular success of a musical whose most memorable thing is not a song but the sight of a helicopter on stage? Or the sight of felines on tightropes above the heads of the audience? Only by recognizing that the the visual has become paramount. Music in megamusicals is no longer the chief dramatic agent. As in film, it has become a mood enhancer, an underscore, acoustic lighting.

Whether the artistic decline is terminal or not, the Broadway tradition since *Show Boat* has had a good run. The best reasons for celebrating the tradition are those rare and brief bursts of creativity marked by musical-dramatic integrity. Each of these is an attempt to respond to a particular dramatic problem, and the artistry and invention of that response allows the play to endure. That is why all of the great Rodgers and Hammerstein shows may be admired even though some stage formula may be clearly discerned. Each has its own dramatic difficulty, and therefore its own unique musical solution. Perhaps the greatest moments of the tradition are those in which the dramatic integrity and musical imagination are sufficient to achieve a musical unity that can be heard, a musical play such as *Porgy and Bess*, *Carousel*, or *West Side Story* that creates and maintains its own characteristic sound that is one with its action. Such integrity assures a life for these plays regardless of the fate of the Broadway theaters in the twenty-first century. They will take their place among the national musical theater traditions of the world as the one that imitates an action through music in its distinctively American way.

Endnotes

Chapter 1: Introduction

1. Joseph Kerman, *Opera as Drama* (New York: Vintage Books, 1956).

2. More precisely, the meaning of a passage of music results from the interaction of a semantic range much wider than that of an utterance of speech with the particular context at hand. Unless that context is purposefully narrow—such as a sung lyric—then the resultant meaning of the musical passage will always be vague and imprecise as compared with speech. See Joseph P. Swain, *Musical Languages* (New York: Norton, 1997), chap. 3.

3. Eric Bentley, *The Playwright as Thinker* (New York: Reynal & Hitchcock, 1946), 284.

4. Francis Fergusson, *The Idea of a Theater* (Princeton, N.J.: Princeton University Press, 1949), 8.

5. Kerman, *Opera as Drama,* 12–13.

6. Eric Bentley, *The Life of the Drama* (New York: Atheneum, 1964), 15.

7. For example, in another activity in which humans extract meaning, listening to spoken language, the mechanism of perception is clearly circuitous. The incoming sounds are at once verified by subsequent ones and at the same time form the basis for the evaluation of the following words. See Swain, *Musical Languages,* chaps. 1, 4.

8. Bentley, *The Playwright as Thinker,* 6–7.

9. Kerman, *Opera as Drama,* 269.

10. See Richard Rodgers, *Musical Stages* (New York: Random House, 1976), 202.

11. One of the applicants for this job was George Gershwin, but Berlin told him that he should be spending his time writing his own music. See Michael Freedland, *Jerome Kern* (New York: Stein and Day, 1978), 57.

12. Bentley, *The Playwright as Thinker,* 6.

13. Ibid., 281.

14. *Poetics of Music*, Lesson Three (Cambridge: Harvard University Press, 1956).

15. Freedland, *Jerome Kern*, 31.

16. "Some Remarks on Value and Greatness in Music," in *Music, the Arts, and Ideas* (Chicago: University of Chicago Press, 1967), 37.

17. "Music: A View from Delft," *Musical Quarterly* LXVII (1961), 439–53.

18. Fergusson, *The Idea of a Theater*, 2.

19. In recent years artifacts of American culture, including musical theater, have become so international in scope that it is increasingly difficult to make hard distinctions of national origin. The Englishman Andrew Lloyd Webber's *Evita*, for instance, opened in London in 1977 and in New York in 1979. However, the producer was the American Harold Prince in both places, and since a Broadway run was undoubtedly planned, contingent on the London success, and since the two cities shared by the 1970s all their musical successes, the opera may be regarded as a product of the Broadway tradition. The original production of *Les Misérables* had nothing to do with New York physically, but everything to do with Broadway in terms of the creators' backgrounds, artistic aims, and terms of expression.

20. For a discussion of some of the problems, see Stephen Holden, " 'Show Boat' Makes New Waves," *New York Times*, September 25, 1988, pp. 1, 27.

Chapter 2: First Maturity

1. Stanley Green, *The World of Musical Comedy* (New York: Ziff-Davis, 1960), 71.

2. "Out of Thin Air," *New Yorker* 30 (April 17, 1954), 116.

3. Miles Kreuger, *Showboat: The Story of a Classic American Musical* (New York: Oxford University Press, 1977), 49.

4. This is obviously a simplified view of the situation, but a more detailed description would not be clearer nor likely more accurate. Edith Boroff summarizes 28 different viewpoints about the origin of the American musical theater in "Origin of Species: Conflicting Views of American Musical Theater History," *American Music* 2, No. 4 (Winter 1984), 101–8.

5. Review of *Show Boat, New York Times*, December 28, 1927, p. 26.

6. Ethan C. Mordden, *Better Foot Forward* (New York: Grossman, 1976), 75.

7. *The Life of the Drama* (New York: Atheneum, 1964), 259.

8. These are the original lyrics of the 1927 version. In deference to black sensitivity to racial slurs, the first two lines were changed to "Colored folks work on de Mississippi, colored folks work while de white folks play" for the 1946 revival, and these appear in the vocal score published by Welk. In the 1966

revival, the lyrics were further toned down to read "Here we all work on de Mississippi, here we all work while de white folks play."

9. Bordman traces this tune back to the entrance music of Act I, One, scene 2 of Kern's *The Beauty Prize*. He also notes several other themes in *Show Boat* that were adapted from earlier works. See Gerald Bordman, *Jerome Kern: His Life and Music* (New York: Oxford University Press, 1980), 291.

10. Oscar Hammerstein II, *Show Boat,* complete libretto (New York: Rodgers & Hammerstein Theatre Library, n.d.), 9.

11. Ibid., 15–16.

12. The choice of keys for the various pieces in the opening scene of *Show Boat* indicates some organization, but it is a very loose one based on pitch height rather than some hierarchical relationship. The opening choral sequence is based on E, the parade sequence on B-flat, Ravenal's first song on D. The 1928 vocal score has "Make Believe" also begin in D and eventually move to E-flat, but the 1946 revision places the beginning in C, which matches the key of "Ol' Man River" in both scores. Clearly the semitone transpositions are supposed to create a limited increase in intensity and have no structural importance. The loose quality of these connections is revealed in the decision to sing "Ol' Man River" in B-flat in the London engagement of 1928 in order to suit Paul Robeson's lower range.

13. The 1946 version of the score contains some equivocation about whether Magnolia and Ravenal are supposed to sing together in that the last phrase is given in small notation in Magnolia's part. The 1928 vocal score (T. B. Harms), however, indicates clearly that they should sing together until the cadence in m. 113. In my view this makes more dramatic sense.

14. Hammerstein, *Show Boat,* 19.

15. Stephen Citron notes that the principal motive of "Ol' Man River" is a melodic inversion of the "Cotton Blossom" motive, thus making the affinity even greater. See *The Wordsmiths: Oscar Hammerstein 2nd and Alan Jay Lerner* (New York: Oxford University Press, 1995), 70.

16. Kreuger, *Showboat,* 50.

17. Lehman Engel, *Words with Music* (New York: Macmillan, 1972), 7.

Chapter 3: America's Folk Opera

1. Edward Jablonski, *Gershwin* (New York: Doubleday, 1987), 287.

2. This story is recounted in Dorothy Heyward, "Porgy's Goat," *Harper's* 215 (December 1957), 37–41, and in Stanley Green, *The World of Musical Comedy* (New York: Ziff-Davis, 1960), 120.

3. William H. Slavick, *DuBose Heyward* (Boston: Twayne, 1981), 9.

4. Ibid., 57.

5. Letter from DuBose Heyward to Kathryn Bourne, December 21, 1931. Cited from Frank Durham, "DuBose Heyward's Use of Folklore in His Negro Fiction," *The Citadel: Monograph Series No.2* (Charleston, S.C.: The Citadel, 1961), 18–19.

6. See Charles Schwartz, *Gershwin: His Life and Music* (Indianapolis and New York: Da Capo, 1973), 60–61, for more details on this piece.

7. Heyward, "Porgy's Goat," 37.

8. Green, *The World of Musical Comedy*, 111.

9. Abe Laufe, *Broadway's Greatest Musicals* (New York: Funk & Wagnalls, 1969), 32.

10. *The American Musical Theatre: A Consideration* (distrib. by Macmillan, 1967), 112. For similar assessments, see Laufe, *Broadway's Greatest Musicals*, 33, and Schwartz, *Gershwin*, 219–20.

11. Green, *The World of Musical Comedy*, 123.

12. It is very difficult to know precisely what Ira contributed to the whole text of *Porgy and Bess*. See Schwartz, *Gershwin*, 261–62, and Slavick, *DuBose Heyward*, 81.

13. See Schwartz, *Gershwin*, 258 ff., for a detailed chronology of the composition.

14. "*Porgy and Bess;* American Opera in the Theatre," *Theatre Arts Monthly* (November 1935), 853.

15. *Music in a New Found Land* (New York: Hillstone, 1964), 392–413.

16. "I Remember," in Merle Armitage, *George Gershwin* (New York, London: Longmans, Green, 1938), 52.

17. For a complete list and discussion of cuts, see Charles Hamm' s "The Theatre Guild Production of *Porgy and Bess*," *Journal of the American Musicologial Society* XL, No. 3 (Fall 1987) 495–532.

18. David Ewen, *A Journey to Greatness* (New York: Henry Holt, 1956), 266.

19. "Todd Duncan," in Robert Kimball, Alfred Simon, and Bea Feitler, *The Gershwins* (New York: Atheneum, 1973), 181.

20. Hamm, "The Theatre Guild Production," 505–7, 514–21.

21. Geoffrey Block recounts such a case in his discussion of the "Buzzard Song," in *Enchanted Evenings* (New York: Oxford University Press, 1997), 70.

22. *New York Times*, October 11, 1935, p. 30.

23. *New York Times*, October 20, 1935, Sec. X, p. 1.

24. Engel, *The American Musical Theatre*, 143.

25. Kolodin, "*Porgy and Bess*," 858.

26. Quoted in Andrew Porter, "Musical Events," *New Yorker* 61 (February 25, 1985), 93.

27. Engel, *The American Musical Theatre*, 144–45.

28. For good introductions to this complex issue, see Richard Crawford, "It Ain't Necessarily Soul: Gershwin's *Porgy and Bess* as a Symbol," *Yearbook for Inter-American Musical Research* VIII (1972), 17–38 and Block, *Enchanted Evenings*, chap. 4.

29. Robert Garland, "Negroes Are Critical of 'Porgy and Bess,'" *New York World-Telegram*, January 16, 1934, p. 14.

30. "Porgy and Bess—A Folk Opera," *Opportunity* (January 1936), 26.

31. "George Gershwin," *Modern Music* (November–December 1935), 13.

32. "Gershwin, Part IV," *New Republic* 176 (May 14, 1977), 25.

33. Kolodin, *"Porgy and Bess,"* 861, and Ewen, *A Journey to Greatness,* 273.

34. Clive Barnes, "Porgy and Bess," *New York Times*, September 27, 1976, p. 40.

35. "Living With Gershwin," *Opera News* 49 (March 16, 1985), 14.

36. Kolodin, *"Porgy and Bess,"* 856.

37. Slavick, *DuBose Heyward*, 10.

38. Ibid., 59.

39. This was cut for the New York production. See Hamm, "The Theatre Guild Production," 530.

40. In "Bess, You Is My Woman Now," Bess sings "Porgy, I's yo' woman, now," and "I's yours for ever," and Porgy sings "you loves yo' Porgy." In the second duet of Act II, Bess sings "I loves you, Porgy." The most explicit statements of Porgy's feelings occur in the same duet when he sings "You got a home now, Honey, an' you got love," and in the "Buzzard Song" of Act II: "Sharin' grief an' sharin' laughter, an' love like Augus' sun." It should be however, that the first occurrence is quite difficult for the listener to catch because Bess is singing the main tune with a different text.

41. Block claims that because Gershwin "indicated in a handwritten notation that a 'Bess theme' should accompany the words sung by Bess, 'Porgy, I hates to go an' leave you all alone,'" the great song "Bess, You Is My Woman Now" is Bess's leitmotif (see *Enchanted Evenings*, 81–82). This contention flouts all principles of leitmotif construction. The first association of that tune is with Porgy who sings it, not Bess, and in building a leitmotif first associations count for a great deal. Furthermore, she has been on stage for over an hour without any association with this tune. Finally, audiences do not see and hear historical sketches and typescripts when they experience the opera, only what it is in front of them. For a semantic theory of leitmotif construction, see Joseph P. Swain, *Musical Languages* (New York: Norton, 1997), chap. 3.

42. Mellers also notes this textual connection, although not the motivic one. See *Music in a New Found Land*, 404.

43. Youngren, "Gershwin, Part IV," 24.

44. The sense of meter derives from regular accents, some of which may be produced by melodic groupings. Here the C-sharp to D motion, because it

recurs insistently, is heard as the beginning of a melodic group, and thus becomes accented. Because each of the groups has only three eighth notes, however, this new accent pattern is heard as a disruption of the prevailing meter, since three eighths cannot divide eight evenly.

45. Lawrence Starr notes that relationship of the particular harmonies used here to the chromatic notes of Porgy's melody. "In measures 7 and 8, the blue notes A-flat and D-flat infiltrate the bass line and are given complete harmonic status as the roots of chords. The result is an intense and colorful precadential progression which also provides a summary of the events related to the blue notes thus far." See "Gershwin's 'Bess, You Is My Woman Now': The Sophistication and Subtlety of a Great Tune," *Musical Quarterly* LXXII, No. 4 (1986), 434.

46. Lawrence Starr also notes this relationship. See "Toward a Reevaluation of Gershwin's *Porgy and Bess,*" *American Music* 2, No. 2 (Summer 1984), 35–36.

47. For an extended discussion of jazz influences in *Porgy and Bess,* see David R. Baskerville, "Jazz Influence of Art Music to Mid-Century," Ph.D. Diss., University of California, Los Angeles, 1965, pp. 486–503.

48. Lawrence Starr also notes this relationship. See Starr, "Gershwin's, 'Bess, You Is My Woman Now,'" 441, 443.

49. In particular, Ronald Duncan, "*Porgy and Bess:* The Work and Its Conception," *Opera* (December 1952), 711–13.

50. Hamm notes that much of this passage was cut from the New York production (see Hamm, "The Theatre Guild Production," 531), but that version still leaves a critical moment in the drama without musical expression.

51. DuBose Heyward, *Porgy* (George H. Doran, 1925), 196.

52. This means that the production failed to recover its investment. It still played 124 performances before closing, many more times than it would have played had the Metropolitan Opera produced it.

53. Ewen, *A Journey to Greatness,* 281. II

54. George Gershwin, "Rhapsody on Catfish Row," *New York Times,* October 20, 1935, Sec. X, p. 1.

55. *A Short History of Opera,* second edition (New York: Columbia University Press, 1965), 545.

Chapter 4: Second Maturity

1. Richard Rodgers, *Musical Stages* (New York: Random House, 1976), 227.

2. There were several revues produced during the period 1919–43 which had significant runs, but none so long as *Oklahoma!: Hellzapoppin* (1938, 1,404 performances); *Pins and Needles* (1937, 1,108 performances); *Stars on Ice* (1942, 830 performances); and *Sons O' Fun* (1941, 742 performances).

3. See his discussion throughout *The American Musical Theater: A Consideration* (New York: Macmillan, 1967). Also see Geoffrey Block, *Enchanted Evenings* (New York: Oxford University Press, 1997), 104–114.

4. Rodgers, *Musical Stages*. 202.

5. Oscar Hammerstein II, *Lyrics* (Milwaukee, Wis.: Hal Leonard, 1985; rpt. 1949), 20.

6. Ibid., 17.

7. Rodgers, *Musical Stages*, 219.

8. Engel, *The American Musical Theater,* 105.

9. Agnes De Mille, *America Dances* (New York: Macmillan, 1980), 188.

10. They are the *Nursery Ballet* (1938) and *Ghost Town* (1939). Stephen Citron records an interview with Agnes de Mille which suggests that she was largely responsible for the final shape of the ballet. See *The Wordsmiths: Oscar Hammerstein 2nd and Alan Jay Lerner* (New York: Oxford University Press, 1995), 141–42.

11. Rodgers, *Musical Stages*, 223.

12. Eric Bentley, *The Life of the Drama* (New York: Atheneum, 1964), 7.

13. Deems Taylor, *Some Enchanted Evenings* (New York: Harper, 1953), 172–73.

14. Oscar Hammerstein, "On Writing 'Oklahoma!,' " *New York Times*, May 23, 1943, Sec. X, p. 2.

15. William Beyer, *School and Society* 67 (June 26, 1948), 475.

16. Rodgers, *Musical Stages,* 229.

17. *Broadway's Greatest Musicals* (New York: Funk & Wagnalls, 1969), 68.

18. Leo Lerman, *Dance Magazine* 32 (May 1958), 17.

19. Hammerstein, *Lyrics*, 8.

20. *New York Times*, May 12, 1963, Sec. VI, p. 30.

Chapter 5: Morality Play as Musical

1. Richard Rodgers, *Musical Stages* (New York: Random House, 1976), 243.

2. Thomas DeLong, *Pops: Paul Whiteman, King of Jazz* (Piscataway, N.J.: New Century, 1983), 269.

3. *Richard Rodgers* (New York: Holt, 1957), 239.

4. Rodgers, *Musical Stages,* 238.

5. John Hutchens, "About a Man on a Tightrope," *New York Times,* May 6, 1945, Sec. II, p. 1.

6. Clara Gyorgyey, *Ferenc Molnar* (Boston: Twayne, 1980), 152–53. 7. This is true insofar as we have been speaking of harmonic rhythm as changes in triads. In other words, "My Boy, Bill" shows only one level of triad motion. Strictly speaking, however, harmonic rhythm is almost always multi-level, as is discussed in Joseph P. Swain, *Harmonic Rhythm* (New York: Oxford, 2002).

8. Rodgers, *Musical Stages*, 241.

9. Ibid., 243.

Chapter 6: Shakespeare as Musical

1. Howard Taubman, "Cole Porter Is 'The Top' Again," *New York Times,* January 16, 1949, Sec. VI, p. 20.

2. David Ewen, The Cole *Porter* Story (New York: Holt, Rinehart and Winston, 1965), 114–15.

3. Taubman, "Cole Porter Is 'The Top' Again."

4. Quote in Stanley Green, *The World of Musical Comedy* (New York: A. S. Barnes, 1974), 177.

5. George Eels, The Life That Late He Led (New York: G. P. Putnam's Sons, 1967), 241.

6. Sam and Bella Spewack, "Much Ado About 'Kate,'" *Saturday Review* 36 (October 31 1953), 55.

7. Eels, *The Life That Late He Led*, 238.

8. Lynn Siebert traces some of the motives in "Brush Up Your Shakespeare" to particular songs. See Lynn Laitman Siebert, "Cole Porter: An Analysis of Five Musical Comedies and a Thematic Catalogue of the Complete Works," Ph.D. Diss., City University of New York, 1975, pp. 310–14.

9. Eels, *The Life That Late He Led*, 254.

10. Anne Barton, "The Taming of the Shrew," in *The Riverside Shakespeare,* textual ed. G. Blakemore Evans (Boston: Houghton Mifflin, 1974), 106.

11. Ibid., 107.

12. Ralph Berry, *Shakespeare's Comedies: Explorations in Form* (Princeton, N.J.: Princeton University Press, 1972), 54–55.

13. Some aspects of this high-level use of half-step motion are also noted in Siebert, "Cole Porter," 265.

14. Sam and Bella Spewack, Kiss Me, Kate in *Theatre Arts* 39, No. 32 (January 1955), 57.

15. Robert B. Heilman, "The Taming of the Shrew," in *The Complete Signet Classic Shakespeare,* General Ed. Sylvan Barnet (New York: Harcourt Brace Jovanovich, 1972), 323.

16. *New York Times*, January 16, 1949, Sec. II, p. I.

17. John Mason Brown, "Kiss Me, Kate," *Saturday* Review *of Literature* 32 (January 22, 1949), 35.

Chapter 7: The Pure Love Story

1. Quoted by Murray Schumach in *New York Times*, April 27, 1956, Sec. II, p. 1.

2. Geoffrey Block traces this genesis in "Frank Loesser's Sketchbooks for *The Most Happy Fella*," *The Musical Quarterly* 73 (1989): 60–78.

3. Burrows was not the first to be asked by the producers Cy Feuer and Ernest Martin to adapt the Runyon stories, but he is the sole author. Jo Swerling's name appears on programs and scores because of contractual arrangements. See Stanley Green, *The World of Musical Comedy* (New York: Ziff-Davis, 1960), 296.

4. Gilbert Millstein, "Greater Loesser," *New York Times*, May 20, 1956, Sec. VI, pp. 20, 22.

5. Eleanor Flexner, *American Playwrights 1918–1938* (New York: Simon and Schuster, 1938), 30.

6. For a discussion of these themes, see Walter J. Meserve, "Sidney Howard and the Social Drama of the Twenties," *Modern Drama* 6 (1963), 256–66.

7. Green, *The World of Musical Comedy*, 298.

8. Flexner, *American Playwrights.* 33.

9. These would include Marie's advice in "The Most Happy Fella" (mm. 232–47), Tony's song "Rosabella," Marie's conversation with Cleo at the end of "Happy to Make Your Acquaintance" (mm. 126–82), "Young People," "Mamma, Mamma," and the trio of Act III, scene 2 (mm. 133 ff.)

10. Frank Loesser, The Most *Happy Fella* (New York: Frank Music, 1957), 262.

11. The metrical ambiguity is addressed by the notion of "hypermeasure," or which measures seem strong and weak in the same sense that beats within measures seem strong and weak. The normal pattern would alternate measures strong-weak, as beats might alternate downbeat-upbeat. This is what happens at the beginning of the phrase. The stable tonic harmony of the first measure establishes a strong measure; the unstable augmented triad of the next brings the sense of weak measure. This works fine until measure four, in which the chromatic harmony of C-flat can be heard as a resolution of the previous G-flat. Does this then become a strong measure? In addition, measure five, which should be strong, has dominant harmony (A-flat), and measure six, which should be weak, has tonic (D-flat). Thus, there is a conflict between the harmony of those measures and the pattern that was established at the beginning, and this conflict causes unresolved tension. For theoretical discussions of high-level meter, see Fred Lerdahl and Ray Jackendoff, A *Generative Theory of Tonal Music* (Cambridge, Mass.: MIT Press, 1983), Chapter 2 and Christopher Hasty, *Meter as Rhythm* (New York: Oxford University Press, 1997).

12. Catherine Hughes, "The Most Happy Fella," *America* 141 (November 10, 1979), 281.

13. David Ansen, "The Most Happy Fella," *Newsweek* 94 (October 22, 1979), 130.

14. Richard Hayes, "The Most Happy Fella," *Commonweal* 64 (June 1, 1956),226.

15. Conrad L. Osborne, "The Most Happy Fella," *High Fidelity/Musical America* (February 1980), 37.

Chapter 8: Myth as Musical

1. Alan Jay Lerner, *The Street Where I Live* (New York: Norton, 1978), 44.

2. K. K. Ruthven, *Myth* (London: Methuen, 1976), 44.

3. William Righter, *Myth and Literature* (London and Boston: Routledge & Kegan Paul, 1975), 34.

4. Eric Gould, *Mythical Intentions in Modern Literature* (Princeton, N.J.: Princeton University Press, 1981), 6.

5. Abe Laufe points out the similarity of Lerner's *Brigadoon* story to "Germelshausen," a nineteenth-century German story by Wilhelm Friedrick Gerstacker. See *Broadway's Greatest Musicals* (New York: Funk & Wagnalls, 1969), 101.

6. This translation appears in Mark P. O. Morford and Robert J. Lenardan, *Classical Mythology* (New York and London: Longman, 1985), 117–18.

7. Arnold Silver, *Bernard Shaw: The Darker Side* (Stanford, Calif.: Stanford University Press, 1982), 181–82.

8. Ibid., 254.

9. Lerner, *The Street Where I Live,* 44.

10. Gene Lees justly points out that while much of the text is Shaw's, Lerner's adaptations are significant: "One of the remarkable things about the play is the fidelity to Shaw in tone and sentiment with which Lerner was able to invent both dialogue and the shimmering lyrics. The flow bck and forth between his materials and Shaw's is almost seamless." See *Inventing Champagne: The Worlds of Lerner and Loewe* (New York: St. Martin's Press, 1990), 128.

11. Alan Jay Lerner, *My Fair Lady* (New York: Coward-McCann, 1956), 85–86.

12. George Bernard Shaw, *Pygmalion*, Act III.

13. "A Directly Sensuous Pleasure," *New Republic* 134 (April 9, 1956), 29.

14. Silver, *Bernard Shaw*, 196–97.

15. "Shavian Musical Notes," *New York Times*, March 11, 1956, Sec. II, p. 3.

16. *T. H. White* (New York: Twayne, 1976), 99.

17. J. R. Cameron, "T. H. White in Camelot: The Matter of Britain Revitalized," *The Humanities Association Bulletin* XVI (1), 45.

18. See William K. Zinsser, "Camelot," *Horizon* 3 (May 1961), 104.

19. Alan Jay Lerner, *Camelot* (New York: Chappell Music, 1962), 130–33.

20. *Words With Music* (New York: Macmillan, 1972), 87.

21. Frank Rich, "Stage: Burton Stars in Revival of 'Camelot,'" *New York Times,* July 9, 1980, Sec. III, p. 15.

22. Lerner, *The Street Where I Live,* 232.

23. Ibid., 228.

24. See ibid., 227.

25. Another factor may be *Camelot's* association with the administration of President John F. Kennedy. See Lerner, *The Street Where I Live,* 250–52.

Chapter 9: Tragedy as Musical

1. "Excerpts from a *West Side Story* Log," *Findings* (New York: Simon and Schuster, 1982), 144. Quotation dated "New York, Jan. 6, 1949."

2. Eric Bentley, *The Playwright as Thinker* (New York: Reynal and Hitchcock, 1946), 160.

3. J. Leeds Barroll, *Shakespearean Tragedy* (New *Jersey,* London, and Canada: Associated University Presses, 1984), 15–16.

4. Ibid., 16.

5. Frank Kermode, "Romeo and *Juliet,"* in *The Riverside Shakespeare,* ed. G. Blakemore Evans (Boston: Houghton Mifflin, 1974), 1055. Harley Granville-Barker shares this opinion, although he remarks that Shakespeare "set out, we see, in the shaping of his characters, to give all likelihood to the outcome. It is by pure ill-luck that Friar John's speed to Mantua is stayed while Balthasar reaches Romeo with the news of Juliet's death; but it is Romeo's headlong recklessness that leaves Friar Laurence no time to retrieve the mistake. It is, by a more subtle turn, Juliet's overacted repentance of her 'disobedient opposition,' which prompts the delighted Capulet to '. . . have this knot knit up to-morrow morning.'" *Prefaces to Shakespeare,* Second Series, "Romeo and Juliet" (London: Sidgwick & Jackson, 1948), 17.

6. Norris Houghton, *"Romeo and Juliet* and *West Side Story:* An Appreciation," in *Romeo and Juliet/West Side Story* (New York: Dell, 1965), 10–11. Laurents on this change: "The thing I'm proudest of in telling the story is why she can't get the message through: because of prejudice. I think it's better than the original story." Otis L. Guernsey, ed., *Broadway Song & Story: Playwrights, Lyricists, Composers Discuss Their Hits* (New York: Dodd, Mead, 1985), 47.

7. Bentley, *The Playwright as Thinker,* 55–56.

8. David Stearns, "'West Side Story': Between Broadway and the Opera House." Liner notes to recording of *West Side Story.* Deutsche Gramophon Gesellschaft 415 254–2, pp. 13.

9. The idea of an unusual musical procedure becoming a norm for a particular composition can be defended with data from the cognitive sciences which

show how humans can learn and accept patterns for a particular situation. See Joseph P. Swain, *Musical Languages* (New York: Norton, 1997), chap. 4.

10. The Deutsche Gramophon recording conducted by Bernstein himself begins as the vocal score given in Example 9–5 does. The original Broadway cast recording produced by Columbia, however, begins with the Jets "whistle motive" which in the "Prologue" does not occur until measure 89:

This is certainly a more arresting gesture with which to begin the musical. However, by beginning with the tritone so brazenly, Berstein's careful motivic development is pre-empted. In addition, by starting with a G-sharp to C-sharp leap, followed by the turn ending on B, the C/A polarity so subtly established and so important to the unity of the whole play is threatened.

11. The consistency of Bernstein's idiom in all his work may be seen in that the melody to "Somewhere" was composed some dozen years before the show as a whole. See Joan Peyser, *Bernstein: A Biography* (New York: William Morrow, 1987), 267.

12. Ibid., 267.

13. Granville-Barker, *Prefaces,* 7–8.

14. Henry Hewes, *Saturday Review* 40 (October 5, 1957), 22.

15. Carol Lawrence, who created the role of Maria, claims that Robbins's control over the production was nearly total, and that Bernstein regularly deferred to his judgment; see William Westbrook Burton, ed., *Conversations About Bernstein* (New York: Oxford University Press, 1995), 172. This does not diminish Bernstein's role as the essential dramatist, however, since he wrote the notes and it is through them that the tragic action is expressed.

16. See interview with Jerome Robbins by Moira Hodgson, *New York Times,* February 10, 1980, Sec. II, p. 4.

17. From *West Side Story* libretto, printed in *Romeo and Juliet/West Side Story* (New York: Dell, 1965), 201.

18. See interview of Jerome Robbins by Moira Hodgson.

19. Harold S. Wilson, On *the Design of Shakespearean Tragedy* (Toronto: University of Toronto Press, 1957), 30.

20. Ibid., 25.

21. Stearns, "'West Side Story,'" 13.

22. Houghton, *"Romeo and Juliet* and *West Side Story,"* 11.

Chapter 10: The Ethnic Musical

1. Quoted in Richard Altman with Mervyn Kaufman, *The Making of a Musical: Fiddler* on *the Roof* (New York: Crown, 1971), 34–35.

2. Dan Sullivan, "A Robust 'Fiddler' Approaches Its 3rd Birthday," *New York Times*, September 14, 1968, p. 25.

3. Richard Rodgers, *Musical Stages* (New York: Random House, 1975), 220.

4. Ibid., 301.

5. Craig Zadan, *Sondheim & Co.*, second ed. (New York: Macmillan, 1986), 211.

6. Rodgers, *Musical Stages*, 295.

7. Eric Werner et al., "Jewish Music," *The New Grove*, ed. Stanley Sadie (London: Macmillan, 1980), Vol. IX, p. 642.

8. See ibid., 642.

9. Sholem Aleichem, *The Tevye Stories and Others,* trans. Julius and Frances Butwin (New York: Pocket Books, 1965; rpt. Crown, 1946).

10. Altman, The *Making of a Musical,* 39.

11. Ibid., 40.

12. Ibid.

13. Ibid., 46.

14. Werner Haftmann, *Marc Chagall,* trans. Heinrich Baumann and Alexis Brown (New York: Harry N. Abrams, 1984), 70.

15. Joseph Stein, *Fiddler* on *the Roof* (New York: Crown, 1964), 1.

16. Butwin, *The Tevye Stories,* 28.

17. See Altman, The *Making of a Musical,* 31.

18. Ibid.

19. See Ibid., Chapter 9.

20. Ibid., 156.

21. Abe Laufe, *Broadway's Greatest Musicals* (New York: Funk & Wagnalls, 1969), 377.

22. Hillel Halkin, introduction to Sholem Aleichem, *Tevye the Dairyman* and The *Railroad Stories,* trans. Hillel Halkin (New York: Schocken Books, 1987), xxiv.

23. Butwin, *The Tevye Stories,* 84.

24. Halkin, "Introduction," xxv.

25. *New York Times*, September 20, 1964, Sec. II, p. 1.

Chapter 11: Religious Experience as Musical

1. Joseph Barton, S. J., "The Godspell Story," *America,* 125 (December 11, 1971), 517.

2. Ibid., 517.

3. The career of Stephen Sondheim, which began so auspiciously with *West Side Story, Gypsy*, and *A Funny Thing Happened* on the Way *to the Forum*, might be mentioned as an obvious exception. In the first two cases, however, he was working with quite a large team of much more experienced men.

4. Stephen Schwartz, personal communication, September 10, 1988.

5. Barton, "The Godspell Story," 517.

6. *Opera as Drama* (New York: Vintage, 1956), 65.

7. Michael Murray, "The Stage," *Commonweal* 95 (February 11, 1972), 447.

8. Tom Prideaux, "On This Rock, a Little Miracle," *Life* 73 (August 4, 1972), 20.

9. Stephen Koch, "God on Stage," *World* 1 (September 12, 1972), 61.

10. Robert P. Ellis, "'Godspell' as Medieval Drama," *America* 127 (December 23, 1972), 543.

11. See H. Elliot Wright, "Jesus on Stage: A Reappraisal," *Christian Century* 89 (July 19, 1972), 786 for details *of* Tebelak's acquaintance with the Cox book.

12. Harvey Cox, The *Feast of Fools* (Cambridge, Mass.: Harvard University Press, 1969), 139.

13. Ibid., 142.

14. Ellis, "'Godspell,'" 543.

15. Cox, The *Feast of Fools,* 147.

16. John Paterson, The *Praises of Israel* (New York: Charles Scribner's Sons, 1950), 59.

17. Koch, "God on Stage," 61.

18. Schwartz, personal communication.

19. Edwin Wilson, "Taking the Long Route to Broadway," *Wall Street Journal,* June 24. 1976, p. 16.

20. Schwartz, personal communication.

Chapter 12: History as Musical

1. Ellis Nassour and Richard Broderick, *Rock Opera* (New York: Hawthorn, 1973), 41.

2. "Sex and Power in the New York Theater," *New Republic* 181 (November 10, 1979), 26.

3. Nassour and Broderick, *Rock Opera,* 37.

4. Ibid.

5. "I have always felt that is the key to musicals, to make them a continuous musical event like opera." Michael Owen, "A London Hit Arrives—With a Controversial Heroine," *New York Times*, September 23, 1979, Sec. II, p. 26.

6. Nassour and Broderick, *Rock Opera,* 99–100.

7. Quoted in ibid., 174.

8. Ibid., 41.

9. "Jesus Christ Superstar-eine Passion in Rock," *Musik und Bildung* 4 (April 1972), 194–99.

10. Ibid., 198. ". . . so wirkt ihr Gesang während des 'letzten Abendmahls' eher wie die Karikatur selbstzufriedenen Monchsschar vorgetragen wird."

11. Ibid., 199.

12. The term applies most frequently to vocal music of the middle ages and Renaissance. Another term for the close adaptation of a vocal piece is *parody*, which is applied to certain Renaissance masses using motets as their models and in recent studies to the music of Bach and Handel. Parody technique allows for freer handling of the original, occasionally even deleting the text altogether to make an instrumental work, while retaining clear identity with the original.

13. Nassour and Broderick, *Rock Opera,* 46.

14. See the latter chapters of John Barnes, *Evita, First* Lady (New York: Grove, 1978).

15. Owen, "A London Hit Arrives," 1.

16. Ibid., 26.

17. Walter Kerr, "'Evita'—A Bold Step Backward," *New York Times,* October 7, 1979, Sec. II, p. 1.

18. See Brendan Gill, "The Theatre: Crying for Eva," *New Yorker* 55 (October 8, 1979), 100; T. E. Kalem, "Vogue of the Age: Carrion Chic," *Time* 114 (October 8, 1979), 84; Stanley Kauffmann, "Theater: Down Argentine Way," *Saturday Review* 6 (November 24, 1979), 49–50; and Kerr, "'Evita.'"

19. Kauffmann, "Theater," 50.

Chapter 13: Frame Story as Musical

1. Mel Gussow, "The Director Who Listened to Chorus Line," *New York Times,* May 23, 1975, p. 22.

2. Jack Kroll and Constance Guthrie, "Gotta Dance . . . Gotta Dance," *Newsweek* 85 (June 9, 1975), 85.

3. Gussow, "The Director Who Listened"; Barbara Gelb, "Producing and Reproducing 'A Chorus Line,'" *New York Times,* May 2, 1976, Sec. VI, p. 20.

4. Gussow, "The Director Who Listened."

5. Stanley Kauffmann, "A Chorus Line," *New Republic* 172 (June 21, 1975), 20.

6. Gussow, "The Director Who Listened."

7. "A Tremendous 'Chorus Line' Arrives," *New York Times,* May 22, 1975, p. 32.

8. Daniel Cook, ed., *The Canterbury Tales of Geoffrey Chaucer* (New York: Anchor Books, Doubleday, 1961), xvii.

9. Ibid., xviii.

10. *The Structure of the Canterbury Tales* (Athens, Ga.: University of Georgia Press, 1984), 25.

11. Clive Barnes does so in his review, "A Tremendous 'Chorus Line' Arrives."

12. Craig Zadan, *Sondheim & Co.*, second ed. (New York: Macmillan 1986), 125.

13. "Theatre," *Nation* 220 (June 14, 1975), 734.

14. Samuel G. Freedman, "332 Dance on a Record 3389th 'Chorus Line,'" *New York Times,* September 30, 1983, Sec. III, p. 5.

15. Measure numbers refer to the published vocal score, *A Chorus Line.* music by Marvin Hamlisch, lyrics by Ed Kleban (n.p.: E. H. Morris, 1977). Unfortunately, Wren Music Co., the print agent for his music, would not permit excerpts to be reprinted here, due to the critical nature of the commentary.

16. Gelb, "Producing and Reproducing' A Chorus Line,'" notes (p. 28) that keys of individual songs were changed in rehearsal to accommodate vocal ranges. It is possible that the individual sections of "At the Ballet" fell victim to such conditions, even though the vocal ranges demanded of the three singers are not extreme.

17. See, for example, Frank Rich, "At the Age of 5, 'Chorus Line' Has Lots of Offspring," *New York Times,* July 20, 1980, Sec. II, p. 4.

18. The removal of one dancer makes possible the rather manipulative "surprise ending," whereby, when Zach comes to make the final selection, he asks eight to step forward, leaving eight on the line. Naturally everyone, including the characters, thinks that the eight coming forward are the winners, until he thanks and dismisses them. If Paul had not been hurt, he would have had to call nine forward, and the trick would have been exposed.

19. Carol Lawson, "Broadway," *New York Times,* August 26, 1983, Sec. ill, p. 2.

20. "Larry King Live," Cable News Network, August 19, 1988.

21. This effectiveness was enhanced exponentially when all past cast members were invited to dance for the performance of *A Chorus Line* which broke the record for longest-running musical play on Broadway on September 29, 1983. For a description, see Frank Rich, *New York Times*, October 1, 1983, Sec. I, p. 13

22. Henry Hewes, "Broadway's Bountiful Season," *Saturday* Review 2 (July 26, 1975), 19.

23. Ibid.

24. Gelb, "Producing and Reproducing 'A Chorus Line,'" 26.

25. Richard Philip, "Michael Bennett and the Making of 'A Chorus Line,'" *Dance Magazine* 49 (June 1975), 65.

26. Arlene Croce, "A Chorus Line," *New Yorker* 51 (August 25, 1975), 78.

Chapter 14: Thriller as Musical

1. Samuel G. Freedman, "The Words and Music of Stephen Sondheim," *New York Times*, April 1, 1984, Sec. VI, p. 28.

2. Ibid., 25.

3. Ibid., 28.

4. It is the only one of Harold Prince's productions that Sondheim inititated. See Martin Gottfried, *Sondheim* (New York: Harry N. Abrams, Inc., 2000), 123.

5. *New York Times*, May 3, 1970, Sec. II, p. 1.

6. Quoted in Craig Zadan, *Sondheim & Co.*, second ed. (New York: Harper & Row, 1986), 230.

7. Ibid., 360.

8. Stephen Holden, "The Passion of Stephen Sondheim," *Atlantic* 254 (December 1984), 121.

9. Zadan, *Sondheim & Co.*, 367. Although this quotation dates from 1973, the statement about the profits is still true through 1988, as long as the profits are regarded as those deriving from the initial Broadway runs of the plays.

10. Freedman, "The Words and Music of Stephen Sondheim," 26.

11. The Broadway production actually began with an organ prelude, reminiscent of the Gothic horror theater. The prelude is built on various important motives of the opera in rather tortured versions. However, the vocal score states that the performance of the prelude is "optional," so that it must not be an important contributor to the opera's scheme, at least for the composer.

12. Freedman, "The Words and Music of Stephen Sondheim," 26. Another facet of this non-functional idiom is Sondheim's penchant for writing melodies that seem bitonal, that is, having more than one tonal center. Typically the sixth degree of a scale serves as the "other tonic," which is the tonic of the relative minor key if the main key is major. A good example is Johanna's melody in "Kiss Me" (Ex. 14-9). The main key is E major but her phrases insist on cadencing on the note C-sharp. Many modal folk melodies have this bitonal emphasis, and it serves Sondheim's idiom because the presence of two perceived tonics weakens the traditional functions that would articulate them.

13. In most of Sondheim's shows, the keys of individual songs were determined at the time of orchestration, when the singer had been contracted. See ibid., 60.

14. The ability of the perceiving mind of the listener to learn such definitions quickly from context is described at length in Joseph P. Swain, *Musical Languages* (New York: Norton, 1997), chap. 4.

15. The lyrics here also indicate the beginning of a new phrase. "Then" is a strong beginning of a new sentence.

16. The four eighths on "lost and oh, so" (m. 241) are not four eighths in the same grouping that has obtained up to that point. The first two ("So lost") are clearly another occurrence of the motives in the previous measure, leaving the last three eighths to carry out the anacrusis. The beaming in the notation should really be two and three.

17. Freedman, "The Words and Music of Stephen Sondheim," 30.

18. *Opera as Drama* (New York: Vintage, 1956), 177.

19. Robert Berkvist, "Stephen Sondheim Takes a Stab at Grand Guignol," *New York Times*, February 25, 1979, Sec. D, p. 5.

20. Montague Slater, Introduction to George Dibdin Pitt, *Sweeney Todd: The Demon Barber of Fleet Street* (London: Gerald Howe, 1928).

21. Stanley Kauffmann, "Slay It With Music," *New Republic* 180 (March 24, 1979), 24. Kauffmann gives no source *for* this information. Joanne Leslie Gordon, in her dissertation, "The American Musical Stops Singing and Finds Its Voice: A Study of the Works of Stephen Sondheim" (UCLA, 1984), writes: "Pitt apparently based his play on the bloodchilling reports of Thomas Peckett Prest. His serial, 'A String of Pearls,' had been published earlier in *The People's Periodical,* a Victorian penny dreadful which titillated and edified its readers with a combination of pious homilies and tales of gore."

22. *Sweeney Todd: The Demon Barber of Fleet Street* (London: Samuel French, 1974), v.

23. Ibid., 5.

24. There is no "original" version of the Pitt original play because it was never published, but rather transmitted through numerous pirated versions.

25. Act II, scene 4. See Slater, ed., *Sweeney Todd,* 135.

26. Mel Gussow, "'Sweeney Todd': A Little Nightmare Music," *New York Times*, February 1, 1979, Sec. C, p. 15.

27. Berkvist, "Stephen Sondheim Takes a Stab," 5.

28. See Joseph P. Swain, "The Need for Limits in Hierarchical Theories of Music," *Music Perception* 4 (Fall 1986), 121–48 for the relationship between musical structure and the listener's limited ability to perceive musical events.

29. Zadan, *Sondheim & Co.,* 250.

30. The term "ostinato" is used rather loosely here, denoting not an exactly repeating bass line, but a seemingly incessant melodic-rhythmic pattern, in the vein of Stravinsky.

31. Even this moment, however, is not allowed for sustained expression. It is broken into sections, between which the judge and beadle arrive and find the two lovers engrossed in one another. Johanna is taken away and Anthony sings the lyric, "I'll steal you, Johanna." All in the interests of pacing.

32. Zadan, *Sondheim & Co.*, 245.

33. Bond, *Sweeney Todd*. Act I, scene 8.

34. Richard Eder, "Critic's Notebook: 'Sweeney''s Dark Side," *New York Times,* March 29, 1979, Sec. III, p. 16.

35. Zadan, *Sondheim & Co..* 245.

36. Clive Hirschhorn, "Will Sondheim Succeed in Being Genuinely Japanese?," *New York Times,* January 4, 1976, Sec. II, p. 5.

37. Zadan, *Sondheim & Co.,* 233.

38. Ibid., 234.

39. Ibid., 28.

40. Ibid., 207.

41. Kauffmann, "Slay It With Music," 25.

42. Geoffrey Block's essay in *Enchanted Evenings* (New York: Oxford University Press, 1997), chap. 13, convincingly argues that the theme of artistic integrity runs through most of Sondheim's work and in that sense makes it autobiographical.

43. Angela Lansbury, who created the role of Mrs. Lovett, is certainly a star, but there is no evidence that Sondheim made any concessions to her in composing the opera, and the opera is certainly no vehicle in the sense that star qualities are highlighted at the expense of dramatic integrity.

Chapter 15: Epic as Musical

1. Sweeney, Louise, "*Les Misérables* bids for World Audience," *The Christian Science Monitor*, December 24, 1986, p. 21.

2. (Cambridge, Massachusetts: Harvard University Press, 1984), 2.

3. Ulrich Müller, "Betrogenes Volk Im Musical? Die europäischen Musicals *Evita, Les Misérables, Miss Saigon*." "*Weine, Weine, Du Armes Volk*": Das *verführte und betrogene Volk auf der Bühne,* ed. Peter Csobadi, et alia. *Wort und Musik*, Nr. 28, 2 vols (Salzburg: Verlag Ursula Müller-Speiser, 1995), 826.

4. Notes to musical score *Les Misérables* (New York: Alain Boublil Music Ltd., 1991), 2.

5. *Victor Hugo* (New York: Twayne Publishers, 1999), 128.

6. For example, there is no mention of it in John B. Wolf, *France: 1815 to the Present* (New York: Prentice-Hall, 1940) and only passing mention in a specialized study: John M. Merriman, ed., *1830 in France* (New York: New Viewpoints, 1975). There we find that the government lost only 70 soldiers dead.

7. Actually the London original cast recording (First Night Records, 1985) begins with four measures of the Jean Valjean ostinato in A-flat minor. Then there is an awkward break before the introduction to "Look down" begins.

8. Frank Rich also noted this resemblance in his review: *New York Times*, 13 March 1987, Section C, Col. 1.

9. This is why the French version is superior to the English. The latter modulates, awkwardly, when it is actually a more intense effect to remain in the key of the bass scale, as does the French version.

For a more precise theoretical discussion of this kind of harmonic tension see Joseph P. Swain, *Harmonic Rhythm* (New York: Oxford University Press, 2002), chaps. 4, 10.

10. Notes to musical score *Les Misérables* (New York: Alain Boublil Music Ltd., 1991), 2.

11. For a detailed theory on how this works, see Joseph P. Swain, *Musical Languages* (New York: Norton, 1997), chap. 3.

12. It could be that the collaborators realized this afterward. Their subsequent opera of 1990, *Miss Saigon*, has comparatively few contrafacta.

13. It is true that the opera brings on stage the two candlesticks that the bishop gave to Jean Valjean to save him, but this excellent bit of stagecraft is overwhelmed by the presence of the two women spirits.

Chapter 16: Epilogue

1. Joan Peyser, *Bernstein: A Biography* (New York: William Morrow, 1987), 267.

2. The early versions of Jerome Kern's *Show Boat* also begin with a prologue. It was not until the 1946 revival that producer Billy Rose insisted on a medley overture to replace it.

3. John Lahr, "Sondheim's Little Deaths," *Harper's* 258 (April 1979), 71.

4. *Words With Music* (New York: Macmillan, 1972), 88.

5. Thelen, Lawrence, *The Show Makers: Great Directors of the American Musical Theatre* (New York: Routledge, 2000), 195, 200.

6. *New York Times* April 19, 1987, sec. 2, p. 37, col. 1.

Index

About the Author

The music criticism of Joseph P. Swain covers topics from show music to liturgical music, from musical aesthetics to music perception, in all periods of the Western tradition. He has written for such diverse outlets as *America*, *The Musical Quarterly*, and *The Journal of Aesthetics and Art Criticism*, among many other magazines, and has published five books. He has taught music theory and history for twenty-five years at Phillips Academy, Harvard University, and Colgate University and is active as a church organist, orchestra violist, and choral conductor.